LIVING WISDOM

LIVING WISDOM

*A Collection of Quotes, Aphorisms
and Insights into Life and Faith*

David J. Riddell

eagle
Guildford, Surrey

British Library Cataloguing in Publication Data. A catalogue record for this
book is available from the British Library.

Published by Eagle, an imprint of Inter Publishing Service (IPS) Ltd, St
Nicholas House, 14 The Mount, Guildford, Surrey GU2 5HN.

Typeset by Palimpsest Book Production Limited,
Polmont, Stirlingshire.
Printed by Caledonian International.

ISBN No: 0 86347 148 X

Warning

This is a dangerous book, especially to those who are afraid to have their current beliefs challenged and to those who, through a complex of psychological defence mechanisms, are hiding themselves from God. Therefore be warned. But also be encouraged. For when the truth is allowed to penetrate and expose the shadows within, it will also heal us and set us free from the destructive end of an ego whose highest loyalty is to itself.

Acknowledgements

The following notes represent the truth about reality as the author has perceived it at a particular point in his journey. As such, they are subject to the limitations of his understanding, and therefore subject to revision as illumination of the truth constantly increases.

They are not new, for, of course, no single person can claim to be the source of *any* new truth, but a great number of them have become clear to the author in times of divine inspiration, after many years of counselling and searching the writings of those who themselves have sought the truth.

Those quotes whose sources are known are identified, but there are some which may have been unconsciously hybridised as the author has endeavoured to clarify and distil truth and in the process of comprehending it, to make it 'his own'. He therefore uses the title 'author' in the loosest sense of the term.

As well as the inspired authors of Scripture, the author wishes to particularly acknowledge with heart-felt gratitude the following teachers (both past and present) who have helped bring the manifold wisdom of Christ into focus for him from their varying perspectives: James Dobson, Charles Colson, John and Paula Sandford, Jay Adams, Derek Prince, Paul Tournier, Dietrich Bonhoeffer, Jack Hayford, Allan Torrance, Jurgen Moltmann, Bill Gothard, Kenneth Hagin, and of course, there are a great many others, too numerous to mention by name.

They are my family, for they also have sought to know the One who is the truth, and to pass on the insights which they have received.

D.J. Riddell
Dunedin

CONTENTS

Part 3   Wisdom in Relationships – Family and Everyday

Part 4   Wisdom for Christians

Contents   ix

Introduction

To recognise the absolute truth about life, both spiritual, emotional and physical, and to know how to apply that knowledge in any given situation, is a scarce and precious ability among us today. To gain wisdom and insight gives freedom from confusion and hope for a better future, by allowing us to live in harmony with a reality that has been pre-scribed.

I have witnessed and heard of the application of truth healing broken relationships, restoring wayward children, enabling avoidance of accident, war and disaster, releasing individuals from addictions, giving purpose to meaningless lives, healing sick and diseased bodies, and prospering individuals and businesses. Equally I have observed so much grief, pain and suffering which could have been avoided if a little wisdom had been available.

Do you have wisdom? Are you concerned about gaining it? Or are you content to drift along, victim of, and vulnerable to, whatever life throws up, hopefully claiming that it was all 'meant-to-be' – a philosophy of fatalism. Most are, but you need not be.

Ultimately, your destiny is determined by the choices that only *you* can make. *You* must accept the final responsibility for your predicament, or at least for your response to it. Your choices in large measure got you there, and only your choices can get you out, or at least enable you to benefit as you go through it.

Now, before the hurting really begins, is the time for you to make the choice to change, and to seek whatever divine and human help which may be needed to make those changes. No one else has power over you, unless you give it to them. You already have the power, you may just need some help. The distilled truths to be found here, in your own hands, are a part of that help.

My earnest desire is that the simple studies and truisms contained within this book will give you a 'way in' to wisdom, insight, and faith, which in turn will give you a 'way out' of your pain. And always remember that Jesus Christ – Wisdom in Person – because of His great love for you, is ready to join with you in reshaping your life, as soon as you make His will welcome. Unlike every other religion or philosophy, He is not a construct of the human mind, but rather comes with His own power to recreate the human spirit and challenge the mind to acknowledge a higher authority than self.

He is, in fact, our 'Wisdom from God', appropriated only when we choose to acknowledge Him – love Him – entrust our lives to Him. The power to accept or reject His loving offer remains with us, but it does not alter the reality of His caring, correcting, presence.

Until that choice is made, we are doomed to abide in the anti-reality of our own self-imposed isolation and condemnation, continually suppressing the knowledge of what we instinctively know, for fear of discovering an authority that we cannot bear. Yet such a fear is forever negated by the sight of God, dying on a cross in the place of His creation, that the fundamental law of selfishness, guilt and death might be reversed through grace.

That is what happened at Jerusalem nearly two thousand years ago, and He did it for you/as you. Now His Spirit waits patiently at your 'side', waiting for your response to His offer of new life, a new identity. Just how long He will wait, you do not know, but it will not be forever.

Today the battle is for the mind. 'Good' thinking, results in 'good' feelings, and 'good' actions. Obviously, therefore, if you are feeling terrible, or you are in a terrible predicament, it is reasonable to assume that somewhere in your thinking you are wrong, i.e. you are believing lies.

Reading these proverbs and short studies may alert you

to a lie that is causing much of the pain, initially, by challenging your own concept of truth, and thereby provoking you to a fresh search for *the* truth. The measure of lies (false beliefs) you adhere to is the measure of just how crippled you will be, spiritually, socially, mentally, physically and financially – and will therefore be the measure of pain you are currently in.

The good news is that grace (God's undeserved favour and power to do what is right) is available. When you know that you are precious – loved – accepted – by God in Christ, before doing anything to earn it, you are freed from inferiority, rejection, bitterness, insecurity, rebellion and every fear. Insight into this grace is the only genuine antidote to a distorted self-knowledge and a 'performance' orientation (nobody can change their behaviour until their image of themselves is changed) and an inner security that is not dependent on circumstances is gained.

You are *unique*. You have only *one* life. In Christ you can live it abundantly. He has promised you His life, His health, His provision. You may have it as soon as you believe it and yield your life to it!

May God bless you and equip you for His service as you read and reflect. I suggest you begin with the chapters on 'Self-Esteem' and 'Exposing Misbeliefs' as the best way in to *Living Wisdom*.

David Riddell, Nelson, N.Z.

Heavenly Father, as I read on, I acknowledge that it was you who arranged that this wisdom should be placed in my hands as an answer to my silent prayer, and it is your love and presence that I sense as I meditate upon the truths found here. You have never been far from me Lord, but now I acknowledge your love and care for me throughout my life, and I open myself to your Holy Presence, to renew my mind to your way and to be cleansed in my heart of any attitude which is not pleasing to you. Forgive me, Father, that I may forgive myself and all others, and forever stand in the loving acceptance of our God and Saviour, Jesus Christ. Amen.

Definition of Terms

WISDOM: The knowledge of things as they function in reality, together with the insight necessary to know how to apply such knowledge to our choices in life.

GRACE: God's unconditional gift of love, forgiveness, acceptance and divine ability, given to humanity through His Son and constituted by the eternal Holy Spirit.

GOD: The Father of Jesus Christ and the heavenly origin of all humanity.

CHRIST: The God-man, to whom is given all power and authority in heaven and on earth.

THE HOLY SPIRIT: God-with-us-now. The one who effects our reconciliation with God. The one who expresses Himself through us.

CHRISTIAN: One who has openly acknowledged Christ as their God and entrusted themselves to Him, rather than relying on the efforts of personal performance. One who has been given the nature of Christ as their new identity.

SATAN: The destroying one, the father of misbeliefs, the perpetrator of anti-reality, the rebellious servant. The mystery of iniquity, now at work among the children of disobedience.

FAITH: The insight and response by which we relate to and entrust ourselves to God through Christ's faithfulness on our behalf.

'IN CHRIST': The eternal position of those who have acknowledged Christ as their own essential identity, and entrusted themselves to union with Him.

Part 1

Wisdom for our Times

Chapter One

Abortion

In 1991 in England and Wales there were 179,522 abortions – more than *seven* times the figure of 1968, Since the 1967 Act was passed, there have been 3.7 million deaths from abortions (including deaths to women who have had abortions) in Britain.

- There are about 50 million abortions performed a year worldwide.

- The status of the foetus is the basic issue in question. The status of the unborn is viewed three different ways in society:

  a. The biological 'genetic' view – there are no changes of a qualitative nature.

  b. The developmental view – according to degree of brain development, viability, or 'quickening'. There are no clearly definable 'stages' in this development, however. (Society in general has a developmental view.)

  c. How society views and responds to the foetus. NB, no society requires that a dead foetus be treated in the same way as a dead person, although, in China, one is dated from the date of one's conception, rather than one's birth.

- Only the foetus' means of support (internal/external) and its size, and its availability to human sight, and its status in society, change. Its essential being does *not* change from conception till death.

- Question: If it's not a human being, what kind of being is it?

If it is really part of the woman's own body, how does she survive without it?

- THE BIBLICAL CONCLUSION is that *no* child is a mistake in God's eyes, and that even unborn babies are made 'in the image of God'. Genesis 2; Genesis 2:7 translates from the Hebrew as the breath of 'lives' (plural for 'life'); Job 3:9–19 speaks of the destiny of those 'short-circuited' into eternity; Psalm 139; Ecclesiastes 6:3–5; Isaiah 44:24 and 49:1; Jeremiah 1:5; Luke 1:41; Galatians 1:15.

- LEGAL STATUS (UK – does not apply in N. Ireland where all abortions are illegal.) Following the 1990 amendments to the 1967 Act, the grounds for termination are now:

  - Risk to the life of the pregnant woman.
  - To prevent grave permanent injury to physical or mental health of the pregnant woman.
  - Risk of injury to physical or mental health of the pregnant woman (pregnancy has not exceeded 24 weeks). Many are performed on compassionate grounds masquerading as psychiatric. Others call it social convenience.
  - Risk of injury to physical or mental health of existing child(ren) (pregnancy has not exceeded 24 weeks).
  - Substantial risk of the child being born severely handicapped.
  - In an emergency – to save the life of the pregnant woman.
  - In an emergency – to prevent grave permanent injury to physical or mental health of the pregnant woman.
  - And a new upper time limit for most abortions of 24 weeks was given but also allowed certain exceptions with no upper limit set, this allowing for some legal abortions up to birth.

- Miscarriage (spontaneous abortion) occurs in approximately one in five pregnancies, while abortions are approximately one in eight to one in ten.

- CONTRACEPTION. Of those women who have abortions, approximately one third were using some reliable form of contraception, one third were using it unreliably, and one third were not using it according to manufacturers' specifications.

- Seven out of ten women do not take the pill strictly according to the manufacturer's instruction, according to their research. The failure rate of the coil (IUD) and dalcon shield is often according to the doctor's experience at fitting it. It is estimated that it has caused thousands of deaths. There are no foolproof methods of contraception; therefore the obvious lesson is *not* to have intercourse if a baby is definitely not welcome.

- Self – its preservation and desires, is the central issue, for it can *never* be said that the abortion is being performed for the '*baby's* sake'. 'I was too afraid to tell my parents', was the most common reason given for those pregnant for the first time and seeking an abortion. Another basic issue is the problem of owning one's own actions, with all its consequences, rather than trying to avoid and escape the consequences.

- Society in general *expects* responsible custodianship of life and nature – poor custodianship is called to public account. Abortion as a means of birth-control is not good custodianship of life from any perspective.

- Most international laws grant human life status at the time of viability, approximately six months, but with new technology this is continually decreasing. What is the lower limit?

- Many give full status to the unborn after the first trimester, but there is nothing magical about twelve weeks.

- Liberalised laws *always* lead to abortion being used as a form of birth control. Infertility has always increased where abortion has been liberalised.

- 'A woman's right to choose' was the slogan coined by a doctor, who now campaigns to save the unborn. Women have *already* exercised their choice at the time of intercourse, to conceive. From that point on there is a new life with new rights. Rape, within or out of marriage, is the exception, and always the red herring for those who do not want to think the matter through. Horrendous though rape is, how will taking the life of an innocent victim help to restore the damage done to the woman?

• The risk of infertility, pelvic disease, perforated uterus, and ectopic pregnancies are all considerably increased as the result of abortions.

• Miscarriage (spontaneous abortion) carries no moral implications, while abortion (induced miscarriage) carries heavy moral implications. The added factor is the intervention of the human will. Nevertheless, even miscarriages evoke grief.

• How can the father have responsibilities towards the baby, without the ensuing rights? The unborn is the responsibility of both the mother, *and* the father, *and* the community, in that it will make demands on *all* their resources for its proper development.

• Just as murder by a wilful and premeditated act of violence is a different legal issue to murder by judicial process, i.e. war, so abortion by consent of those responsible is a different legal issue to abortion by violence.

• 'Every baby a wanted baby' is a goal, not a legitimate basis for extermination. Such an argument if extended, could have been appropriated by the Hitler regime, 'Every person a desirable person'. Note; there are *no* unwanted babies, there are *many* couples who want babies and are unable even to adopt.

• The medical dangers to a woman's health following an abortion are much more severe than if she carries the child to term, so, in fact, abortion itself is the *real* danger.

• A mother is required by her own instinct to care for the baby while in the womb, *and* this instinct is reinforced by *society's laws* to give responsible care to the child, *after* birth.

- Propaganda calls a baby a 'product of conception', and an abortion a 'termination of pregnancy', to prevent personal identification with the baby.

- It is paradoxical that the same health departments which spend money instructing pregnant mothers not to smoke, in order to protect the health of the baby, *also* spend money to purchase the tools with which to kill babies at the same age and stage. What kind of society does this? What kind of society closes hospitals while building abortion clinics?

- A doctor, while sucking a baby from its mother's womb at 20 weeks, heard it scream in pain when a bubble in the birth fluid floated over its mouth. It shook him so badly that he instantly vowed never to do another abortion. What was it that shattered his rationale?

- More than half of the abortions performed are during a woman's first pregnancy.

- IUDs are not contraceptive devices, they are abortificants, because they prevent implantation of the fertilised ovum.

- Secular reasoning says, 'Why can't a physician, with the best interests of both the baby and the mother at heart, intervene just as God or "nature" has so often done?' Humanistic reasoning is not afraid to act like God.

- Pro-life and Pro-choice. Pro-choice is a deceptive term. Those who call themselves by this name are actively trying to make women conform to their way of thinking, in order to validate their own moral stance and possibly assist their own denial. They must also, of necessity, be pro-abortion if they take such a view. Pro-choice is not the neutral stance it first appears to be. The Society for the Protection of the Unborn Child (SPUC) is sometimes portrayed as compassionless, moralistic, even cruel, by media images of vulnerable, reluctant, frightened mothers being confronted with placards at the point of abortion. Placard-waving is seen as an 'action of alienation – 'below the belt' and not appropriate to

Christians. The 'method of approach' is sometimes seen
as wrong by those who would otherwise be supportive.
This frame of reference is *dualistic* – to support *either* the
baby *or* the mother, and is at the heart of this difficulty.
To reach the baby, one must go *via* the mother's needs,
and her immediate supporters. It is certainly true that
working to prevent unwanted pregnancies is a wiser
activity than battling over the fate of the unborn, but
it is never too late to intervene in an escalating chain
of foolish decisions.

• In a nation with many differing belief systems, no one
group should be able to force its minority opinion of
truth on the rest, no matter how much it may be
convinced of the justness of its cause. Government of
a democracy is always on the basis of consensus of what
is right and wrong. If pro-life could dictate change, so
then could the humanists. Consensus demands that we
work to educate the majority to the true nature of the
action, for the murder of the innocent can never be a
case for consensus. The church certainly does have a
vital educational role to play in a democracy.

Counselling

• The unwanted pregnancy is *not* the primary problem
– the problem is poverty, or relationships, or sexual
identity, or fear, or ignorance. It may be a woman
looking for love in all the wrong places.

• That consent be 'informed', requires pro-life counselling
also, but could a pro-life counsellor ever recognise the
right of the mother to do wrong? Can a pro-lifer *ever* be
neutral in the face of the helpless unborn? God gave us
the freedom to choose between right and wrong, but He
did *not* give us the 'right' to choose to do wrong. He
does not help us to do wrong, quite the contrary. Some
women may choose to abort their babies, but we cannot
help them in that choice by civil laws or material help.
The right of conscience means that we must accept that
a woman has the freedom to follow the dictates of her

conscience, even when that is morally abhorrent to us, but such a conscience should be informed, not ignorant. (A booklet is needed to outline the debate and possible consequences for unsure mothers.)

• Women contemplating abortion often feel that they have no other choice. In this they are always wrong, but they need to be told about the resources available to them.

• Professor Simpson, in his address entitled 'Directive Counselling in the Post Rogerian Era' showed that non-directive counselling is actually harmful to the patient, because what she is really looking for is guidance, and this is not to be confused with overbearing direction which the counsellee is unable to own as her own. (Consider also the myth of neutrality in counselling.)

• A newly pregnant woman at the point of decision is extremely vulnerable and not always thinking rationally. She can easily be talked into, or out of, abortion. Those in the abortion chain seem to take advantage of this fragile state.

• The majority of women don't understand that they are killing a fully formed baby and change their minds when they become better informed. Most are told it is just a piece of tissue, and simply asked if they want their menstrual cycles re-established. If wombs had windows, there would be no abortions.

• Women who say they can't face having a baby are not saying they want an abortion, but an abortion clinic invariably interprets it that way, and begins the process of termination. The 'pro-abortion' people who advocate a woman's power over her own destiny, themselves may rush a woman through her abortion, because the abortion staff have their own hidden agenda. They don't necessarily talk about the abortion or the baby, neither do they always give post-abortion support. Pregnancy is treated as a sickness.

• How is it that people are heroes who sit in trees to save forests, but are despised and imprisoned for sitting in clinics to save motherhood and babies? 'Be a hero, save a whale. Save a baby, go to jail.' How are we to understand the pacifist who yet advocated abortion?

• Those who are advocating protection for the unborn should remember that social change never comes from the top, but from the grass roots, because those in power usually have, as their first priority, the maintenance of the status quo, otherwise they would not have been invited up by those already in power, in the first place.

• Our concept of who we are lies at the heart of everything we do. Having an abortion dramatically changes a woman's image of herself, and consequently, her behaviour changes also, taking on a tendency toward self-destructive habits.

• Many mothers become pregnant again soon after an abortion in a subconscious effort to make amends. This is the 'replacement' or 'atonement' baby.

• Mothers who have had several abortions often find they are unable to provide their children with the nurturing love which they need. Their God-given 'motherhood' has been seriously damaged.

• Abhorrence of pregnant women and new-born children is a symptom of a repressed consciousness of the wrong of abortion. So is depression, nightmares and self-destructive behaviour. For the mother, the period of denial is usually about five to seven years, then the 'walls' begin to bulge.

• Mothers who encourage their daughters to go through with abortions also carry a great load of guilt. There is a post-abortion syndrome for *all* involved.

• No one tells the new mum when she's contemplating abortion, that at the birth of her first baby she will be grieving over the death of 'the other one', and spend the days after her birth crying. Then the doctors will merely prescribe Valium. Dad also will often remember and regret. If they have only girls, they will torture themselves with the thought that the other one could have been a boy. Imagine how the infertile mother feels when she discovers that that particular child was the only one she could have, and that it died at her own hand?

- A woman 'in denial' has feelings of guilt, depression and sadness, often with weeping and nightmares and doesn't know why – hasn't made the connection. She may hate to hear the sucking of a vacuum-cleaner, or be unable to use a pair of kitchen tongs, things which elicit subconscious abhorrence. Connections often come via nightmares. 'As time went on I slowly began to realise what I had done. I wondered what the baby would have been like – how old it would have been.'

- Denial is dangerous to the development of the personality; it introduces a life of avoidance, escapism and deceit, and begins with the earliest efforts to escape the consequences of one's own behaviour.

- The mother, in finding forgiveness, will also need to forgive the clinic's counsellor for misleading her, and anyone else she feels is responsible. Ultimately though, she must accept the responsibility for her own actions.

- An able, caring counsellor is vital to the mother's recovery of her mental health.

- Having an abortion will not, and can *never*, nullify the knowledge of, or the fact that, pregnancy and motherhood has indeed taken place.

Conclusion

- The freedom of abortion on demand brings its own particular kind of enslavement.

- The oppressing knowledge of a past abortion leads many women to come to Christ in their search for forgiveness and emotional freedom.

- If you were the doctor, would you, by means of a vacuum pump, break up and suck out, piece by piece,

a baby from its mother's womb, and drop the limbs into
a rubbish bag? If not, then why, by your silence, do you
support those who do? If we do not actively resist evil,
then we become party to it!

• Evil, seen too often, can eventually be embraced. This is
  how abortion became respectable. But the words of Jesus
  cut across such a view . . . 'Inasmuch as you did it unto
  the least of these, my brethren, you did it unto me.'

• Though God 'allows' someone to injure another, this
  does not release us from our responsibility of forcefully
  trying to stop them. Christians everywhere have a moral
  obligation to oppose unjust laws that are contrary to the
  law of God. The time for talking is never over, but beliefs
  held to without actions are useless.

• Parents should confirm to their daughters that, should
  they *ever* become pregnant, they would always have the
  parents' complete support to carry the baby to term.

• Although abortions are carried out on the grounds of
  health, abortion itself is the *real* danger to the mother's
  physical and mental wholeness.

• Ethicists who begin their 'neutral' consideration of abortion by viewing it as a situation of conflicting rights
  have already predetermined their conclusion because of
  their (a priori) pre-supposition. They are beginning their
  argument from a pro-abortion stance.

• 'If you believe that abortion is murder, why aren't you
  doing something about it?' is the inescapable challenge.

Further Reading
Sacrifices of the New Age, by Paul De Parrie & Mary
  Pride.
Abortion: Questions and Answers, by Dr Wilkie.
Sanctity of Life, by Chuck Swindoll
When Does Life Begin, by John Ankerburg and John
  Weldon.
Book and resources are also available from CARE, 53
Romney St, London SW1P 3RF.

Post-Abortion Blues

Possible physical effects of abortion
Miscarriages • Sterility • Stillbirths • Incompetent cervix/-ruptured uterus • Ectopic pregnancies • Hysterectomy • Shock • Coma • Perforated uterus • Peritonitis • Various degrees of haemorrhage from moderate to life threatening • Fever/cold sweat • Intense pain • Vomiting • Passing blood clots (incomplete abortion) • Menstrual disturbances • Loss of other organs • Gastro-intestinal disturbances

Psycho-physical effects of abortion
Nervousness • Constant swallowing • Constant tiredness • Crying • Sighing • Insomnia • Loss of appetite • Anorexia • Weight loss • Frigidity • Decreased work capacity • Seizures, tremors

Psychological effects of abortion
Personality disorders – ranging from depression and general unhappiness to obvious neurosis • Obvious personality changes • A loss of the joy of living • Conscious or subconscious guilt • Withdrawal • Despair • Helplessness • Lowered self-esteem • Frustration and inner turmoil • Loss of confidence in decision-making capability • A sense of feeling unfulfilled • Thwarted maternal instincts • Hatred for those connected with the abortion • Desire to end relationships • Loss of sexual interest • Feeling of dehumanisation • Feelings of having been cheated or exploited • Overall sense of insecurity

Subconscious psychological effects of abortion
Mourning/grief • Regret & remorse • Anger/rage/hostility • Nightmares • Pre-occupation with death • Desire to remember date of abortion • Pre-occupation with 'would be' date • Intense interest in babies • Internal frustration taken out on children born before the abortion • Over-protectiveness towards those children born following abortions • Fear of future sterility or miscarriages • Fear of not ever becoming a mother • Desire to end one's life

Chapter Two

DEBT

No one is ever secure by virtue of finance. Consider Howard Hughes, the multi-billionaire who died an unhappy recluse.

- Debt is a primary cause of divorce and marital fights, due to the pressure it puts on the couple.

- Men go into debt to achieve significance, whereas women prefer security. Husbands should learn to heed their wives' cautions.

- Why is it that so very few people are debt free, even though everybody wants to be? Have you ever thought about the reasons that lie behind that phenomenon?

- Scripture does not condemn debt, it says go into it carefully and keep out of it wherever you can.

- Like a well-designed trap, getting into debt is *much* easier than getting out, but there is great wisdom to be gained in the escape.

- The debt squeeze is caused by *presuming* on the future.

- Where there is debt, there is conflict and a clash of loyalties.

- Learning to be *content* is the great need. 'Always wanting more' is symptomatic of a spiritual void that is going unheeded.

- Debt is actually a symptom of another, deeper problem.

- A debt consolidation loan only hides the problem, and debt invariably recurs three to four years down the road.

- Pay off the smallest debts first, (while drip-feeding the big ones) and the satisfaction will create its own momentum.

  Have you/can you face up to your need to reduce your life-style and live more austerely?

- *Some* amount of giving to the church and/or to those in need, even while in debt, gives recognition that God owns it *all*, and forces us to get our priorities in order.

- Every spending decision is a spiritual decision, and reveals the priorities of our hearts. (Perhaps our cheque stubs will be in the next life for all to see!!)

- Christ's teaching to 'take no thought for tomorrow' must also be balanced against 'who among you would build a tower, without first sitting down to count the cost'.

- Young mothers, whose children still need them, don't have to be away from home all day to get out of debt *God's* way. Look for Him to reveal another way.

- In Chinese, the characters that spell 'crisis' represent both danger and opportunity.

- To cope with financial worry, first externalise it. List out the commitments, and talk it over with a counsellor. Organisation is a good defence against needless anxiety.

- Don't waste your life trying to fulfil *all* of your desires.

- Even after death, each one must face the day of assessment. How have you used the resources available to you in this life?

- 'The borrower is servant to the lender.' Whose servant do you want to be?

- Will all your worry change the interest rates? Use the additional emotional energy constructively to get proper control of your finances.

- You'll think more clearly after you share your burden with the Lord.

- Borrow only on non-consumable and income-increasing investments.

- Be diligent to locate the primary lie in your thinking which underlies your present predicament.

  Remember that no predicament can harm you, unless you choose a wrong response to it. What can you learn about yourself and God's faithfulness from this experience?

- Debt can wedge a couple apart or draw them closer together, depending on the attitude they choose to adopt.

- Before God can trust you with wealth, He must teach you to find your security in Him before all else, and poverty is the way if you will not heed His Word.

Chapter Three

Drug Abuse

- Drug abusers are usually sensitive people with a poor self-image, who find the pressures of life, the painful memories of the past, or the guilt of his or her conscience, intolerable to live with. Only by deadening their mind by alcohol or drugs can they enjoy any sense of wellbeing.

- Young people are particularly vulnerable to drug abuse because they are impressionable, adventurous and usually ill-informed. They also have not yet learnt the coping skills needed to respond positively to stress, anger and frustration.

- Doctors, when prescribing drugs, always have to balance therapeutic benefits against side effects and risks to the patients' health.

- One factor common in heavy users is a *low tolerance* for distress, anxiety, pain and frustration, together with the desire to escape, or experiment, or just have fun.

- Teach the abuser *how* to face up to pressure and pain. 'To face it or escape it', is their constant option.

- A child from a home where alcohol is used is *many* times more likely to become an alcoholic than a child from a non-drinking home. The lesson is surely obvious.

- Physical dependence occurs when the withdrawal symptoms cannot be tolerated.

- Alcohol in the bloodstream hastens the speed of absorption of other drugs, or else combines its effect as a central nervous system depressant, and death often occurs accidentally.

Symptoms of drug abuse: A loss of interest in life •
School, work and sport performance is decreased •
Disinterest in personal appearance • School and work
absenteeism • Old friends dropped, a 'new group' associated with • Secrecy about friends and activities • Stealing
cash and readily saleable goods • Tranquillisers taken
from home • Evasiveness and lying • Long periods spent
alone • Physical signs.

- Blanket rejection by parents usually reinforces drug taking behaviour. (Such rejection is not to be confused with
  the pressure which 'tough love' may bring to bear.)

- Until a user actually realises and admits that he or she
  has a problem, there is little you can do to help. There
  is no hope until they realise that the pain in their lives
  is actually being caused by drugs.

- Find someone the user *trusts* and enlist their help.

- Most drugs can cross the placental barrier and enter the
  unborn child's system, particularly in the first few weeks
  after conception.

- At birth, the babies of women who smoke more than
  ten cigarettes a day during pregnancy are lighter and
  their heads and brains smaller than average, and even
  in primary school they continue to lag behind in general
  achievement.

- For some addicts the choice is to stay on drugs or commit
  suicide in order to escape their unbearable inner pain, a
  pain that began with broken relationships. The initial
  breakdown in communication between parent and child
  needs to be restored with humility and forgiveness *from
  both sides*.

- Giving forgiveness to all those who have hurt him or
  her is the first step in ridding the addict's subconscious
  mind of all negative material.

- If it will make one feel good, whatever it is, it will be
  abused by the vulnerable in our society. (Lithium does
  not fall into this category.)

- Sitting your child or grandchild on your knee, and making them promise you that they will *never* ever start smoking, is a very good thing to do, to 'drug-proof' them in later life.

- Iatrogenic symptoms are those caused by a doctor's prescriptions. It's easier for them to reach for the prescription pad, than to talk the patient through the problem.

- Were we to remove alcohol and tobacco from our society, we could reduce the size of our hospitals by 70%!! It is not the *illegal* drugs that are the priority problem in our society. Society must be re-educated.

- 'What has the straight life got to offer me?' is the first question that needs to be answered for the addict.

- It isn't the presence of drugs that is the primary cause of usage, but dysfunctional families, cultural norms, and an environment geared to rejection.

- Legislation still pours money into the end of the line, rather than at the beginning, where the young are most at risk. Yet *everybody* knows that prevention is better than cure. When will we ever learn?

- Since Western men are not 'supposed' to get into expressing feelings, they often self-medicate by drug and alcohol abuse to deal with the pain.

- If drug users (not suppliers) were merely fined and the money used for preventative work, instead of their being criminalised, then they could be much more easily rehabilitated into the community, and the supply could be halted.

- Three joints a day *will* result in paranoia. Twelve cups of coffee, or twenty cups of tea, *will* result in anxiety disorders.

- Amongst the drug-abusers are often found the most dangerous and evil people in society. They may have completely forgotten the qualities of love, honesty and compassion. Escaping the truth is a way-of-life.

- When you work with substance abusers, you must understand the issues of adolescence.

  If the brain is being artificially stimulated by drugs, then when the stimulant is removed, the mind will 'crash'.

- Society concerned about drug rehabilitation needs both an easy access, needle exchange programme to combat the threat of AIDS *and* a 'tough love' rehabilitation programme.

- The sense of wellbeing, or relaxation obtained by using alcohol or drugs is the way a normal person feels most of the time. It just seems to be a high by comparison to their normally depressed or anxious state.

- More common addictions can include TV, radio, hard rock music, sugary foods, gambling, spending, reading love stories, cleaning, promiscuity, sports etc. Anything that pretends to meet an unmet emotional need, is suspect.

- Do not shield or protect the addict from any of the consequences of their behaviour, but rather help them to make the connection between cause and effect. Drugs are not a *relief* from their daily problems, they are the *cause* of them.

- The addict must be removed from the so-called unconditional acceptance of his or her 'mates'.

- Diaphragmatic breathing is a better tension relief than smoking.

- Sudden removal of tranquillisers is dangerous, and may result in seizures.

- In some senses, tranquillisers may be regarded as solid alcohol.

Chapter Four

JEHOVAH'S WITNESSES

- 'Any organisation which assumes itself to be the way of salvation for all should be willing to submit to scrutiny and criticism.' AWAKE, August 1984.

- Your own Bible teaches that no one can work towards or improve upon their own salvation (from Ephesians 2:8–9; New World Translation).

- Christ's sheep are everywhere, not just in the Watchtower Society (from John 10:11; New World Translation) but why do you hate Christians?

- You have worked so hard for Jehovah, but what about Matthew 11:28–30 and John 1:12?

- Are you living in frustration, anxiety and fear of impending judgement? If that is not the kind of life you wish for your children, how could you think that that is the kind of life which Jehovah has for you?

- Are you trusting in Christ, or in elders and supervisors to save you?

- Do your elders live for their own advancement, or for the welfare of the flock?

- The 'Governing Body' have predicted the end of this system and the arrival of God's kingdom at least five times *wrongly*. How many errors can they make without losing their credibility in your eyes?

- You may remain in the Watchtower Society only on the condition that you don't start to think and reason for yourself. What happens if you openly disagree with any of the preset answers in the 'Book Study'? If you don't

want to think for yourself, you should ask yourself
'What need are they meeting in my life which might
be jeopardised if I start asking too many questions?'

• If you have 'earned' your salvation by preaching, then
  you have no share in God's kindness, for you have no
  need of it – salvation has become your 'right'. Your great
  efforts are only distancing you from His grace. Look at
  Romans 3:20 and Ephesians 2:8–9 for yourself.

• You expect religious tolerance in the lands where you
  work, but do you love or treat as untouchable your previous members? Is your 'dis-fellowshipping' according
  to Matthew 18:15–17?

• Did you know that your 'Governing Body' reserve the
  right to lie to you, if *they* do not feel that you are entitled
  to know the truth? Refer to 'Aid to Bible Understanding'
  p 1061.

• When the Governing Body have changed their teaching
  – which they have done *many* times – they say 'We have
  new light now.' How do you reconcile that with Malachi
  3:6 and Titus 1:2?

• Acts 1:8 calls us to be witnesses to whom? Check the
  original text if you can.

• What was Christ's attitude to the 'black sheep' who
  wandered away from the flock? (Luke 15:4). Is Christ's
  attitude the same as your group's?

• When/if you renounced the religion in which you were
  brought up, did it occur to you that you were throwing
  the baby out with the bathwater? Did you really understand the 'salvation by faith in the God-man' teaching of
  the Protestant church?

• Dare you ask yourself why you have *really* become so
  dependent on the Society? (When people agree not to
  think independently, they invariably do so for some
  kind of return.) Dare you study the New Testament
  on your own, relying only on Jehovah's Spirit to help
  you understand?

- Do you believe the accusations against other religions and their ministers without checking them out for yourself? Remember that Jehovah warns you against prejudiced judgements (see 2 Corinthians 13:1).

- Are you aware that the changes made to the translation of the 'New World Translation of the Hebrew Scriptures' are totally unsubstantiated and that *no* Hebrew or Greek scholar will endorse the alterations made in the following verses: John 1:1; Hebrews 1:8; John 8:58; John 10:38; John 14:20; John 17:3; John 17:26; 1 Corinthians 10:4, Galatians 2:20; Ephesians 3:19; Colossians 1:16,17; Hebrews 1:16 plus *many* more. Find an Amplified Bible and do some comparisons *for yourself*. There were no Hebrew or Greek scholars on the New World translation committee at all.

- Are you aware that Johannes Greber who did the translation was a self-acknowledged spirit medium who relied on his spirit guides for the 'true' translation? Compare *Watchtower*, February 15, 1956 with *Watchtower*, April 1, 1983 (p 31) *if you dare to know the truth*.

- 'The truth shall set you free.' But what do the public talks *actually set you free from*? Can you even remember what you sat listening to last year, last month, or even last week?

- Even when you can win all the arguments, is your heart filled with love, joy and peace, or are you becoming filled with suspicion, distrust, contempt and nervous frustration?

- When was the last time you prayed to God and felt His loving reply? If your 'truth' is in fact false, then you will *never* feel His loving approval of you, only an emptiness of heart. Surely something is lacking.

- Do you *really* know what the orthodox Christian churches teach about the topics listed below. Find a Bible and look *for yourself*.

1. THE TRINITY: Genesis 1:26; 11:7; 18:2–3; Isaiah 6:8; 48:15; Matthew 28:19; John 14:16; 2 Corinthians 13:14.

2. THE DEITY OF CHRIST: John 1:1; 5:18; 8:58; 10:28; 17:15; Philippians 2:8–11; Colossians 2:9; Hebrews 1:1–4.

3. THE ATONEMENT: Leviticus 17:11; John 1:29; 2 Corinthians 5:20; Colossians 1:20; Hebrews 9:22; 1 Peter 2:24; Revelation 13:8.

4. THE VISIBLE RETURN OF CHRIST: Zechariah 12:10; Matthew 24:30; 1 Thessalonians 4:16,17; Revelation 1:7.

5. THE BODILY RESURRECTION OF CHRIST: Mark 16:14; Luke 24:39–44; John 20:27,28; 1 Corinthians 15:15.

6. HUMAN GOVERNMENT: Romans 13:1–7.

7. THE EXISTENCE OF HELL AND ETERNAL SEPARATION: Matthew 5:22; 8:11, 12; 13:42, 50; 2 Peter 2:17; Jude 13.

8. SATAN – THE DEVIL: Matthew 25:41; Revelation 20:10.

9. THE EXISTENCE OF THE SOUL: Genesis 1:26; 5:1; Job 32:8; Acts 7:59; 1 Corinthians 11:7; 2 Corinthians 4:12.

10. THE KINGDOM OF HEAVEN: Luke 17:20–26; Revelation 22:1–5, 14.

Further reading:
Thirty Years A Watchtower Slave, by W.J. Schnell.
Jehovah of the Watchtower, by Walter Martin.

Chapter Five

Feminism

- Liberation is not a place, or a position of dominance, or even an 'equality' but rather a state of mind and attitude, where we are liberated to be what we were created to be. To achieve their 'liberation', many women have become enslaved instead to anger, rebellion, sexism and painful memories.

- Is it necessary to prove yourself the equal of a man at all costs? If you are free, are you free to accept your limitations – free to accept help from a man? Are you, for example, free to reciprocate a male employer's concern for your welfare?

- Does being **equal** to a man, mean being the **same** as a man? If not, where can the roles complement each other?

- Domesticity is no less valuable or fulfilling than any other career. It is, in fact, the *one* career upon which society itself is utterly dependent, and should never be devalued by political, commercial, ecclesiastical or legal authority.

- When the desire for liberation robs a woman of the joy of her wedding day, or the joy of new-found motherhood – perhaps the two greatest moments in a woman's life – something is desperately wrong. When the props are taken or given away (independence, figure, status etc) where can she find a new source of self-esteem?

- 'Who am I – who has the right to validate me – to tell me who I am?', is the central quest. At its heart, the crisis is one of faith.

- A clear distinction needs to be made between loving service and subservience. There is no element of coercion or self-depreciation in healthy service.

- Feminism worldwide generally has the common elements of reactionary anger, victimhood, jealousy and resentment from previous experience of discrimination and injustice. 'Can such energy be harnessed in a positive way?' is the challenge.

- Concerning men, 'Give them an inch and they'll take a mile' is the oft repeated lie. Though men at times can be opportunists, women can gain their respect if they will first respect themselves as beloved daughters of God.

- 'Domestic' and 'femininity' are only loaded terms for those with 'loaded' pasts. If domesticity merely means brimming nappy buckets and last night's dishes, then your thinking has been damaged and your view has become distorted. What unnatural environment bruised you in the first place?

- In finally becoming aware of your own needs, can you remain sympathetic to the needs of the men in your life? Don't damage others with the anger you feel at your own past naïveté.

- The greatest thing one can do for the feminine cause is to help educate males to the thoughtful exercise of their responsibilities and power.

- We can only be healed from the anguish of victimhood when we first become aware that our oppressor is also a victim.

- When the oppressed liberate themselves, they often become the oppressors in their turn. Beware reverse sexism.

- Is your attitude proactive, or merely reactive to the manhood you have so far experienced? No man ever had the power to tell you who you are, but then neither does a group of angry women.

- Both depending on a man, *and* depending on yourself

for self-esteem, is futile. Christ's love for you is the only reliable objective source of a healthy self-image.

- Women abused by men are not healed by having their angry reaction indulged or by associating only with other women. Such behaviour only reinforces the misbeliefs and stereotyping that continues the pain.

- God is not male, any more than God is female. Words of gender in religion become loaded terms only in the ears of the bruised. As the old proverb states, 'Ill nature sucks poison from the sweetest flower'.

- No one is automatically a 'natural' mother. Such mothers have simply had opportunity to observe role models and practise mothering skills during formative years. If you feel inadequate in this area, remember competency comes the same way in any field, that is by training, so don't be bound by any premature conclusions.

- Only when we first leave the safeguarding of our 'rights' with Christ, can we then avoid the resentment which embitters the soul, and only then can we safely and genuinely call to correction those who would oppress us.

- Will the removal of generic terms in Christendom heal the hearts that have been damaged by the misrepresentation of patriarchy? Only God can define what genuine 'maleness' and 'femaleness' is, and He has done so two thousand years ago.

- It is not male or female chauvinism that damages people primarily, but the inhuman desire to gain at another human being's expense, in a word – selfishness.

- Is your distrust of God directed at God 'as He is', or against your own hideous homemade parody of Him (God as you perceive Him to be)? He is certainly pleased with your rejection of such a chauvinistic, divinely autocratic being, but your preoccupation with your own false concept also means that your attitude denies to both of you each other's love.

- Can a woman find the liberation that can free her to

also enjoy domesticity, femininity, male protection and complementary roles?

- When used in God's presence, all God talk becomes subject to definition by God, not by those who speak or hear, so it is in fact impossible to speak of God in a sexist fashion simply by using male or female pronouns.

- The alternative to open hostility and silent resentment is to 'speak the truth in love to one another', and to accept responsibility for ourselves – our attitudes and responses, if not our predicaments.

- Part of the pain inherent in a democracy is the discrimination that occurs against minorities, but it's only a man's world if half the populace (the women) allow it.

- The New Testament reveals that a woman's place is first of all 'in Christ', and from there she can find liberation in any place she may choose.

- Do men really want power over women, or are they also simply trying to escape the same sense of powerlessness and victimhood?

- Do you need financial reward to enable you to take a pride in your mothering? Have you left your self-esteem in a pay-packet?

Chapter Six

Managers

- In spite of all our education, those with real people-handling skills *still* remain in short supply, yet a proved motivator will always accomplish far more than a proved genius.

- Everyone has to be a motivator in some capacity or other, and the ability to enthuse can be taught and learned – it is never an accident.

- A true leader can bring out the potential which lies dormant in all of us. To be 'believed in' is to be enabled to believe in ourselves. Even gifted people first of all needed someone to believe in them before they could exercise their own ability.

- Don't confuse the motivator with the manipulator. The manipulator has only one agenda – themselves, whereas the motivator is seeking the best for all.

- At the leadership level, technical expertise is much less important than ability in human relations.

- Can you defuse a tense and difficult situation between and within groups of people? Avenues for communication will relieve the pressure before it becomes destructive.

- Get enthusiastic people together and they will create their own momentum.

- Always remember that attitudes are of far more importance than facts because attitudes can change facts, but facts need not change attitudes.

- Can you identify the strengths of your people and

build on them? Everyone believes they are capable of something better and greatly appreciates the one who helps them achieve their full potential.

- When you put people in close touch with their faults their behaviour will often become worse. Focus on their strengths throughout your corrections.

- Does the individual's personal welfare count? Many are watching how you treat the one in trouble.

- Your first assumption should be that people *want* to do a good job. Ultimately, people would rather work hard at something they believe in than spend their time in idleness.

- To persuade someone, first connect with them by using the right questions. What do they really want, and how can they get it? Where are they going, where are they hurting, what do they love and hate? What do they attach supreme value to? Everything they do is motivated by something.

- Do you seek to be served, or to serve? Those who serve best, lead best. Achieve your objectives by helping others achieve theirs.

- The true leader wants those under him to become better at what he does than he can be himself. How secure are you?

- People act in accordance with their beliefs about life and what is certain. Do you know what your staff's are? Do you know what your own are? Don't assume that what motivates you will also motivate them.

- It is people's desire for more and better which lies behind the complaints, but this is also what enables the leader to lead.

- People cannot help loving those who are continually interested in discovering more about them. (This is a key to healing many broken relationships.) Notice them and you affirm them. Take them for granted and you denigrate them without saying a word. The real leader says 'Tell me about yourself.'

- Choose your critics carefully.

- Have your staff discovered the pride and pleasure of doing something to a high standard of excellence? Have you?

- A laid-back attitude undermines morale by communicating that this endeavour is not really worth their best. Leaders who run a tight ship produce the most secure staff (the same applies for parents and children).

- Share your dream with others who are of like mind whenever possible and it will never die, for with enough presentations to enough people, some will pick it up and run with it.

- If you care about your staff, then you will care about how successful they are and you won't need to apologise for pushing them.

- Dedication has to come from somewhere and if you lack it yourself, you cannot enthuse another.

- Do not sanction incompetence. A good reprimand is brief, specific, verified and passionate. We all need a poke from a sharp stick called truth now and again, but get your facts straight first of all.

- It's good to be popular, but if you can't risk being disliked, you will not be able to correct when the occasion calls for it.

- First spell out the price to be paid, for every challenge has a power to evoke our best.

- Ultimately, people need to work for a cause more than merely retain a job, yet today most people are bored with their lives.

- Are your objectives clearly defined? They also need to be attainable.

- Accomplishment feedback is what hooks the sportsman. What means of feedback do you have for your staff's accomplishments?

- Failure is one of the most helpful experiences we can have providing its lesson is identified. Teach them how to fail well and in doing so you will create an environment where failure is not fatal.

- In the face of failure, your staff need your support. Teach them that failure is never permanent. To say 'I have failed', is totally different from saying 'I am a failure'. (Always admire those who attempt great things, even though they fail.)

- What is more important than to help someone else succeed in their own lives? It begins by telling them of their possibilities, and there is no reward quite like it.

- The more specific the goal, the more motivation it produces. Can your staff own *your* goal as their own?

- Get in touch with what's going on in your inner world, for if you are in conflict with yourself, you will also be in conflict with others.

- Do you push people into roles they do not want, or simply help them to clarify their options and make up their own minds?

- Never be inconsistent, either with yourself or with your staff.

- When people make a public commitment, they will then go on to ensure its fulfilment in order not to be inconsistent, for we do what we do in order to affirm the person that we think we are.

- Most people are disappointed in who they see themselves to be, but people are inclined to become whatever they are encouraged to be.

- Great persuaders stir the emotions with great stories of 'if he can do it, then so can you. Great success came to people who were just like you'. (See Hebrews 11.)

- When you find yourself succeeding, begin to duplicate the process in a larger setting.

- Don't take others' successes for granted. Cultivate an attitude of gratitude, especially in front of their peers, and be specific about your credits. When you praise good quality, you ensure a repeat performance.

- Monitor the musings of your mind; you are only as strong as your grasp of the truth.

- Your aim should never be to pressure or control others, but to point out consequences and give choices to people. That is not manipulation, but motivation. Is it clear to your people that you are devoted to the good of all?

- Harness people's inclination to compare by introducing some healthy competition.

- Don't hide your anger, but be sure it is directed against the problem, not the person.

- Two people are three times as difficult to stop as one. Encourage partnerships.

- Can you cultivate a sense of 'belongingness' in your staff? There are many factors that will engender loyalty.

- Don't make promises you can't keep.

- Be sure that everyone is playing on a level playing field – indulge no favourites.

- The manager who can teach his or her staff to enjoy their work is welcomed by all concerned. Remember to have fun. Ultimately that's why people will want to stay in your group.

- Keep working on the quality of in-house communication, it will save many misunderstandings and upset feelings.

- How do you cope with troublemakers: with ease and assurance, or by going for the bottom line? Take them aside and hear them out before doing anything else and you may not need to do anything else, for grievances must have an outlet.

• Is the troublemaker really disruptive, or is she/he just the group's ventilator? Perhaps his/her contribution far outweighs the trouble she/he causes, but sometimes some people simply have to be asked to leave.

Before you get anything else, get enthusiasm. Keep successful and positive company – those who can stimulate and inspire you. The company you keep *will* have its influence on you and the reverse is also true. Do you spread excitement and energy around, or doom and gloom?

• Followers need leaders, and leaders need time alone to think and plan, to set goals and make decisions for the future.

• If you don't manage your own time, others will manage it for you.

• Are you free in your task or driven to it? Driven people will sacrifice friends and family alike for the sake of achievement.

• Remember the Sabbath, it will enable you to keep all else in its proper perspective. If God needed it, so do you.

• Your voice can be your greatest asset, or your greatest liability, when working with people.

• Qualifications are no substitute for proficiency and experience. Sometimes they merely paper over the gaps.

Chapter Seven

NEGOTIATION

- A contract represents an exchange, but a total imbalance of power is not a bargaining situation. Can you correctly identify your own power?

- You must know your own worth to bargain from a position of strength.

- Can you identify a position of strength? It comes from authority, power, goodwill, indebtedness, information or circumstance.

- Don't allow one party to assume authority, position or power which they don't have. Power is as power is perceived to be.

- The choice may be either to conflict for scarce commodities with a no-win or win-lose result, or else co-operate to achieve similar goals.

- Always think through the possible deals *before* going in to bargain. The one who tries to think on his feet usually loses.

- The life of a contract should always be limited to a certain period, for the pressures of time and circumstance can tear it apart.

- Ideally the bargainer needs an aid as a witness and as added strength.

- In order to survive, the powerless usually resort to manipulation, blackmail or bullying. They would be better advised to build up goodwill by service.

- Be realistic, and be prepared to move on your initial position. Remember you have to live together.

- Never concede anything without getting something in return. What is not costly to you may be highly prized by the other.

- Take time to identify and define exactly what it is you want, and exactly what it is that the other wants.

- 'Can we negotiate on that' is a good response to an unreasonable or unexpected demand. So is 'no', when accompanied with alternatives.

- Sometimes the perfect response to a demand is no response at all.

- 'It's not *my* problem, it's *our* problem' is more likely to be the truth when you're being 'dumped on'.

- *Never* negotiate with confirmed bullies, despots, and liars. Such 'deals' will *always* cause you pain, for an agreement is only as useful as the reliability of the parties to it. A deal with an untrustworthy party is no deal at all.

- An 'I win, you lose' kind of contract is not in *either* party's long-term interests. 'Be not unequally yoked', the Bible reminds us.

- Wordless expectations that are not met, are the hidden cause of most disputes.

- Can the contract cope with changes in supply, demand, circumstance, or shifts in power?

- A good contract combines the resources of two or more parties to work together in a common interest.

- A good match is only achieved by honest discussion of what is actually wanted.

- Any agreement is only as good as the faithfulness and reliability of the parties who sign it, and that can only be known from history.

- Do not confuse poverty with powerlessness. Though the poor may be powerless, it is not *primarily* because they are poor, but because they have a 'poverty conscious-ness' of their own value and an inability to recognise their real value and resources.

- God does not strike bargains with His children. He promises to supply everything we need, and we are to respond by abiding within His revealed will.

- Errors must be apologised for in the same arena in which they were made. A quiet apology will not undo a noisy insult.

Five phases to bargaining

PREPARE. What do you actually want – the maximum and minimum. Prioritise your desires.

PROPOSE. Each states their position, 'as things stand'.

NEGOTIATE. Tentative offers – signalling of flexibility and willingness to negotiate.

AGREEMENT. If you . . . then I will . . .

RATIFICATION. (Documentation.)

Chapter Eight

THE 'NEW AGE'

Its basic presuppositions are that we are all gods, rein-
carnation is our destiny, there is no death, and that each
person has the power to define their own reality or 'truth'.
The New Age belief is *eclectic*, i.e. it draws its beliefs from
paganism, Eastern religions, occultism, quantum physics,
psychology, etc.

Six Main Beliefs

1.   A new age (Aquarius), a new spirituality, a time of
conscious evolution, a time of crisis and opportunity. The
ascendence of a new world-view giving and bringing peace
and harmony.

*The Christian hope is in the promise and power of God who
works in all things after the purpose of His will. Hope is not in
evolution, but in God's reign and Christ's manifestation/return.*

2.   All is one. This is known as 'foundational monism'. It
is supposed to be *the* great liberating truth. There are no
boundaries between God, man and nature. There are no
real dualisms, only apparent ones, and the ultimate state
of consciousness transcends all boundaries. There are not
many selves but one self. All current world problems are
caused by non-holistic world views.

*The Christian view is that God has created distinctions, i.e. a
plural order that is held together by Christ. Neither is God an
undifferentiated unity but a tri-unity. Good is 'in relationship'
with God, and evil is 'alienated' from God.*

3.   'All' is God. Synonymous with pantheism. Brahman and
Tao are synonymous with the 'force', an impersonal energy
– an 'it'.

The Christian view is that God stands beyond and distinct from His creation. Although present, He is not to be confused with it. When God created, He caused things to be 'other than' himself. God is not an amoral entity but a moral agent. The great 'I am' is not the great 'It is'. God is a personal being of infinite power and holiness.

4.   We are all God. We are 'deity unawares'. Kneel to your own self, honour and worship your own being, God dwells within you as you. (Atman IS Brahman . . . as above, so below.) Pray to the best in yourself. Self-actualising psychologies claim that all power, knowledge and truth lie within. 'You are unlimited, you just don't realise it.'

The Christian view is that we are not God, we are not infinite, all-powerful or everywhere-present. We are finite, personal and sinful. We are creatures. We may reflect God but we are not God. Our contact with God comes as we acknowledge our spiritual deprivation and entrust ourselves to God's acceptance in Christ.

5.   Our consciousness must be transformed. An 'awakening' must trigger a new awareness. This may come through meditation, yoga, drugs, bio-feedback, sensory deprivation, visualisation, martial arts, hypnosis, or consciousness-raising seminars which all employ methods to bring this about. At this point, 'higher' powers are activated. Reality is whatever you perceive it to be – you create your own reality. You are lord of your own universe. There are as many real worlds as there are people. NB Many realities contradict the concept of 'all is one', but the intellect is said to misunderstand, it is the error. (Therefore all statements are false.) This higher consciousness puts us beyond good and evil. In 'truth' therefore, there is no morality – no good or evil.

The Christian view is that our problem is not ignorance of our divinity but our rebellious and sinful nature that separates us from God. Within we find the problem, not the answer. When fully trained we will clearly distinguish good and evil (Hebrews 5:14). Psychic power is warned of in the Bible again and again as being the way to open a Pandora's box of psychological destruction. These are all realms that God declares 'off limits'.

6. All religions are one. The new-age Jesus is a figure of the new-age imagination. Their 'Christ consciousness' is not Jesus of Nazareth in the biblical sense, but a self-consciousness in a mystical sense. It may be anything that mediates my 'god' to me, or which acts as an agent in self-actualisation.

'The scandal of Christianity is its exclusivity.' No other figure than the one we know as Jesus Christ combines the being of humanity with the being of God in a simultaneous act of judgement and reconciliation, God's 'Yes' and 'No' to us. No other figure than Jesus of Nazareth claims to be the only way in to the knowledge of God.

Questions

If all is one, how can individual souls exist and receive reward or punishment? If the cosmic oneness is neither good nor bad, how can there be good or bad karma? (If we create our own reality there would be no karma imposed on us, because we are in charge.) If karma is a universal system of justice, how is it that we must be punished for lives we cannot even remember? If all is one, how is it that it has no connections with the Christian faith? What does evolvement depend on? Surely not right and wrong!!

Conclusions

There is only one scripture in the Bible where humans are told they can become gods. See Genesis 3:4–5. New Age taps into many spiritual sub-cultures including pantheistic philosophy, New Thought, Christian Science, Unity, Spiritualism, Transcendentalism, and Theosophy. Holistic education appeals to all kinds of experiential learning and is often part of the phenomena. It is an eclectic religion which teaches the age-old lie; that we can find fulfilment, (eternal life) *within ourselves* . . . that we can be 'like God'. (Human pride and selfishness cannot be dismissed by a self-centred change of consciousness, self cannot save itself *from* itself. It *must* have outside help.) The New-Age world-view can be called 'Cosmic Humanism'. The old 'secular humanism' which has expanded to cosmic dimensions. Its God-talk has *no* objective controls. It is like a monkey insisting that it is God – until it discovers itself locked in a zoo. (New-Agers may be difficult to reach until they discover that things have got out of hand and they are no longer in control.)

IT APPEALS TO: Our quest for spiritual experience and meaning – our desire to understand ourselves as something more than animals. ('You are God' is better than 'you are dust'.) The central focus and self-aggrandisement of man – Its appeal to mystery and secret knowledge. Refer to Gnosticism. *Self-actualisation in a Christian sense will include self-denial in a human sense.*

Chapter Nine

THE UNEMPLOYED

- Your own attitude is your greatest asset, or your worst liability, and is of *far more* importance than the state of the economy. Your powerlessness comes not from your circumstances, but from your misbeliefs.

- Assess your resources; interests, skills, locality, tools etc and seek to make the most of what you *have* got, rather than focus on what you haven't.

- Keep hoping for the best, but be prepared to do the worst meanwhile.

- Most firms no longer advertise, but simply contact those who have already contacted them, and begin by offering them casual work only.

- Are you waiting for the perfect job? There isn't one. Look for possibilities first of all.

- Work experience is of far more value than money in the long run.

- To develop a sense of hopelessness, simply do nothing. Beware complacency, it can erode your life while you sit in front of the TV.

- Structure your day *the day before*, and you will have something to get up for. The first hour of every day is the critical one.

- A goal will motivate you where nothing else can. Everyone needs a cause they can live for.

- Have you asked your Heavenly Father for His help? If not, what are you waiting for?

- Nothing to do? How is the state of your house and garden – your parents' house and garden – your elderly neighbour's? There is *always* plenty of work about, the problem is in how we perceive it.

- Society always has, and always will reward those who *make themselves useful*. Don't give up, keep knocking. Eventually it *will* pay off.

- Everyone has marketable talents – what skills did you use to do the things you have enjoyed doing in your life?

- Others can decide whether or not your *job* becomes redundant, but only *you* can decide whether or not *you* are redundant.

- Your natural incentive is undermined by the presence of subconscious lies which continually betray your cause. Counselling will help you identify and replace them with the truth.

- Circumstances have no power to affect you in a negative way unless you *choose* a negative response, but the attitude you choose depends on how you perceive your resources. Is your assessment really correct?

- Do your relatives a favour – ask them to *help* you in your search for meaningful work. They will have contacts and resources which you know nothing about, and they can spread your net much wider than you can spread it yourself.

- Your feelings automatically follow the attitude you adopt, so monitor your thoughts carefully and don't ever allow despair to go unchallenged.

- Get any outstanding debt repayment structured quickly, for the knowledge of it will continually undermine your enthusiasm. Go and explain your predicament, *before* the situation gets out of hand.

- Some people draw their self-esteem from their job or occupation, some from their house or car, some from their wife, husband or children. The one thing they all have in common is that they are all vulnerable to life-crushing disappointment when these things fail or are taken from them. The love of God found in Christ is the *only* sure foundation for one's sense of self-worth.

- If you can't find a job that fits, design your own job, and then locate the key people who need your services. *Take charge*.

- What is your mission in life? Your fantasy can come true, at least in part, if *you* will organise it.

- Your initiative is your best friend during a time of unemployment, but it must be developed by taking a creative approach. Put it to work today.

- Keep your dress and appearance tidy, it will help you to believe in yourself, and also enables others to believe in your willingness to try.

- Work on your voice – it conveys as much as everything else taken together, and may be a great asset, or a great liability.

Chapter Ten

WAR AND PEACE

- Militant aggression by *any* governmental authority for expansionist reasons destroys the peace and victimises weaker countries. It is unjust, and therefore by divine command (given to the office of government – the State – to maintain justice) must be held in control by peace-loving allied governments who act in accord with *just* principles – viz:

a. That hostilities be as limited and focused as possible to crippling the military might of the aggressor, attempting always to limit civilian casualties, who themselves are the victims of their ruling tyrants.
b. That offensives stop just as soon as the aggressive government is stripped of its military might and power.
c. That peace-loving nations act in accord, and are constantly in communication with each other concerning their movements and beliefs.
d. That all offensives are ultimately for the purpose of restoring peace and stability to friend and foe alike.
e. That aggression will be entered into only if the war is deemed winnable, and that maximum effort will be immediately put forward against the aggressors military machine to do this in as efficient a manner as possible.
f. That every effort to negotiate with, and/or pressurise the aggressor by embargoes etc is first of all exhausted, and seen to be exhausted, and that, by the prayers of believers everywhere, application to Christ is made for divine intervention, in order that all may be assured that the tragedy of war is indeed necessary. As many as possible of the allied nations should be in agreement

on just *when* the time for talk becomes superseded by the need to control with force.

g. That the lines of communication be kept *open* with opposing hostile nations in order that negotiations may re-convene whenever desired.

- Remember that all war is first of all an *ideological* conflict. Every effort therefore should be made by peace-loving nations to warn governments that certain attitudes likely to end in aggression should not be promulgated within their administrations, e.g. Anti-semitism, apartheid, utopianism, nationalism (my country, right or wrong) triumphalism, fascism, racism, expansionism, sectarianism, tyranny, totalitarianism, etc. The battle is against *wrong beliefs*, so in a very real sense, *every* armed force mistakes its real enemy.

- When the situation begins to deteriorate to open slaughter (when the innocent are taking more pain than the aggressors) then military action should *cease completely* to prevent *total annihilation of both sides*. At this point a policy of total non-violent, non-co-operation with the enemy should be adopted and a truce called for. (This should occur *before* the use of nuclear weapons is even considered and before the environment is made uninhabitable.)

- Beware the power-hungry opportunists waiting in the wings to take advantage of the situation.

- Every participant has hidden knives and friends with hidden knives. Beware of escalation – it knows *no* winners.

- Do *not* use a sledge-hammer to crack a nut, least you destroy the entire banquet. *Nuclear* devices are just such a hammer.

- '*Never* go to war with one hand tied behind your back.'

- To use physical force in the name of Christ is *always* a contradiction in terms. Christ's power is not 'of this world'. The state however, 'bears the sword' as necessary to fulfilling its mandate to maintain order and justice, within its own area of authority.

- 'The revelation of Christ crucified redefines our understanding of power and success, and challenges our use of human force to achieve anything' (Maltmann). Can you imagine Christ carrying an AK47?

- The follower of Christ *always* sides with the oppressed, but the oppressed are *always* found on *both* sides.

- Every inch you give the aggressor makes him stronger. 'Evil flourishes when good men do nothing.' If you love your enemy, do not indulge him in his evil way, but do whatever is necessary to stop him adding to his guilt.

- There are no pacifists amongst law-enforcement agents, nor does anybody expect them to face aggressive gunmen without weapons of their own. 'Do they *serve* Christ's cause or *oppose* it?', is a question which every Christian should face up to.

- The need of the self-righteous to be guiltless before God underlies the appeal of pacifistic philosophy. (Even Bonhoeffer, in his effort to kill Hitler, did not try to justify himself or his actions, but left the question of his justification entirely with the One who alone can justify.)

- For what *cause* would you die? In defence of your family, your ideals, your land, your faith, civilised society, or other peoples' rights? If there is nothing that you would die to protect, then what do you have to live for?

- The *profit* motive is behind most wars – the lust for resources and power – and which nation has not contributed to the aggressors strength? Do not assist the tyrant, or you will share in his guilt.

- In a world where *every* decision affects our neighbour, there is no longer any room for unilateral decisions about war.

- *Don't* become so mesmerised by the Israeli cause that you give it unqualified and unquestioning support. If you love her, you must also oppose her injustices. Criticising Israel must *never* become off-limits, or forces of mind-control will be unleashed.

• If Christians may not bear arms, then they may not support the police ever bearing arms or the army, without being inconsistent. The result however, will be the loss of all law and order.

• 'Pacifism is an unrealistic sentimentalising of the Christian view and will result in the loss of all liberty and justice' (Reinhold Neibuhr).

• 'God talk' is very dangerous in times of war. Always ask 'what are the objective controls on it', for God's will is claimed by every king with an ulterior agenda (Alan Torrance).

• Employing professionals to do our killing allows us to wage war without emotional involvement, and we become isolated from our own deeds. To avoid doing evil our soldiers must come from all levels of society.

• Beware of the technology that allows us to wage war without the need to identify with the pain of our victims.

• Could the beliefs of the 'justified' army be wrong? There is an arrogance endemic to power which will sacrifice others rather than admit to its own mistakes.

• If governments lie or cover up, it proves they know their decisions are unacceptable to the people in whose names they govern.

• To wage war is always a deliberate choice, and killing in order to prevent tyranny or greater killing will always be an uncomfortable decision.

• No officer or enlisted man should fight in a war the issues of which he knows little.

• All children should be taught how to recognise imperialism, the escalation of revenge, and uncritical submission to authority as the chief causes of war.

- Before we judge another nation we should first judge ourselves.

- A fatalistic attitude to war will always prove fatal.

Further reading:
People of the Lie, by M. Scott Peck
Nuclear Holocaust and Christian Hope, by Ronald J. Sider and Richard K. Taylor.
The Peace of Christ in a Nuclear Age, by Ray Galvin.

Chapter Eleven

Working Mums

- Living fully extended as you do, leaves you little emotional reserve to draw on in emergencies. Be honest with your family in times when you're struggling. It will help them make allowances and take some of the pressure off you.

- Household tasks – are they really important? Get your priorities right and let the non-necessary things go, to spend what free time you have with your family.

- It's true – just being physically present all day with your child is not what makes you a good mother, but an absent mother is no mother at all.

- Why are you working? Was it financial circumstances? Or was it because you've never known or been enthused by the rewards of child-raising? Whatever your reason, you yourself must be fully persuaded, or else there will be double-mindedness, guilt and confusion.

- Where is the pressure coming from? Is it people's demands on you, or is it your own unrealistic expectations for yourself?

- Are you working as well as trying to cook and clean just like your Mum did? Perhaps your expectations are unrealistic and you are being swamped by false guilt. Come out of conditional love, and live in grace.

- Spend time balancing expectations with your husband to avoid any resentment creeping in. Do it *now*.

- Remember, there will *always* be bills to pay, but you only get a few short years to enjoy shaping the basic personality of each child, and a few more to enjoy them before they have gone. If at all possible, don't spend them working for the fickle pound, or some kind of transient status, for neither will comfort you in your old age.

- We live in an age that has devalued the role of mother-hood in comparison with the dubious concerns of 'status' and materialism. How has such cultural conditioning affected you?

- If you have no inspiration to make a home, then the smallest chore can result in resentment. Don't forget to own your own decisions, and remember your ability to change your mind about what you do and don't enjoy.

- The tax structure has pushed many mothers out into the workforce, but not as many as has materialism and the devaluation of motherhood.

- Home-making and child-rearing do not come naturally to many women, but we can all learn. Our attitude and personal security have a lot to do with how we cope.

- Going to work may be a way of escaping from feeling incapable or ignored. Motives need to be examined carefully.

- If you are convinced that home-making is worthwhile, then you won't need to apologise. If you can't be proud in saying what you do, then you may need to re-evaluate what you are doing and why.

- The investment you make in your child's life is totally underrated by most teachers in society. Even the 'church' can seem condescending and take motherhood or home-making for granted, but this is *not* God's attitude, so your own attitude may need to change.

- If you must work, then choose your work carefully. How much night-time and weekend time will be taken up? How much energy will be needed? How much stress does the job cause?

- Remember your partner. You working is putting extra

demands – both physical, mental and emotional – on him too. How is he coping?

- If you work, be assured that *your* influence – if you give *quality time* to your child – *will* prevail. You are your child's most significant person in his/her early years, so *be* significant.

- Be aware of each child's different moods and personality. Baby No 1 may be socially well-adjusted and love daycare etc. Baby No 2 may not be the same. This must be a major consideration in coming to a decision about a job that is right for you.

- *Every* job has times of monotony, boredom or loneliness. It's *how you respond* to those times which determine whether yours will be a positive or negative experience.

- Identify the pressures on you, and then work out for yourself what it is that you are really looking for.

- Who do you trust to be 'mum' to your child? They should have your unqualified approval, in order that you may be free from anxiety.

- After additional clothes, petrol, fast foods, daycare, taxes, increased hire-purchases, parking tickets etc. etc. have been paid for, are you *really* going to be better off by working? And if not, then what is it that is pushing you?

- Is mothering a real bind? Take some time out to find out why. Does your husband encourage and affirm you as a mother?

- Do not simply expect gratitude from your husband for working, for in becoming more independent, you may be striking at the very heart of his fundamental need to be a good provider to you and the family.

- An empty house always breeds insecurity in a child.

Ideas for earning from home

There are many ways to supplement the family income while working from home. Such endeavours enable home-makers to fulfil family responsibilities as well as developing their talents, character, independence and, most impor-tantly, their self-respect. Consider the biblical account of the industrious woman in Proverbs 31.

- Crafts: sewing children's clothes, wedding dresses, hand and machine knitting, leather jackets, cushions, quilts, wooden toys. Market these anywhere possible (including a roadside stall).

- Take in outside work: ironing, washing (shirts, rugby jerseys, curtains), typing theses, caring for neighbours' children, accounting, assisting with tax returns, design-ing (e.g. garden plans or clothes), poster painting, sign writing, wedding bouquets, cake decorating.

- Rent yourself as a: party cook, grocery gatherer, com-puter operator, word processor, cleaner, dog walker, gardener, lawn-mower, window cleaner, animal feeder, pot plant waterer over holidays, car valet, removal packer, counsellor, hairdresser, exam supervisor.

- Make and sell: vegetables, home baking to professional friends on a fortnightly basis, propagated plant cuttings. Make jam annually and freeze veg on contract. Make toys, dog kennels, bird tables, wind chimes, garden furniture.

- Garage sales on main roads or near universities, etc. (Old plates, pot plants, cutlery, clothing, furniture, etc.) Or let your high-profile garage out to others to have their garage sales in.

- Direct Marketing.

- First learn, then teach, using: polytechnics, W.E.A., colleges of technology, university extension, teachers' colleges, art schools, Access, YWCA, correspondence courses, Open University, library books.

'When your output exceeds your intake, the upkeep will
be your downfall.' Your choice is always either to decrease
your expenditure or increase your earnings but remember:
living beyond your means will always catch up. (See also
chapter on *Debt*.) Remember, your problem is not so much
one of predicament and lack of opportunity, but in the
attitude you take to your own talents and the opportunities
that are all around you. (And try to be gracious to the
person who teased you, when they come back begging for
a loan!)

Further reading:
The Working Mother's Guide to Sanity, by Elsa Howitz.

Part 2

Wisdom for Healing in Heart and Habit

Chapter Twelve

ANGER

Anger is a sudden release of emotional energy needed to make change. It *must* be mastered and channelled, or it can control and damage us and those around us. To be controlled however, it must first be understood. Because it is neutral in itself, it is what we *do* with it which determines whether it is positive or negative in its influence in our lives and families. You can slam a door or call a conference – shout abuse or write a letter of complaint – strike out or go for a walk.

Anger and frustration are experienced in varying degrees by *everybody who feels threatened,* and everybody has developed their own way of handling them. (Having a Christian faith is *no guarantee* that a person will be any better at handling them than anybody else.)

Question:
- *How do you express anger?*
- *Are you an erupter or a stifler?*
- *Which way do you react?*
- *Are you a wrestler or an accommodator of life's problems – uptight and inflexible or relaxed and easy-going?*

Both 'clamming up' and 'blowing up' are unhelpful. We can ventilate by yelling, smashing something or attacking somebody, but this stimulates further aggression and damages relationships. (Remember, 'for lack of fuel the fire goes out'.) Alternatively, 'clamming up' can internalise the anger, resulting in an active (rebellion) or passive (depression) mind-set. Resentments, having accumulated over time, can suddenly boil over in an uncharacteristic act of violence. (Look out for the kid that is picked on,

and becomes full of pent-up frustration. Buried resentments can tick like a time bomb for many years, until
something triggers its rage.) Such suppression can also
result in physical sickness, e.g. ulcers, indigestion, high
blood pressure, skin diseases. Refusal to face the conflict
or analyse the problem leads to habits of escapism which
ultimately leave us hiding from life and love. We usually
refuse to face the problem because *we do not know how to
tackle it without making it worse.*

There are, in general terms, two kinds of anger; **Reactionary** and **Life-dominating:**

- REACTIONARY ANGER is caused by actions and incidents; e.g. a child disobeys and the parent reacts; the
  shop assistant is rude and the client reacts; the car won't
  start, one's spouse won't co-operate, the boss makes
  an unfair accusation. These are incidents . . . incidental
  anger. All these things represent a disappointment of
  expectations . . . the greater the disappointment, the
  greater the anger. This kind of anger doesn't last long
  and is easily defused by making a space, e.g. doing
  something else for a while.

- LIFE-DOMINATING ANGER. A bitter root of stifled
  anger which runs through all one's thoughts and actions.
  (Often present in marriages.) Again the causes must be
  located, e.g. **Self-hatred** can come from parental rejection
  (whether real or perceived) at an early age ('My parents
  hate me, therefore I am rejected.'). **Life's injustices**
  stimulate us to respond in deep-seated anger and frustration at life and God. (Someone you love died and deep
  down inside, you feel that God let you down, and you've
  never forgotten.) Stealing and withdrawal from intimacy
  are often caused by an underlying anger.

DEEP DISAPPOINTMENT in self or others means we
can carry a perpetual grudge, which flares up with any
minor provocation – touch a tender spot and the pain is
magnified.

UNREALISTIC EXPECTATIONS from an unconscious need for others to be 'perfect' – which is continually bringing disappointment to the 'victim'. (People who have been 'hurt' by the church, and who have concluded that Christ is not to be trusted and that all Christians are hypocrites come in this category.) Perfectionists have a deep-seated insecurity, and need to see that they are 'setting up' other people for failure, and themselves for disappointment.

A LEARNED RESPONSE. Because of parents who might tease their children, or indulge temper tantrums (both their own and their children's) that person believes their ventilation is acceptable and gives it unbridled expression. 'Blowing up' simply becomes a well-entrenched habit which must be confronted and opposed by those who love them and the person themselves. Remember, thoughts activate one's emotional response. Change your thinking habits to get proper control – e.g. when something doesn't go the way you want it to, instead of fuming, fussing and cussing, try just reminding yourself that, really, it doesn't matter, and then let it go. We all need to learn to lay down our rights and learn to do what is best for the other person. Here are some do's and don'ts to help you.

DON'T

- DON'T indulge your mind in angry thoughts of bitter accusation and defensiveness, or violence.

- DON'T dump your anger on others – stay with the source of the problem.

- DON'T make excuses for your angry and destructive behaviour. Instead, choose to channel it in a constructive way.

- DON'T see everybody else's anger as a personal attack on you. You may not be the real cause at all.

- DON'T forget that nobody else can make you angry. You choose to get angry all by yourself. (Taking responsibility for yourself.)

- DON'T continue the argument if it is escalating rather than moving to resolution.

DO

- DO forgive yourself as well as others for past disappointments.

- DO learn to lower your expectations when appropriate. (Is it their behaviour or my expectations that need to be adjusted.)

- DO try and understand the provocateur's behaviour, e.g. 'He must be really under pressure/hurting to overreact like that.'

- DO try and identify the *real* source of the conflict. Where is it really coming from? Why did I overreact like that? What is there in me that's hurting? Why do I feel threatened?

- DO value your anger as the energy you need to make the necessary changes.

- DO learn to distinguish between trivialities and serious injustice.

- DO ask yourself, 'Am I enjoying my anger?' If so, why continue to indulge it?

Helpful ways of expressing anger are:

- Calling a conference of the affected people to talk the issues out.
- Writing a letter of complaint, factually stating your case and what you expect to have done.
- Forgiving the offender by realising that they also are a victim.
- Reflecting upon the real reasons for your own overreaction, e.g. unrealistic expectations or a threat.

WARNING. When seeking to talk the matter out, or venting it, be careful of merely rehearsing it. Discussion can lead to practical solutions, but it can also become obsessive and self-perpetuating, 'fuelling the fire' as it were.

Finally, take note of God's advice to Cain (history's first murderer) 'Look, sin is crouching at the door, and wants to overcome you, but you must master it' (Genesis 4).

Further study may be done from the scriptures listed below.

Proverbs 14:29 The even-tempered are wise.

Proverbs 19:11 To overlook an offence is to our credit.

Proverbs 29:11 The fool 'blows up' (25:28). Like a defence-less city.

Isaiah 26:3 Keep your mind focused on God's providence.

Mark 3:5 A display of Jesus' anger.

John 14:27 A peace beyond our circumstances.

Ephesians 4:26 Be angry, yet do not sin. 4:15 Speak the truth . . . lovingly.

James 1:5 God's patience with us.

James 1:19 Man's anger not like God's.

James 4:7 Submit to God, resist the destroyer.

Further Reading:
How to Really Love Your Teenagers, by Ross Campbell.
Caring Enough To Confront, by David Augsberger.
Emotions – Can We Trust Them? by James Dobson.

I trust that as you have followed this study you have gained insight into this important and neglected topic. I hope that parents who have gained insight into dealing with anger will pass on their wisdom to their children – it may well be one of the best things they ever do for them.

Chapter Thirteen

ANOREXIA

Description

It is self-imposed starvation for a 'better' self-image and self-assertion and is almost always confined to young Western women. It begins as a self-imposed discipline and progressively becomes a dominating concern. It is the one thing which they can do well – better than anyone else. It is a 'refuge' from pain, a distorted way of acting out repressed inner hurt. It is a tyranny which replaces another tyranny in the girl's life. It is really an exercise in 'reclaiming' her body, and her control over it. It is self-control gone berserk and usually involves an obsession with calories, dieting, exercise, avoidance of meals, looking for fat, feeling fat, and social isolation. The normal amount of food is interpreted as far too much. Eating feels disgustingly greedy to the victim. They are pursuing a feeling of lightness and purity and control. 3% of teenagers are anorexic to some degree, and 80% of teenage girls generally believe that they are overweight, thus it is a popular myth which becomes a controlling misbelief in these girls. (5–10% of young girls get bulimic at some stage. Alternate fasting and bingeing with purging is more often a separate condition, in which the patient, unlike the anorexic, is well aware of the nature of their problem.) Frequently they are the 'good' girls who conform in every other area of their lives, the perfectionists for whom 99% is not good enough. The victim begins to fragment in person, as she begins to pull in two different directions. Which is right? Her own sense of perception becomes distorted, making her unable to judge her own body size. Losing weight gives a much needed sense of achievement and control which becomes addictive. The desire to diet gets out of hand and finally masters the girl. Being thin becomes the main object of life. Their own sense of reality – their perception – their 'interpreter' – is damaged, making them unable to judge their own body size. 'It was weird, the jeans just fell off me, yet I still felt really big in them. It was strange, because I know that when I used to wear them, I wasn't fat then, I was really slim.' The anorexic risks cardiac arrest followed by death, starvation or suicide, becoming infertile, or doing irreversible damage to their health. In one sense anorexia is a subconscious defence against a more immediate suicidal desire. It is a defence mechanism against something much more threatening – the fragmentation of the psyche. In general, the sooner the condition is caught, the sooner they recover.

Causes

The causes are many and varied, and each case should be treated on its own merits, rather than considering it as a stereotype. However some general comments may help provide a way in to the epidemiology. Self-loathing generally is a kind of death wish for that part of one's character which has been determined as deserving of it. It is often triggered by sexual or mental abuse, or conclusions that one is a failure. (A man who hates himself will in turn hate the girl he 'loves', who in turn will learn to hate herself.)

Childhood and teenage conclusions about themselves, reactions against parental control, rejection, sexual abuse, or not developing social acceptance, is usually at the root of it. As she thins down, she gets admiring comments, which all reinforce her desperately needed feelings of success. It may be a reaction against the womanhood that has got her into so much trouble – a return to the safe neuterdom of childhood. An over-powering fear of fatness causes the mind to misinterpret and to reinterpret everything it sees. 'I'm already far too fat.' There is a subconscious desire to destroy that part of oneself that one hates so much. Sometimes the dirtiness they feel inside gets projected onto

the world around them and they become 'germ phobic'.
(Sexual intercourse in a context of manipulation, where the
girl is deeply ambivalent in regard to her willingness, has
the same destructive consequences as rape.) Some anorexics
were abused or felt rejected as children, and have learnt
to hate their bodies as the only reason for it that they
can find. These wrong conclusions about themselves often
come from peer, sexual or parental abuse. Such need to
be reconciled with their parents in order to help them
forgive and reinterpret what happened. Most anorexics are
very sensitive to criticism. Feelings of guilt or failure are
common to them. So is a fear of eating in front of people.
The thought of eating and putting on weight can reduce
them to panic.

The Way Forward

The need for her to recognise that she has a serious problem,
is the first step to healing. She must realise that she does not
in fact want to die. Then she must, if at all possible, submit
herself to her parents' care and guidance, re-learning to
accept herself. She should place the right to interpret her
own image in another's hands. This might require the
healing of damaged relationships in the family, which
occurred in childhood, in order to again submit to an
authority other than self. Remember, her refusal to eat
food is only the symptom of a previous problem. It is not
the cause and should not be treated as the real issue, so
stay off the subject of eating, and do not try to force feed.
Self-hatred, evoked by every pound regained, is scary for
it brings the girl back to face up to the original threat.

Questions to begin with

- Who imposed on her the image she has of herself?
- What previous experience is she trying to starve out of
  her body?
- When and why did she first experience the feelings of
  being out of control of her life?
- Whose approval was she trying to gain in the first
  place?

- What factors precipitated the vulnerability to manipulation etc?
- What makes up the list of things she couldn't do properly or well, when she first began to diet?
- Is there a controlling or manipulating mother who dominates her?

Male therapists (good ones) are essential to helping women work through their threatened feelings about men in general. The girl must learn how to accept her body *as it is*. Try to guide her out of the passive 'victim' role. Help her to regain her power over her own life. One-to-one with a therapist, a support group, reading books by other sufferers, keeping a journal and art work are all useful tools in externalising the pain and achieving cathartic release and reintegration. When this new awareness comes, forgiveness of self and others comes with it. N.B. Forgiveness can only come after insight, catharsis, expressed grief, etc. Confession of that which is disgusting and of which she is deeply ashamed may be needed to enable her to recognise her defence mechanism for what it is. New skills for protection and nurture need to be learnt, to replace the armament of anorexia. N.B. If 'treatment' for the anorexic, via institutionalisation, is rendering her powerless, those feelings which triggered her condition in the first place will be strengthened. Losing her power over her own habits, while it may be necessary for her short-term survival, is in fact enforcing her resolve to rigidly control the only thing she can, the intake of her own body. Would you eat a plate of cold, lumpy porridge under duress. Of course not – especially under duress, but that's how it feels to these girls when you insist that they eat. Allow her to choose the food she can eat.

Conclusion

Never care for the anorexic as a stereotype; she is an individual and her way in to the addiction is not the same as anyone else's. Once she is no longer afraid and ashamed, she must also then re-learn to eat three balanced

meals per day. Those who work with anorexics are highly
prone to burn-out, because of the low rate of recovery. But
recovery is always possible. Pray that by then it will not be
too late. Parents of anorexics, and especially mothers, must
throw away their guilt, it is not in any way helpful. They
should also look to their own care, for they often become
surrogate anorexics. The family goes through the stages of:
denying that there is a problem, then arguing and stormy
scenes, then a very bad patch of guilt, shame and worry.
Parents must realise that during this time, understanding is
more important than getting her to eat more. Again it must
be said that anorexia is a symptom of earlier problems.

Relevant Scripture:
James 5:16. Confess your faults one to another and pray.
James 1:8 A double-minded man is unstable in all his
    ways.
Psalm 32. When I kept quiet about my sin . . .

Further Reading:
Starving for Attention, by Debbie Boon.
The Anorexic Experience, by Marilyn Lawrence, published
    by the Women's Press.
'Beating Anorexia – A Survivors Story' *MORE Magazine*,
    November 1990.
Puppet on a String, by Helena Wilkinson.

Chapter Fourteen

DECISION MAKING

Notes

- The need does not always constitute the call. You may be surrounded by demands on your time and services, but what are you particularly gifted at or interested in? Do that, and do it well.

- Learn to say no to demands on your time and resources that are not in harmony with your own God-given priorities.

- 'Yes' is a good servant, and a bad master, but then so is 'no'.

- Time is your most limited, and most precious asset. Don't allow other people to use yours for you, unless you can give it wholeheartedly.

- The decision to walk in self-denying love at all times should undergird *all* our decisions about how to speak and act and decide. (And love can be tough, on both the giver and receiver.)

- The first question which you should ask yourself is: How does this decision affect those things that are of most importance to me? e.g. relationships, values, goals, self-image.

- When decisions are to be made, learn to think in terms of long-term consequences, instead of merely short-term reward.

- The Christian's daily guidance is to allow Christ to live His life, through their person – and He will always live for others.

- Bad decisions are caused by either never having had a clear goal or sense of direction in the first place, or else through not having the necessary information available.

  Any decision is only as good as the information that goes into it.

- Remember, you can't actually make a decision until all the facts are in, but don't keep procrastinating indefinitely. For better or worse there comes a time when you must make a move. Move ahead slowly.

- When praying for something, remember that 'no' and 'not yet' are also answers.

- Without access to the divine self-giving Spirit, how will you ever gain freedom from the power of a lifetime of conditioned, self-serving desires which constantly influence your judgement?

- Great opportunities are often disguised as troubled situations. Look for the opportunities to learn new lessons.

- Get training, the best you can. In this complex civilisation, it's too dangerous, too difficult, too time-consuming, to teach yourself. But choose your teacher carefully, to obtain the benefit of many years of past failures and painful mistakes. (Remember also, that when fully trained, you will become like your teacher.)

- Only God has all the facts. Your decisions will always have an element of the unknown in them. Take one step at a time.

- The ultimate objectives of the group (according to the constitution) must remain uppermost in the leadership's mind, in order to maintain unity of direction. But remember, the constitution must not oppose the will of God, or else it has no legitimate place in the world.

- Looking for a new direction in life? What things do you really feel strongly about/enjoy doing? They will be your clue to new endeavours.

- Never do anything at odds with your own conscience. It can be your cruellest and most persistent opponent. If in doubt, wait.

- To discover that you are not, and can never be, in over-all control, is a good thing, providing you also discover that your Heavenly Father is.

- Bad waiting says 'When the situation is perfect, then I'll move.' Good waiting says 'First I'll do all that I can do, then I'll wait expectantly on God to come through.'

- Getting your guidance clear is difficult, for your own desires are always entangled. Are you open to the advice which you don't want to hear?

- If you have to break down every door, God is probably not 'in it'.

- Beware of impulsive, 'feel-good' decisions. Feelings do not make reliable guides.

- If you make the wrong choice, don't get mad at God. Mistakes, even serious ones, are a natural part of growing up, and have already been allowed for.

- Mistakes and pain are merely feedback on how you are doing. They are an essential part of the learning process.

- To hear God's voice of direction, you must first want to know His will.

- Having made the decision, will you accept, and continue to accept responsibility for the consequences, or will you try to escape the result and avoid cause-and-effect?

- Before you can deal with your situation, you must first face up to it, and before you do that, you must dispense with all methods of avoidance, which may include drugs and tranquillisers.

- Every decision is a stepping-stone, they are only truly foolish if you don't learn from them.

- Always carry a metaphorical 'letter of resignation' in

case of certain decisions which may be foisted upon you, otherwise you have no bottom line, and are therefore vulnerable to manipulation and complete control.

- If you get the early decisions right to begin with, the future will simply get better and better.

- A problem, clearly identified, is half solved. What exactly is the dilemma?

- What is your mission in life? Your dream can come true, at least in part, if you will organise it.

- Divine guidance is not a tightrope. Adopt a positive 'green-light', rather than a negative 'red-light' attitude toward life and guidance. 'In all your ways, acknowledge Him.'

- Do not go on a mission until you have first built up your resources. ('No man builds a tower . . .')

- Guidance is not like walking a tightrope. If you truly love God and people, then do what you will and it will please Him.

- Do not confuse faith with fatalism. There are no 'straight lines' between God and circumstances.

- Procrastination has many possible causes, and all of them exist because we are afraid to face up to our fears – failure, responsibility, criticism, etc.

- Divine guidance is not like walking a tightrope; it is more like an open field with a fence around it, within which failure is not fatal.

- Living is not for spectators. To live abundantly demands that we take risks in coming down from the grandstand and getting involved.

- Your feelings are not a reliable guide to what you should and shouldn't do. They merely reflect subconscious beliefs.

- Your future is not determined by your parentage, but

by your own choices – the choices you make today and tomorrow.

Decisions: my four-step check

1. Define the problem, and the goal, on your knees.
2. Gather information on the alternatives. 'What is the worst case-scenario if the decision is wrong.' Test your decisions out on advisers, family or friends.
3. Select the alternative.
3. Action it, then evaluate it.

Six questions to help identify the will of God

1. Is it in harmony with scriptural principles? e.g. service before self and relationships before materialistic advantage.
2. Is it ethical? (Does it consider others?)
3. Are circumstances providential? (Not a factor to be considered in isolation.)
4. Is it reasonable, ordered, and rational?
5. Are you still open to hear other alternatives?
6. Do your parents/teachers/employers/advisers/spouses approve? They can often see things which you can't.

Chapter Fifteen

Discouragement

- Can you list the thoughts and conclusions that are working against you to undermine your incentive and enthusiasm? Trace them and face them one at a time.

- Those who are vulnerable to discouragement and faint-heartedness often have four things in common:

  1. They were not verbally encouraged as children and are therefore not able to call to mind the truths necessary to defend themselves against negative conclusions.
  2. They lack any clear idea of what they want to achieve or how to go about getting it.
  3. They feel trapped and unable to see a way out of their situation.
  4. They play too passive a role in their own lives, perhaps because of a faulty concept of God where their faith is bordering on fatalism.

- If negative thoughts are dirty thoughts, how hygienic is your thought life? 'Stink' feelings follow 'stink' thinking. Remember that your mind can grow thistles or roses.

- Is the goal still worth the effort? We become reluctant to pay the price only when the rewards no longer seem sufficient.

- A society geared by qualifications presents a seemingly impossible barrier to an unqualified entrant or unemployed who wants to better themselves, yet cannot survive without an income, but where the will is strong enough, there is a way. Find some people who have done it and ask for advice.

- What are you telling yourself? Is it the truth? Will you test it against the wisdom of another who has broken through the hopelessness syndrome?

- The first priority should be to find someone to believe in you when you can hardly believe in yourself. Though you believe in Christ, are you also aware that He believes in you?

- Have you identified what your Creator wants you to do with your life? Your discouragement may simply be a warning that you are going in the wrong direction.

- It's OK to say no to a job if it really conflicts with an opportunity to train in your chosen field. Go for the best you can.

- 'Where hope is often deferred, the heart becomes sick' (Proverbs). Don't play such a passive role in your own life, if your desire is a good one, and the door won't open by itself, give it a good shove.

- If the way seems too difficult, perhaps it's simply because the resolve is weak and really needs strengthening. What is undermining it?

- Whether to 'face it or escape it', is often the issue, and the answer depends on the strength of one's resources – money, enthusiasm, wisdom, time, etc.

- What would it take to make you happy? Remember that, ultimately, happiness is your choice.

- Wisdom is knowing when to hang on and when to let go, and there is, of course, a right time for both.

- Are you suffering from a 'mental wrinkle?' Beliefs that conflict with each other need to be reconciled by the discovery of a third integrating insight, else you will remain jammed tight by intra-personal conflict.

- What you tell yourself will either invoke or quench the presence of the 'Comforter'. (You are His child and He is deeply in love with you.)

- Your concept of yourself – did it come from God or did you invent it? It will either encourage you or cripple you – bind you or free you.

- Wrong conclusions have the power to shut you out of the abundant life. Misbeliefs must be traced, faced, and displaced.

- Are you struggling with a bad habit or desire? Remember that God will only deliver us from our enemies, not our friends.

- If a thing's worth doing, it's OK to do it badly, *while I improve*. (All beginnings are hard.)

- Is there something within you that wants to hang on to your anger or fear or depression? What need are you trying to meet?

- Who were your childhood mirrors? Were they damaged? Don't look in cracked mirrors to determine your own value or self-worth.

- Behind every angry and unhappy moment there's a wrong belief. Trace the lie, face the lie, replace the lie.

- The momentum in a group can help you progress in a way you can never achieve on your own. To achieve your goal, first find those who are like-minded.

- Some learn by theory before practice, and others learn practice before theory, so some are disadvantaged in the classroom and others in the workshop. Neither should take failure personally.

Chapter Sixteen

FEELINGS AND EMOTIONS

'A rut in the mind produces a mood in the heart'

- To choose to take responsibility for our moods rather than to be subject to them, we need to first of all realise that we are not our moods. Moodiness occurs in the soulish realm, whereas we are 'spirits' who have a soul (the mind, will and emotions) and who live in a body.

- Feelings make good servants but bad masters.

- To learn to say 'no' to a mood is a mark of maturity.

- Child tantrums, if allowed to continue, grow up to become adult tantrums which result in dismissal from work, being charged with assault or just sabotaging relationships.

- If you don't feel like being civil, or controlling your anger, self-pity etc., you need to learn how to subject your feelings to discipline, or you will always remain a baby in your mental and emotional life.

- Unconditional loyalty to doing what feels good, always results in a particularly nasty form of enslavement to self.

- The goal is not to ignore our moods, or to pretend that they don't exist, but to submit them to objective assessment and to discover where they are drawing their energy from.

- To change your mood, you must first change your thinking – about who you are, about the nature of life, and about what God requires of you. Today the mental wards and jails are full of people who, through lack of insight, are in the habit of giving free reign to such moods, whether anger leading to rage, self-pity leading to depression, or selfishness leading to social isolation, with the result that as they 'go with' these changing moods, they begin to 'fly too high and fall too far'. At this point the volitional aspect is diminished and the moods take on a momentum of their own.

- In most (though not all) cases we can choose our mood just as Cain was challenged to do in Genesis 4.

- Moods are merely the appropriate feelings we have in response to the kind of thinking we have been indulging ourselves in.

- Female bio-cyclic emotions can be anticipated and pre-pared for by scheduling less-demanding activities and being careful to monitor one's own thoughts during the vulnerable time. It is also a time to draw closer to God in prayer and reflection.

- Men can learn to do the opposite of an habitual incli-nation to withdraw and internalise their thoughts and feelings in moody silence, or else 'blow up' in a rage if things don't turn out the way they had expected. Oppositional behaviour very soon weakens the strength of moods and forces new patterns of feelings to take hold. Nevertheless, the old habits have dug for themselves deep ruts and it will take some time for the new thoughts to become second nature.

- The Bible teaches us to oppose the unrestrained moods that try to govern us: '. . . do not gratify the desires of the sinful nature' (Galatians 5:16). '. . . like a city without walls' (Proverbs 25:28).

- Moods, whether good or bad, are contagious. They can spread easily to a family or group.

- Where a mood will not submit to discipline, it is likely that the trauma of a past experience needs to be 'exhumed', reinterpreted in the light of new wisdom, and allowed to find expression through the emotions.

'Don't mind me, I'm just feeling my feelings to see if my feelings are feeling the same as the time I felt the feelings I think that I'm feeling now!'

Chapter Seventeen

GOAL-SETTING

- People need goals, and any goal is better than no goal. Even a wrong goal is still a valuable learning experience.

- Not so much the goal, but the journey you take in the process, is the really important thing.

- It is important and necessary to set your goals, but remember to set them while on your knees. Involve the Lord-who-loves-you.

- Return often to your goals. They will keep you going and monitor your course.

- What might you become in the pursuit of your goals?

- Setbacks and mistakes are an essential part of the growth and learning processes. Don't miss their vital feedback.

- Define your goals by writing them down. Why do we make lists for everything except the goals of our very lives?

- It is not where you start that counts, but where you choose to finish.

- Set your goals in harmony with what it is you would like to be remembered for, long after you've gone.

- Remember that those who have succeeded 'overnight' have usually been slogging away quietly for years.

- It's scary to set goals, but all the best things in life are out on a limb. Fear of failure is itself a cause of failure and must be faced up to.

- A purpose is not a goal until it has a time limit in which it must be done.

- Are you failing? Remember that only the finish counts, and you aren't finished until you have finished.

- Winners always take more risks than losers.

- Total and absolute commitment releases assistance from a host of unexpected sources, but you'll never know it until you decide to go for it!

- Whatever you can do, or dream of – get started. Knowing and dreaming is no substitute for action.

- There is a world of difference between the statement 'I'll try it' and 'I'll do it'.

- Here's how to get whatever you want – do whatever it takes!

- No talent, or education, or opportunity can take the place of persistence. (A big shot is simply a little shot that kept shooting.)

- Quitting can easily become a habit. When you quit, do so with care!

- Your first goal should be to discover those areas God has gifted you in and cultivate them.

- Is your 'reason' for quitting, the truth, or is it merely a cop out? Such rigorous questions need to be asked.

- If all your goals are entirely restricted to this life, what will you have when you pass over?

- There is a 'wickedness' in refusing to develop one's full potential for achievement (from Matthew 25:25).

- It is achievement, rather than 'success' which is God's will for you.

- In realistically assessing your own capabilities, don't be proud or ashamed of your 'givens', for everybody is both superior and inferior in some area of their lives. It is only your character that you are responsible for.

- When you are fulfilling both a great need in your own life, as well as a need in society, you have found your vocation.

- While stubbornness doesn't guarantee success, a weak will will always guarantee failure.

- The momentum in a group can help you progress in a way you can never achieve on your own. To achieve your goal, first find those who are like-minded.

Chapter Eighteen

GRIEF

- Grief is a process – the process of letting go. If one cannot, for any reason, let go what is lost, then there will be no end to it.

- Grief sours to despair when its natural course is obstructed by avoidance or a lack of recognition. To face the loss, first trace the obstruction.

- To continue on in life, you must first accept your loss. To face your loss, you must first be sure of your resources. 'In Christ' you have all the help you need.

- Grief is your friend, encouraging you to ask the questions, without which you may never find the true meaning of life. Let it call into question your entire worldview and philosophy.

- Any loss, from a loved one to a little finger, will cause grief and will require adjustment. Traumatic bereavement may take years just to accept the fact of the loss, and years more to return to life.

- One may not relinquish what is lost, until one has something else to replace it with.

- It is love that combines two people, and when one dies the other mourns the loss of something of themselves. Grief is part of the price we pay for love.

- The funeral is an opportunity to begin to face up to what has happened, to give thanks for what that person has meant to you, and to commend him or her, to God. Never avoid the funeral of one you have loved.

- Every death needs a 'place', a memorial, a point-of-contact, at which the bereaved can mourn. This is generally the place of committal.

- Always encourage children to attend the funeral of those they knew. (Be quick to assure them that the death was 'nobody's fault' if you sense the need.)

- If you cannot attend the funeral or committal of one you love, try to get it videoed or taped. It will be of comfort and assistance to you in your grief.

- That 'time heals' is a myth. Time has no innate healing quality, it only blurs the pain. The source of the pain itself must be faced up to and dealt with.

- You are not, and have never been, alone. Jesus has always shared your pain.

- Do not expect that things will quickly get back to normal and do not run from the pain, whether by taking a trip or hiding yourself in your work – it will only postpone having to face up to it.

- A bereavement is like an amputation; it means that we must 'let go' some hopes and dreams, and it calls for a whole new approach to life.

- The 'if only's' indicate the need to pray and turn those things over to God, who alone can transform tragedy and bring life out of death.

- When the tears come, don't repress them – don't struggle to 'be strong'. Tears are part of the way we are designed, and if you don't cry on the outside, the crying inside doesn't stop.

- Don't be reluctant to share your memories of the one who has died with those who knew and loved them.

- After bereavement, don't make any hasty decisions, it's never wise to jump from a train while it's travelling through a tunnel. This is not the time to leave what is familiar.

- Several years may elapse before the grieving ceases and one feels able to return to life and living. It is always longer than expected, but it does 'come to pass'.

- 'Having faith' does not mean we will not experience anger, fear or depression. But those feelings do confirm that we are truly human.

- God is not evil. He does not plan tragic deaths, neither does He control our destiny as if we were robots, but He does promise that He will be there for us through it all. (Remember the Lord's prayer . . . His kingdom – total rule – has not yet come!)

- We all must die, and from eternity's vantage point, the length of life is not nearly so crucial as how it was lived.

- Knowledge of this world cannot be projected to tell us about life in the next. Our only source of insight into that realm must come from the One who overcame death on our behalf, and faith is the only way in to His teaching and life.

- Though you can not know the future, you may know the God to whom the future belongs. There are some things which human beings simply may not know.

- The community of people that make up your local church are an important part of Christ's answer to your prayers for hope and friendship. Ministers and priests, especially, have sought to know the truth about the meaning of death and bereavement, and they are there for you.

- If you are grieving over a miscarriage, it is helpful to name and prayerfully dedicate the baby to the Lord, and look forward to meeting that child again.

- To retreat into, and become comfortable with grief, does no honour to the memory of the one you have lost.

- From the day of her abortion a woman can be surrounded by a cloud of regret, and fearful of what God's attitude to her is. Self-destructive behaviour is often the course that her grief will take. Contrary to popular opinion, there is a need to acknowledge her guilt, and there is also a need to accept God's forgiveness in Christ specifically for that action.

- Even the mother of Moses had no choice but to give her baby up for adoption. Her act was acceptable for she dedicated the child first to the Lord. Hannah also did the same, and Samuel grew to become a man of God.

- Replacement (atonement) babies do not help alleviate the pain of abortion. Children are not interchangeable.

- Sometimes the question 'why?' has no answer, but that the kingdom of heaven has not come yet. In this world we will have tragedy, but take heart, Christ can transform all tragedy (from John 16:33).

- At the root of false guilt are emotional and mental lies. Even if our own hearts condemn us, God is greater and He alone can judge objectively.

- Most miscarriages are caused by a malformed baby, and are not in any way the fault of the mother. Such babies are short-circuited into the immediate care of God (from Psalm 22:9).

- There is a severe blessing in grief, in that it forces us to ask questions about the spiritual world which otherwise we might never ask.

- Never be afraid to touch and pray with those who are suffering; they need it more than they may care to admit, and you are giving of yourself.

- A diary is a good way to express one's thoughts and feelings if there are none to listen.

- Fatigue and exhaustion are not something to be ashamed of, but the body warning us that something is wrong, and needs some attention.

- In the midst of sorrow and pain, look for wisdom rather than pat answers.

- Be patient with, and forgive others for their insensitive remarks and actions. Holding a grudge will only magnify the pain and prolong the grief.

- Search aggressively for the answers to your questions. The more you can reduce the unknowns, the less room there will be for fear, anxiety and misconception.

- In the case of a stillbirth, parents are wise to ask to see the baby, to hold it and to say goodbye, and to keep something of the occasion.

- You can't go to God for comfort if you believe that *He* is the source of your pain. Jesus alone reveals the will of God and He identifies with us in referring to death as His enemy also, but on our behalf He has reversed its cruel effect (from John 16:33).

- God does not punish us with the death of loved ones; Christ's death on the cross has cancelled all talk of punishment (from Romans 8:1; Hebrews 2:14).

- Your feelings are your friends, listen to what they are trying to tell you.

- There is no right or wrong way to grieve – what was a 'description' of grief should never become a 'prescription'.

- Guilt is often indicative of unexpressed anger. Are you angry with the one who died?

- What were you taught about grief as a child? Was it correct?

- You can only help your children face grief to the extent that you have learned how to face it yourself.

- The tasks of grief:
  1. To accept the reality of the loss.
  2. To experience the pain of the loss constructively.
  3. To adjust the environment in which the person or thing is missing.
  4. To let go and reinvest our emotional energy.

- Grief includes our total response to loss.

- A grief response delayed or suppressed, will accumulate, and can be triggered by minor loss later. Then it erupts in anger, forgetfulness or depression.

- The grief counsellor's work is chiefly to provide a safe place and a listening ear.

- Children lack the necessary vocabulary to express how they feel, and need an adult's assistance in this.

- A child who loses one parent may in fact lose two, for the surviving parent may never be the same again.

- To lose a loved one is to lose a source of personal affirmation. In this we grieve for the loss to ourselves.

- Every bereavement is a divine invitation to place our lives in the eternal care of our heavenly source, and to discover afresh how much we rely on him.

- The 'abundant life' does not include heart-crushing disappointment from the loss of expectations. (The grief of God is never hopeless.)

- Unforgiveness is always linked to a sense of victimhood, so victims must ask, 'What can I learn from this experience?' before they can forgive.

'I thought I saw you today
My heart lunged toward you as you disappeared
Leaving a total stranger standing there.
How could I have imagined that you were still here?
You shall not come to me again, but I shall go to you.'
                                                      (*Author unknown.*)

Further Reading:
Good Grief, by Granger E Westberg. A description of all the stages in the grief process.
Grief, by Haddon Robinson. A practical, personal and inspirational response to bereavement.
A Grief Observed, by C S Lewis. A deeply personal

account of the author's reaction to the death of his wife.

Give Sorrow Words, by Terry Creagh. This book is designed for those who minister to the dying and the bereaved as well as for those who grieve and wish to understand more about what they are going through.

On Death And Dying and its sequel *Questions and Answers on Death and Dying*, by Elisabeth Kubler-Ross. These deal primarily with terminal illness and the responses of both patient and family or friends.

Chapter Nineteen

GUILT AND CONSCIENCE

- Shame, remorse, depression, anxiety, alienation, internal conflict, hostility and a sense of worthlessness can all stem from a condemning conscience.

- To be free of all guilt, first acknowledge your feelings to yourself and to God, and then to someone who knows the principles of God's forgiveness in Christ (from 1 John 1:9).

- Until guilt is acknowledged and grace is understood, there can be no assurance of forgiveness (from Luke 18:13).

- Objective guilt must be distinguished from subjective guilt. The conscience is not an infallible guide, nevertheless it is always wisest to obey it (from Romans 2:15; 1 Timothy 1:19).

- Your conscience is your friend, reminding you when you are not walking in love and goading you into action. Suppress its nagging pain at your peril (from Acts 23:1; 24:16).

- Capacity for guilt is closely related to capacity for love. Those who never knew any love, cannot feel for, or identify with their victims.

- During childhood we learnt to abide by our parents' conscience, but during teen years all these values have to be tested and then adopted as our own.

- The pain of guilt can bring hope if we search for the true cause. A correct response will bring instant relief and healing. Guilt is not an enemy; just a painful signal that something is wrong.

- Work, sport, alcohol, drugs, even religion and charity, can be an attempt to escape the quiet nag of an offended conscience, but avoidance ensures that the pain continues.

- A conscience stifled on a major matter will over-react on minor issues (often involving the behaviour of someone else) and all in a quite subconscious manner (from John 8:9).

- That you feel guilty at all about what happened, shows that it was never typical of you in the first place. But to disown it completely you must try, as much as lies in your power, to put it right by asking for forgiveness and making restitution.

- A permanent feeling of guilt may have been produced by growing up in conditional love where, no matter what you did, it was never enough.

- It takes reserves of inner acceptance to face and examine your own feelings of guilt. Discover God's grace before guilt can be faced up to.

- Pathological guilt may indicate the need to evict an unclean spirit, an 'alien' entity (from Titus 1:15).

- A confused conscience occurs when mixed messages come from parents, society or church. (from Titus 1:15).

- Guilt is your ally for it brings you to grace. (Christ's unmerited favour towards you.) Those who have sinned greatly are ripe for great grace (from Hebrews 10:22; 1 Peter 3:21).

- We have no objective past. All our conscious memories are selectively stored and edited by pride.

- Our own guilt should never be the motivation for condemning another (from John 8:9).

- The renewed conscience works with the Holy Spirit and is subject to His justification (from Romans 9:1).

- The internal peace of a good conscience is a better

motivation for keeping the law than the external threat of being fined for breaking it (from Romans 13:5).

- A faulty conscience comes from faulty knowledge. Allow for, and deal very gently with those who suffer under it (from 1 Corinthians 8:7; 10:28).

- For God's sake we must subject ourselves to others' ignorance in order to win their confidence (from 2 Corinthians 4:2).

- Even if our hearts condemn us, only God can judge truly (from Hebrews 9:14; 1 John 3:20).

- Those whose trust is not in their own effort, but in their place in Christ, will never be judged guilty of wrong (from Romans 8:1).

- Deal very gently with those who have a sensitive conscience; they are apt to condemn themselves at the least provocation (from 1 Corinthians 8:12).

- The conscience 'knows with us' what is right and what is wrong.

- Guilt is the intra-personal conflict created when my concept of myself is in conflict with the memory of my actions.

- What the psychologist calls 'cognitive dissonance' the Bible simply calls 'guilt.'

Further reading:
Guilt and Grace, by Paul Tournier.

Chapter Twenty

HOMOSEXUALITY

- Homosexuality – 'if God really made me like this, why don't I have peace about it?' is the very real dilemma.

- Never forget that some of Christ's harshest words were reserved for those who burdened others with difficult demands, without being in the least bit willing to help them bear those burdens.

- Our sexual desires return for fulfilment to whatever awakened them in the first place. This 'imprinting' must be consciously acknowledged before change can take place.

- 'Who' and 'what' we are is not for us to decide. We are to affirm by our actions and by the confession of our mouths, who God says we are, until our minds are renewed and His identity is fully formed within us.

- The belief that one is born homosexual is held on to in order to relieve one of the responsibility and difficulty of changing a subconscious orientation. The first step out is to agree with God that homosexual activities are sin which one is morally accountable for, and which one can and must be freed from.

- No one factor alone causes homosexuality, there are a number of root causes, not the least of which is the person's own personal choices. But what pressure or unmet need lies behind the choice?

- There is a vast moral difference between experiencing temptation, and choosing to indulge ourselves in it – but what need lies at the heart of the desire?

- People grow into labels. Once the homosexual label is accepted, the implied characteristics begin to develop in that life, because what we believe about ourselves is of absolute importance in determining everything that we do and say. God labels nobody as a homosexual. He knows them as His children who are trying to meet their needs in destructive ways.

- Homosexuality is not a simple description. There are many kinds, variations and levels of involvement, and each must be treated according to its roots.

- The way out of same-sex orientation is not a system or method, but a relationship – with Jesus Christ. It is the relationship which can change all our relationships, the identity which can replace and restore every other identity.

- The depth of submission to Christ as Lord equals the degree of victory gained over gayness, but be warned, one is never far enough out to regain control of one's own life.

- Co-operation with God's Spirit, obedience to His Word, persistence, and insight into the causes, are the essential ingredients to change.

- When did you first start to feel different? What was going on in your life at that time?

- Acknowledging your 'wholeness in Christ' aloud, will feel hollow and mocking, if you have not yet achieved it, but it drives the misbeliefs to the surface where they can be identified and dealt with.

- Christians acknowledge that God hates the sin but loves the sinner. Sometimes though, they themselves are not quite so generous. To receive help, first forgive them for their ignorance and fear with the same grace that God gives to you.

- Until the Lord is called upon to reveal and cut the root, you may strive in vain to change. The 'freewill' is only free when the subconscious pressures on it are exteriorised and in balance.

• Are homosexuals born that way? I have yet to meet a homosexual who has a good, strong father and an affectionate mother.

• All anger and bitterness, fear and suspicion of the opposite sex needs to be negated by prayer and forgiveness, with appropriate actions, in order that bitter expectations can be annulled.

• One of the most powerfully healing things a homosexual can do is to give their same-sex parent a big hug, telling them they love them and asking for their forgiveness for past resentment and bitterness. Such an action will begin to demolish all sorts of psychological and spiritual obstacles – in both parties.

• We all need non-erotic same-sex love. It is necessary to learn how to distinguish between our sexual need and our non-erotic need for affection.

• Any learned behaviour is weakened by non-practice.

• Yes God does condemn your immoral acts, but in no way does He condemn you. Your choice is whether or not to become identified with your acts, or with Jesus' own holy identity.

• Is a self-centred heterosexual act any less condemned than a homosexual act? They are both responses of the same carnal nature which we all share, and from which we can all be freed.

• We have all looked for comfort in the wrong place at some time or other, and we should all discover that the best source is our heavenly Dad. Emotional dependency is not confined to the homosexual community.

• Latent homosexuality can be triggered by the death of a parent, unsatisfactory heterosexual experience, separation/divorce, or same-sex friendship which degenerates into reliant attachment.

- Premature emotional disengagement between child and same-sex parent, for whatever reason, is the most common cause of homosexual orientation, but not the only one.

- *Anyone* who is insecure, in grief, depressed, rejected, or otherwise severely stressed, is vulnerable to becoming emotionally dependent on another of *either* gender.

- Sexual orientation should be distinguished from sexual behaviour. Even if the behaviour is disciplined, the orientation will remain until the emotional need is addressed.

- God doesn't tease. If He condemns it, He doesn't cause it. If He causes it, He won't condemn it. If He condemns it, He can also provide the way out if called upon to do so.

- Suppression of a homosexual desire for the rest of your life is not the abundant life that Jesus promised; neither is enslavement to it.

- The reparative drive is the desire to repair and possess through sexual experience (sexualisation) the masculinity or intimacy which the homosexual does not feel in possession of. They are trying to self-medicate for a developmental disorder.

- Male homosexuals should work with male therapists to work with some of the father/son issues never resolved in younger years.

- Therapists should focus on the homosexual's subjective experience by analysing the attraction/idealisation of the third person, not the behaviour or lifestyle of the person.

Further Reading:
Reparative Therapy, by Dr Nicolozi.

Chapter Twenty-One

Mental Health and Happiness

- I will always try to identify the *true source* of my anger/frustration and not be content merely to blame others.

- I will acknowledge and own up to *genuine* guilt and seek to make restitution in word and deed where necessary and possible.

- I will acknowledge His involvement and rely on God's help in *everything*. (Including holding to lists like this one.)

- I will monitor my personal thought life, focussing on the *positive* and cultivating an attitude of gratitude.

- I will submit my gifts, and the use of my talents, to the oversight of the Giver lest they assume God-like status in my life.

- I will look for the divine lesson in every situation, past, present and future, and treat my regrets as cause for me to search out and correct my misbeliefs.

- I will remember that God is not the author of every situation, but He is *always* the master over it, and therefore can transform it if invited to.

- I will monitor my thinking and examine my self-talk and ways of coping in times of trouble and stress to see if they are ultimately positive.

- I will not take every attack and critical word against me as a true reflection of who I am, for I know that often people hurt others simply because they themselves are hurting.

- I will examine my parents and role-models to iden-tify where they have wrongly conditioned me and/or deprived me of emotional nurture, in order to compen-sate in my own life and lay down my old survival kit.

- I will remember that my mind alone contains no source of life or well-being in itself, therefore I will not try to live out of it or rely on it as my 'centre'.

- I will speak the truth to others when necessary, but always out of love and respect for *both* of us.

- I will remember that encouragement is far more effective in effecting change in others than criticism, therefore I will not focus on their vices but rather dwell upon their virtues.

- I will accept my true share of the responsibility for my current predicament in order to regain the power over my own destiny.

- I will learn to critique my own thinking, knowing that from these decisions stem my eventual predicament and personal state.

- I will endeavour to recognise when I am turning to an *external* or anti-social source of comfort in order to escape emotional pain, and identify such as 'false-comforters', which ultimately work against my cause.

- I will combat insecurity, defensiveness and a feeling of insignificance by learning to find all my security and significance in God's personal love for me as revealed in the crucified Christ.

- I will learn to accept the volitional (chosen) nature of my attitudes and accept full responsibility for my own moods and emotions.

- I will remember that both states of happiness and pain are conditional, and that if I have understood and applied the truths, blessing and peace will *always* follow.

- I will remember the lesson of Joseph: that nothing in

life can harm me or do me ill unless I choose a wrong
response to it, for 'if God be for me, who (or what) can
be against me?'.

- I will work less on improving others and more on
  improving myself, for I know that their attitudes are
  often merely a response to my own.

- (And I will diligently pass on all such truths to my
  children, that they also may learn how to enjoy all the
  blessings that life and God bestow.)

Chapter Twenty-Two

EXPOSING MISBELIEFS

'Once there was an army unit which never won any battles, because one of the soldiers was a traitor to the cause. His presence had to be identified and removed before the army had any sucess.'

Neither will we have success in life and relationships until our 'traitors' have been identified and removed from our belief systems. Daily, many conclusions, both correct and incorrect, present themselves for our adoption or rejection. Any wrong conclusions which we have taken on board as reality will betray our cause and cause us and our families repeated pain, sorrow, failure and frustration. The extent of their influence depends on what level they lie in our layered belief structures.

How did you choose the right from the wrong? Did someone else choose it for you? Is it and its effect on you now 'sub-conscious', influencing your behaviour from 'behind the scenes' of your conscious awareness? What is the truth? What should I believe – what should I accept to be the truth? The Spirit of truth leads us into all truth, if we will yield to Him. In St Paul's words, 'we have the mind of Christ' (1 Cor 2:16, Phil 2:5) but if we remain loyal to a lie, we will be unable to appropriate or live in it. We need outside help to challenge our belief systems. A myth or delusion is a fixed, but false belief. It does not correspond to reality. It is not confirmed by Scripture. (Our 'normative' frame of reference – our window on reality.) Are you living in fantasy or reality? (Consider Hollywood 'special effects', where the senses are deluded.)

Your question needs to be: 'What lies am I still loyal to as being the truth? Am I willing to search them out as traitors to my cause?' Dare you ask yourself, 'What misbelief am I maintaining right now? Do I still insist that all my conclusions reached so far must be correct?' That it must be the truth simply because I believe it, is often the lie that underlies them all. All of us, somewhere in our thinking, have brought lies on board, at some time or other.

These lies prevent us from fully acknowledging who we are 'in Christ', and cause chaos in our relationships, our families, our business and professional dealings. 'Buy the truth and do not sell it!' we are exhorted in Proverbs 23:23.

Question: How to know if you have believed a lie? Answer: Somewhere in your life you will be hurting! You will be frustrated, either mentally, emotionally, financially or socially. Lies always prevent growth, both in ourselves and in our relationships. What you believe about yourself and about life, determines how you act, and how you act determines whether you are living or hiding from life. Be prepared to test everything. 'Is what I believe to be the truth, really the truth?'

We all need to be de-conditioned from the misbeliefs which we have believed about ourselves and our world. Scripture, pastor, parents, counsellors and friends are all able to identify your 'pet' lies if called upon to help. We are safeguards for each other. You might try asking your spouse or someone whose judgement you trust, to tell you honestly if they are aware of any lies that you are believing. Bring your lies to the one who is *the* truth. It will be the most threatening, and the most rewarding activity you will ever engage in.

Lies that cause pain

(As identified and collected from hundreds of counselling events.)
N.B. Lie defined as synonymous with misbelief. Something formerly believed in and included in one's belief system which is proved by reality to be incorrect. Such a list must remain in the subjective category, but this is not to infer that all truth is subjective. Most lies are usually

held to subconsciously. Some are primary, some secondary in their effects, depending on how early in life they were adopted.

That as a child, I interpreted life's events and adults' actions – including those of my parents – correctly.
I am unloved/unlovely/ugly/no good/a failure/a reject.
God doesn't love me/isn't with me/doesn't care about me.
I'm a hopeless mother/father/wife/husband/worker etc.
My child/parents/boss/pastor ought to be beyond fault or error.
I can get away with immorality without getting hurt or hurting others.
I can break the law and escape the consequences.
Nobody has the right to tell me what to do.
Love isn't genuine unless it's soft and sentimental.
The other person should seek my forgiveness first.
My survival is entirely up to me, and I am in constant danger/under threat by others' words and actions.
It's my lot in life to be sick/poor/lonely/in meaningless work.
Loving and helping people is not worth the pain.
I could never speak/pray in public.
Black/brown, is inferior or powerless in comparison to white, or vice versa.
My brother/sister/neighbour, wouldn't want to get a visit from me.
Other people have the power to make me unhappy.
Other people are totally to blame for my predicament.
If I had a new car/house/wife/husband/anything, I would then be truly happy.
Getting my own way is the most important thing in life.
I'm better off alone.
I don't have the right to correct my parents.
One never knows what the will of God might be.
For God to love me or be pleased with me I must act just right – talk just right – think just right.
Other people should attend to my needs without my having to ask.

T.V. can be on every day in my house without damaging my family's communication and moral standards.

A double standard can exist in my marriage without causing pain to both of us.

New ventures should be easy.

I can change another's mind if I can just put enough pressure on them.

I have to be the best at what I do.

God doesn't want to heal me.

If I say something I'll only make a fool of myself.

My opinion doesn't count for much.

Love does not involve discipline and correction.

I was responsible for my parents' divorce/death/sickness.

My parents didn't want me, I am a 'mistake'.

I'll never be able to comprehend or recall what I study.

I can't do anything for God unless He directs me personally.

I should not 'burden' someone else with my need.

Right or wrong, my first loyalty is to my family's beliefs.

Christians should be doormats.

Love is a feeling, if you don't have it, you're not in love.

Christians should obey authority without question.

I can't discover why I'm like this.

Some things/people never change.

My children/spouse are my property to do with as I wish.

Fantasy is more enjoyable than reality.

Suicide is an easy way out of the pain.

Some people are especially favoured by God for His blessing.

I can please God by trying to please people.

I can be blessed just by knowing something, rather than by doing something about it.

Abiding pleasure will come from attaining perfect co-ordination of mind and body.

When I've reached the top, I will at last be satisfied.

The pleasure of eating/drinking etc., can make the feelings of anxiety and emptiness go away.

Others' values should be the same as mine.

I should look like the images presented in the media.

If we love each other it must be right.

Most of my problems have been caused by men (or women).

I can follow Christ on my own terms.

I can indulge myself in immorality and still enjoy normal family relationships.

When my potential is fully actualised I will know as God knows.

I can find God by looking within myself.

I must withdraw to protect myself from danger/a hostile world.

My friends'/neighbours'/family's morality is none of my business. (Everything we do has social consequences.)

What I do will not affect my family or the society in which I live.

Guilt is always a negative and should be avoided at any cost.

I should always have to cope. I should never lose control of my emotions.

I must not overlook the smallest detail.

I must always please everybody.

I must always be in complete control, or at least know exactly what's happening.

I am ultimately responsible for the success or failure of my children.

This habit which I despise in myself belongs to the real me.

I can still retain the old beliefs when new truth is revealed to me.

I do not need to check my own understanding when opposed or offended.

My refusal to forgive will not affect me.

There is only my side to the story.

Sex will get better without us both taking responsibility for it.

If I apologise to my children, I will lose their respect.

Pleasure comes by being first of all concerned with myself.

A baby is not a human being until it's born.

Discipline is an end in itself.

My love for order and tidiness is more important than my love for people.

(Your turn now, there is room for some of your own . . .)

Further Reading:
'I am the truth' John 14:6
'The witness to the truth' Genesis 3:1–7; Proverbs
    8:7; Proverbs 8:32; 1 John 2:20–27.

Remember, to hurt and cripple you, all the destroyer has
to do is to mislead your thinking/belief system. Test
everything. N.B. If truth seems threatening, even myths
and ill-founded beliefs seem preferable. That is why fear
and anger are the immediate response of someone whose
personal lies are being threatened by the proclamation
of truth.

Chapter Twenty-Three

RESTORING MENTAL HEALTH

- What we are feeling is determined by what we are thinking. Our emotional life *follows* our thought life (from Genesis 4:6).

- Our own response to the events of life is the only thing that can harm our personality, and our response is determined by what we believe about life and God (from Philippians 4:4).

- All my thoughts and actions have been chosen by me, whether consciously or subconsciously.

- All actions begin with conclusions. Which conclusions are false? Am I feeling myself the truth? (from Proverbs 4:23).

- Are you preoccupied with the past or future? Peace of mind can only be found by living in the present (from Matthew 6:34).

- To improve your situation, first accept responsibility for it. Your choices led you into, and can lead you out of it (from Luke 15:17).

- Make your peace with what you cannot change, or you will wrestle with it to your own ruin. But remember, with God, nothing is impossible (from 1 Thessalonians 5:18).

- Your outlook is interpreted from within, in the light of your past experience (from Proverbs 15:15).

- Whatever gets your complete attention eventually gets you. Whatever is not submitted to God in your life, will seek to become your God (from 2 Samuel 11:2).

- Misbeliefs are all that give the destroyer 'right of access' to our lives and the lives of those within our realm of influence (from John 14:30).

- Learn to value your anger as the emotional energy needed to make changes (from Proverbs 16:32).

- Take charge of your mind by monitoring your thoughts and quickly rejecting the useless ones (from 2 Corinthians 10:5).

- Fear of fear's symptoms adds fear to fear, and may well culminate in a panic attack. Don't resist it – go with it – allowing it will allow it to pass, but don't run from the feared situation (from Psalm 23:4).

- Decisions – face them, make them, learn from them – then leave them behind. 'I did what seemed right at the time' (from Philippians 4:6).

- Peace comes with the assurance of adequate resources. In Christ's care you will always have enough (from Philippians 4:19).

- The grief process, when obstructed, degenerates into withdrawal and despair. To enjoy life again, first locate the obstruction (from Proverbs 13:12).

- Anger accumulated too long turns sour, becoming resentful and bitter (from Ephesians 4:26).

- Worrying about your needs is as insulting to the 'God-who-provides' as blasphemy (from Philippians 4:6).

- The power of the will – the power to choose the good – is released *after* externalising the sub-conscious conflict.

- It's not what you are achieving, but what you are becoming, that is of lasting importance, for it is *you* that God will inherit (from Ephesians 1:18).

- Having fun is a God-given need, don't suppress or deny it, but subject it to the Giver (from Proverbs 17:22).

- Receive comments at face value; love gives the benefit of the doubt (from 1 Corinthians 13:7).

- Sow a thought, reap an act. Sow an act, reap a habit (from Proverbs 4:23).

- Before they spring up, look for and remove the seeds of destruction, planted in your thinking in days gone by (from Song of Solomon 2:15).

- Uncontrollable thoughts and severe mood swings may indicate the need to evict a foreign influence – a spiritual 'squatter'. Seek out pastoral help, and seek out the original wrong belief in your heart.

- Compulsive thoughts may be drawing their strength from our fear of them. 'So what, they can't hurt me now', is the response of those who know and understand Christ's atonement (from Romans 7:5).

- Retrain negative thoughts and self-talk by thinking and talking only positive things. Fill in the ruts of the mind (from Psalm 42:5).

- Resistance to sickness requires emotional reserves – don't live in emotional overdraft (from Proverbs 17:22).

- Complaining of your lack may be contradicting the 'God who provides' (from Philippians 4:13).

- Discouragement comes with focusing on problems rather than on your resources (from Matthew 14:30).

- The eyes of the self-righteous are focused on themselves and their performance. Discouragement will always be the result (from Galatians 2:16).

- A personal verdict of complete failure, rejection and guilt, brings with it an inclination toward death. The cross spells out forgiveness and new hope (from Matthew 27:3).

- Without a goal, what is there to live for, yet anyone can seek God's purpose for their lives (from Matthew 6:33).

- Living in emotional overdraft always results in depression (from 1 Kings 19:4).

- An angry person is one who doesn't know when to 'let go' their loyalty to justice, for the sake of love.

- Where there is human pain, you may be sure there are misbeliefs in residence.

- 'What a person thinks is determined by *where* they think and *why* they think' (Cox).

- There are no formulas in the kingdom of God.

- When you start thinking 'What did they really mean by that comment?' evil will come looking for an opportunity to work its mischief. Don't indulge in second-guessing or over-interpretation.

- Once it is understood that fear always exaggerates the dangers in order to warn us, it can be accepted – even welcomed – as an ally and friend.

- Life will change for you when *you* change. Christ's belief in you can motivate you when you have run out of internal incentive.

- Always picture in your mind how you want to be, rather than how you are, or the old image simply gets reinforced.

- 'Dis-ease' of the mind, often becomes disease of the body.

- Plan for the future, but live in the now.

- Today, make a choice to be happy for the rest of your life. If you want to be happy, then be happy. If you can't or aren't, make it your business to find out why.

- Don't take yourself too seriously! It's O.K. to 'stuff up' or 'make an idiot of yourself' occasionally.

- A salvation experience with Jesus is not a short-cut to mental health. Our thinking must still be conformed to His (from Romans 12:1).

- Are you remembering the things you should forget, and forgetting the things you should remember? Don't dig in God's graveyard! (from Psalm 103:12).

- You are always moving towards what you are thinking about, so think about your goal.

- Cherish your imagination, your ability to dream. It is a gift that marks you as one 'made in the image of God'.

- Combine your inspiration with perspiration to make your dream come true.

- Mentally rehearse whatever you want to do, before you do it. You will always move towards your pre-conceived goal.

- Remember that thinking about taking the bull by the horns is always more frightening than doing it.

- 'I know that what I believe must be right simply because I believe it' is the misbelief which underlies all other misbeliefs.

- When truth seems too threatening, even myths and ill-founded beliefs are preferable.

- A 'free' will is never free until the subconscious pressures have been conscientised, externalised and balanced.

- Many are the offended, and many are the 'offences', but few are they who pause to test their own conclusions.

- Arrest your angry thoughts before they sour your personality and quench the spirit of forgiveness.

- If you lose your joy while seeking justice, how are you profited? Do not become one more victim of revenge and bitterness.

- Can you spot the opportunity in the problem, the heavenly lesson in the earthly circumstances?

- Mistakes and errors are merely feedback on how you are doing. Can you welcome them as an essential part of the learning process.

- Laughter relieves pain, so always look for the humour. You can't laugh and get a stomach ulcer at the same time.

- To build your confidence, first replace your negative self-image by picturing yourself as bold and persuasive.

- Cope with stress by doing one thing at a time, the important things first.

- Fear of failure is negated when pride and insecurity are laid down.

- Don't run from the problem. Collect up your resources and then confront it.

- Worry produces 'paralysis by analysis'.

- Have you ever met a person who loves to hate? It is a 'survival kit' which rots the soul and embitters the spirit.

- The mind set on fulfilling sensual desire, *and* on pleasing the Lord, is divided against itself, and cannot remain whole.

- Never underestimate the destructive power of an outraged conscience.

- If minds were washed of misbeliefs as often as bodies are washed of soil, what a most wonderful place this world would be.

- No one can ever take from you your freedom to choose your own attitude in response to what has happened.

- Don't be so concerned at what you can't do, focus your attention on what you can.

- An attitude of helplessness and hopelessness can eventually become a self-fulfilling state.

- Aggressive anger leads to bitterness, passive anger leads to self-pity. Speaking the truth in love to those who have wronged you leads to peace.

- Being happy is not the result of getting things the way you want them. The 'if onlys' will negate contentment every time.

- Before trying to understand a new topic, be sure to put your conceptual shelves up first, or all the new information will have nowhere to 'land'!

- What makes you think that you'll be any happier in the next life, than you are in this one?

- Ruts in the mind soon cause moods of the heart.

- Real mental health comes by a commitment to live in reality by consistently avoiding fantasy and the 'soft options'.

- To exercise your self-awareness, try verbalising every thought and fragment of thought for just sixty seconds. *Then* you will know what you think.

- Fear of what others think always cripples your ability to learn, for self-improvement is a risky business.

- 'She'll be right' is a biggie on the list of misbeliefs and the cause of enormous human misery.

- An over-active mind can indicate a permanent state of 'red-alert' as the result of childhood trauma. Yet if God be for us, who can threaten us now?

- Anger and panic are closely related, for anger is usually the consequence of feeling threatened.

- The degree to which a person only hears what they want to hear indicates the degree of emotional pain they are in.

- When you are angry, you should ask yourself: 'Are my expectations realistic?'

- Ambivalence (double-mindedness) creates tension and needs to be resolved before you crack down the middle. What is the insight that will resolve your dilemma?

- Before you get anything else, get organised. It will always save you time and trouble and unnecessary anger.

- Deep happiness is conditional; it doesn't simply happen. Mental/emotional health must be worked at.

When angry, you can either lower your expectations or use the emotional energy to make changes.

- The more you give in to your fears, the more they will grow. Avoiding all risk is not the way to peace.

- You are more than just your thoughts; therefore you can monitor and change them when necessary. But first get more insight.

- Your situation was caused, at least in part, by your choices. Accept responsibility for your predicament, to regain the reins of your own life.

- True freedom is found in deliberately choosing to do those things in which I have no choice. In this way I 'own' my own activity.

- Do you have a problem with anger? Do you know when to say: 'So what, it doesn't actually matter' and then *let it go?*

- You don't have to be perfect. Sometimes 'good enough' is good enough. (Good news for a performance-based society.)

- Is every one of your beliefs and opinions correct? Those that aren't will be causing you pain, anxiety and frustration.

- Are you telling yourself the truth? Not if you're feeling frustrated or fearful. Your thoughts must encourage you, not attack you.

- This life isn't fair. If you always insist on justice you'll be angry all your life. (Don't make a god out of justice.)

- A vital part of emotional growth is the process of bringing feelings and emotions to word and expression.

- If you resort to any activity to mask problems, hide from people, or as a substitute for love, then that activity will become compulsive. It is your 'security'.

- False guilt blames us for things beyond our control.

Helpful guilt enables us to accept responsibility for our choices.

• Self-control is the ability to postpone immediate pleasure in order to confront less attractive tasks. (Willpower comes after insight.)

• Accepting responsibility for your own responses and choices is the first step to a healed life. (Christians call this repentance.)

• Take time to understand the motivation behind your desire, or in time that desire may become your dictator.

• If you only tolerate ideas that agree with your existing beliefs, how will you ever discover new truth or identify your own error?

• Helpful guilt assists us to identify our own beliefs as the culprit when we are going wrong. Destructive guilt is non-specific.

• When stress levels rise, do three things: Relax. Breathe deeply. Tell yourself the truth.

• Stay in your own territory. Do what you can do and leave the miracles to God.

• Don't be like the beautiful swan who kept insisting she was really an ugly duck. You are made in the image of God.

• Though you fail, you are not a failure unless you fail to learn something from it. (It is your beliefs that have failed you.)

• Stress is directly related to fear. Is anxiety accumulating in your life? The Comforter is always near, but first you must adopt His perspective.

• Freedom is not found in doing what you want, when you want. That simply results in slavery to self.

• Are you comfortable with nothing but your own thoughts for company? Vices only hide the pain; they never heal it.

- When next you overreact in anxiety, loneliness or anger, try to distinguish between present reality and the echoes of past experiences.

- The degree to which you can forgive is largely dependent on the degree to which your insights have released you from all sense of victimhood.

- To grow we must first let go. Those who cannot let go a mistaken belief cannot progress.

- Harness the power of your regrets to help you dig for greater wisdom, and so your pain will be transformed.

- Adults regress to a child's response whenever they lack the wisdom to deal with a particular difficulty.

- When your beliefs and your actions don't agree, it's time to locate and reconcile the contradictions in your belief bank (paradigm).

- The painful double bind of contradictory beliefs stops personal growth. Greater understanding is required to integrate your 'cognitive discord'.

- Face it and deal with it. Escaping it will only mean you'll hit the pain again tomorrow. (Old survival kits must be traded in.)

- Don't judge your value by your past actions. They merely reflect your past beliefs. Your true worth comes by virtue of who created you, and is fulfilled by better choices.

- Don't try to dispel a wrong belief. Rather, displace it with a better insight. The truth sets us free.

- Your future is not determined by your parentage but by your own choices – the choices you make today and tomorrow.

- Procrastination has many possible causes, and all exist because we are afraid to face up to our fears – failure, responsibility, criticism, etc.

- Your intellectual ability, however perceptive, is only

as good as your skill at retrieving what you know. Understanding the memory should precede all formal learning.

- 'I'll do it later' and 'I don't need to read the instructions' are two 'biggies' in the world of misbeliefs.

- Living is not for spectators. To live abundantly demands that we take risks in coming down from the grandstand and getting involved.

- 'There are no dumb questions.' Without this insight your learning will be inhibited.

- When all is considered, my beliefs and ideals are really the only thing I have that I can truly call mine.

- Mental passivity, once identified, needs to be actively opposed by questioning everything. Initiative, like a muscle, must be exercised.

- As a magnet influences a compass, so a spiritual entity interferes with the minds of those in proximity. Counsel the mind, but confront an evil spirit.

- While stubbornness doesn't guarantee success, a weak will will always guarantee failure.

- The stronger the character, the greater the need for God, for a powerful ego, harnessed only to itself, is yet unharnessed. Eventually it will self-destruct.

- Those who would grow old gracefully must give up control and ready themselves to leave this place. The alternative is to grow old angrily.

- Transcendental meditation calls for focus on a sound; Christian meditation calls for focus on the Creator of sound.

- A sense of destiny can be a heavy burden and must give way to the need to become properly centred.

- Are you utterly and unquestionably certain you are right? If so, beware. For so were the cruellest men history has ever known.

- The challenge of youth is to become independent. The challenge of middle age is to become inter-dependent. The challenge of growing old is to accept your dependence again.

- Healthy self-control is really proactive reaction – it allows choice of expression.

- Neuroses are our 'soft option' survival kits, formed in the face of reluctance to experience any emotional pain. (Pain avoided becomes unavoidable pain.)

- The journey into total mental health begins with a commitment to come out of 'hope so' into reality, at any personal cost.

Chapter Twenty-Four

Personal and Emotional Healing

- No one can ever take from you the freedom to choose your own response and attitude towards the events of your life.

- Knowing God's unconditional approval, is the only completely reliable source of self-esteem (from John 12:43).

- Are you focusing on your lack or on your resources? Concentrate on making the most of what you have, rather than what you have not.

- A temporary foundation laid for self-worth (from skills, looks, sporting prowess, others' approval) ensures a later crisis. What does your self-esteem depend on? (from Luke 6:48).

- People who are themselves damaged and hurting, invariably damage and hurt others. Don't take it so personally (from Matthew 12:35).

- Healing of memories is founded on forgiveness and a new, better-informed response to past trauma (from Genesis 33).

- Self-esteem is nurtured or damaged by the words of parents (from Proverbs 18:21).

- To know God as Father, first distinguish Him from your image of your natural Dad (from Hebrews 12:10).

- The pain of rejection is well-known to the heart of our heavenly Father. (Refer to the whole Bible.)

- You have never suffered alone – God always shared your

pain, for He lives and exists 'in intimate relationship' with all humanity (from 2 Samuel 18:33).

- Children are excellent recorders of their past experiences, but poor interpreters. Later, they must reinterpret with an adult mind, conscious now of the loving providence of God (from 1 Samuel 3:5).

- Healing of memories is re-discovering the trauma in the context of the resources and purposes of God for your life (from Psalm 139)

- To forget the past, first ensure that the conflicts are resolved. 'We must trace it, face it, then erase it' (Adams).

- Being 'rejected' by others, whether real or imagined, is the bitter complaint of those who are always down on themselves (from Exodus 4:1).

- We go to extremes to compensate for unmet emotional needs in our own life's development.

- Wrong conclusions arrived at in childhood must be consciously identified and exposed in the adult mind, in order to be freed from compulsive, destructive behaviour. Use a pastor, counsellor, or *Living Wisdom*.

- Were you 'set up' for a repeated sense of failure by parents' unrealistic expectations? (from Romans 12:3).

- Any corrective comment spoken 'threatens' the ears of the bruised in heart. Their hurt psyche distorts the way they interpret you (from 1 Samuel 18:8).

- We can dwell on our hurts, or find our healing while helping others. It is more blessed to give than to receive (from Luke 9:23).

- Until they are renounced, words spoken to us in the past can continue to influence us on a subconscious level today (from Proverbs 18:21).

- Inner healing of past trauma comes as we relate the bitter memories to God's eternal, loving purpose for our lives (from Romans 8:28).

- For every painful feeling, Scripture has an ointment (from Psalm 119:25).

  No one is supposed to cope in every situation. Realising this enables us to call for help.

- Hindsight is only valuable if we learn to shine it on the pathway up ahead.

- You can only face your fear – your suppressed memory – your opponent, when you know, first of all, that 'in Christ' you are completely secure.

- Identify the lies you have believed, before you can take new truth on board.

- Negative thinking and talking invokes weariness, discouragement, and depression. Put off a negative mind-set (from Philippians 4:8).

- Our self-image underlies all that we do or leave undone, yet we are made in the image of God, and made acceptable 'in Christ' (from Genesis 1:26; 1 Samuel 16:7).

- Learn to gain all of your self-esteem from the knowledge of Christ-crucified-for-you.

- Question: When did the breakthrough come for the Ugly Duckling? Answer: When it acknowledged its true identity as a beautiful swan.

- Subconscious hurts lose their power and pain as soon as they are identified. It is knowing the truth that sets us free.

- Insecurity or childhood habits are usually at the root of stubbornness.

- Your feelings are your friends. Don't deny them appropriate recognition, or they will put great pressure on you.

- Frightening dreams warn us that something is wrong within and is needing some attention/expression.

- To stop hurting, first take your hand off the stove. (from Stop dwelling on the painful thoughts.)

- If you have had a miscarriage, you need to name the child, dedicating it to God, and be confident that in Him nothing is ever lost. You will therefore be sure of meeting the child again.

- It is not time that heals, but understanding the truth and, where necessary, making restitution. Time alone has no healing qualities.

- If you have had an abortion, you need to acknowledge honestly your guilt and learn of the forgiveness that is found in Christ. Receive His forgiveness, dedicate your life to Him, and forgive yourself and all those involved. Until you do, you must go on living in denial and all the pain that that suppression involves. Find a counsellor and get help.

- The key to a healthy self-image is to stop considering your own needs only, and to begin serving God by serving others. What was 'useless' then becomes 'useful'.

- Addictions and eating disorders are symptoms of personal discomfort with oneself, often from guilt, rejection, or an ugly self-image.

- 'I couldn't do that, it's just not me.' Yet only your Creator knows who the real 'you' is.

- Unfinished business won't stay buried. First resolve the conflict, then put it behind you.

- Even St Paul had to reconcile what he had done as a persecutor of the church with who he became as its patron. He did this by discovering the hand of God on his whole life, rather than just from his conversion (from 1 Timothy 1:16).

- The past will keep hurting, until you ask Christ to redeem and transform it from meaningless experience to preparation for your future life and service.

- The pain of those past mistakes will be redeemed (from transformed) when it motivates you to seek help for yourself and others.

- What is your earliest memory? It may have set the course your life has taken, by shaping your image of yourself.

- To come to terms with a situation or feeling will demand that we find its name and thereby bring it to understanding.

- If you always do what you've always done, you'll always get what you've always got.

- Dismantle your negative, history-based feelings. They are telling you lies about the present.

- What were the unspoken rules of your childhood home? They remain powerful forces in your psyche today.

- No, life is not fair. But God is, and your security does not rely on life being just, but on God's love for you.

- The primary goal of self-improvement is not happiness but loving others. Happiness will follow after.

- Remember to stay in God's comfort zone. He *is* looking out for you. Remind yourself to calm down and relax in His loving care.

- To shift a truth from your head to your heart, speak it out loud, speak it often, and make a deliberate choice to believe it. For example, if God be for me, what can threaten me?

- Christ's great love for you is the only reliable foundation for good self-esteem (and the only one that continues beyond your last heartbeat).

- To hate myself is to reject what God created and calls precious. (Rather I must reject the indulgence of my mistaken beliefs.)

- What you tell yourself will either invoke or quench the presence of the Comforter. (You are His child and He is deeply in love with you.)

- Your concept of yourself – did it come from God or did you invent it? It will either encourage or cripple you, bind you or free you.

- The root of inferiority and pride is the human inclination to compare ourselves with one another. (The result of ignoring the divine mirror is always insecurity.)

- The motto your family lives by will nurture you or cripple you, and will probably never be clearly identified. Yet it is one of the most powerful forces in your life.

- The truth will set you free to enter heaven, but first it will hurt like hell.

- To genuinely think for yourself, you must first distinguish your beliefs from those of your parents, and cut the intellectual/emotional apron-strings.

- 'I'm not good enough' and 'I mustn't cry' are two mistaken beliefs which give rise in their turn to mistaken emotions.

- Unresolved pain from the past causes an over- or under-reaction today. The past must be reframed/reinterpreted.

- Reality is often not what we perceive, especially when we have been hurt and betrayed in our formative years,

- 'I've left it too late!' is a cry God will want to qualify. If you have learned from it, then it was worth it, no matter how long it took.

- Don't confuse identification of your pain with the healing of it. It must yet be followed by the application of truth and the adoption of new practices.

- The priority of your feelings is to be safe and comfortable, but the divine priority for your life is to risk and grow. Which will it be?

- To really forgive yourself, you need to understand fully why you did it, and to become assured that you aren't likely to make that mistake again.

- Emotional pain results when life's experiences go beyond

the answers we have available. Dig deeper for more wisdom or go on hurting.

- Have you *ever* felt valued and secure? The Comforter is available to you any time, but first you must tell yourself the truth.

- Emotional echoes need not be feared when recognised for what they are. Acknowledge them, then lay them aside. They can't hurt you now.

- You must make friends with your past, for it will always be a part of you. New insight alone will enable you to reinterpret your regrets and leave the pain behind.

- Have your feelings died, or are they just obstructed by walls built too high, to protect them?

- You can only forgive when you first understand why there are no victims in the family of God.

- Do not look to your parents for that which Christ alone can give. Your sense of identity is sourced in no other than your Creator.

- Self-esteem cannot be self-generated. Left to ourselves we do not know who we are, or what we are worth. (from Refer to Calvary for a true reflection of your value.)

- Labels. We either grow into them or compensate for them. What label or nickname was given you and how did it form your concept of yourself?

- Trying to control other people and every situation is *not* the way to feel safe or avoid being hurt. Attending to the basis of your own self-worth is.

- Reacting badly? A trauma from the past causes an over-reaction in the present. Acknowledge and compensate for it in order to carry on.

- Sometimes you just need a 'big' person to give you permission to fail, or to quit. We all need a kindly mentor.

- A desire within you is not necessarily *your* desire until you indulge it. (It may simply be an echo from the past.)

- Resolve the feelings by acknowledging emotions and reinterpreting old conclusions. *Then* bury the past.

- Let the pain from your past trauma motivate you to increase your insights in the present. Only then is the experience truly redeemed.

- Sometimes I need to call my feelings 'liars' and choose to side with reality *against* my own emotions.

- Ambivalence (double-mindedness) creates tension and needs to be resolved before you crack down the middle. What is the insight that will solve your dilemma?

- The feelings you experience outside your comfort zone will be identified as threatening or exhilarating, depending on how your parents labelled them when you *first* experienced them.

Chapter Twenty-Five

PHOBIAS

- Phobias are irrational, debilitating fears which generate uncontrollable panic. Fear of crowds, lifts, flying, water, snakes, spiders, public speaking and thunder are among the most common.

- Fear of fear's symptoms, is what adds fear to fear, producing a full-blown phobia or panic-attack.

- Heart palpitations, shortness of breath or hyperventilation, chest pain, sweaty palms, 'jelly legs' and dizziness symptomise a phobia and may lead the victim to mistakenly conclude that they are going crazy, or that death is imminent.

- Panic-attacks are usually stress-induced, following a major or minor crisis, as far back as childhood, or else can occur while coming off certain types of drugs such as anti-depressants.

- Anti-psychotic drugs, tranquillisers, shock treatment and psychoanalysis may not be the way to healing. Rather, they can actually worsen the condition.

- How much you want to overcome it is what will determine your success.

- When you find yourself avoiding certain situations for fear of panic, seek help – it is the thin edge of the wedge which can ultimately leave you hiding from life.

- Everybody has a level of anxiety. Learning to manage a high level is necessary for the phobic-prone.

- Phobias are no respecters of class, education or upbringing. Those with a background of secure, sensible parenting are less at risk.

- A sympathetic and understanding person is a vital resource in overcoming fear.

- Knowing why you are fearful doesn't usually help.

- Avoid avoiding your fear, or you will only feed it!

- Time doesn't heal fear. In fact, if coupled with avoidance, it actually strengthens it.

- Don't resort to tranquillisers, or you will give away your power over the situation. Instead, find a sympathetic friend to help you.

- Learn how to relax, and then confront the fear in your imagination first.

- Work out a programme to gradually and systematically face your fear, with two or three exposures every week for practice.

- Endure the symptoms for 30 seconds while thinking 'I feel terrible now, but it will pass,' and the panic will subside.

- Try to never leave a feared situation until the fear is reducing.

- Our autonomic nervous system cannot be directly controlled, it can only be influenced via our thinking. Think on the care that Christ has for you.

- Feelings of fear, though acutely uncomfortable and thereby alarming, are actually harmless. Allow them to occur, even expect them, in order not to overreact to them, and wait for them to pass. They do not mean that something disastrous is about to occur, they simply overstate the danger.

- Repeat successful endeavours in order to establish your success. Expect setbacks as part of progress, and don't be discouraged by them.

- Peace comes from the assurance of adequate resources. In God's loving providence, you have all the resources you need to face every threat and to overcome it.

- What is the source of your security? The balance in your bank account or the promises of God to care for those who cooperate?

- Remember to stay in God's comfort zone. Remember that He is looking out for you. Remind yourself to calm down and relax in His loving care.

- Instead of asking God to comfort you, acknowledge that you are being comforted right now. You are not, and never have been, alone, uncared for, or unloved.

- To shift a truth from your head to your heart, speak it out loud, speak it often, and make a deliberate choice to believe it, e.g. 'If God be for me, what can threaten me?'

- In the quest for popularity one risks the loss of one's own soul. It is not for others to decide your value or identity.

- God is not a tease, but the blessings of God (unlike his love) are still conditional, and your life's task is to understand them.

Chapter Twenty-Six

SELF-CONTROL

- 'I can't help it', often really means 'I can, but I don't want to'. The next question to ask is 'Why don't I want to?'.

- Negative habits cultivated over a lifetime require incentive, effort and time to change. Where will such motivation come from, if not from the love of God?

- Happiness is a by-product of living a self-controlled-by-God life.

- Those who never learn self-control will spend their lives paying for previous acts of self-indulgence.

- Immediate self-gratification is the ever-present, ever-popular, path to sorrow.

- We are paralysed by the misbelief that happiness 'just happens' – that we don't have to work at it, or suffer for it.

- Self-control is the sacrifice of a short-term pleasure for a long-term goal – the 'tough option'.

- At the point of temptation, 'actual' beliefs can be distinguished from 'professed' beliefs if one asks 'what am I telling myself at this moment?' (See Proverbs 23:7.)

- A defeat is not a failure. A failure is one who stops trying. A lapse is not a relapse until it's repeated.

- Self-control is a natural consequence of having the Holy Spirit present in one's life.

- Self-control needs incentive. It is a by-product of having been captured by a higher goal. 'Without a vision the people dwell carelessly.'

- All beginnings are difficult. If you always expect otherwise, frustration will pressure you to quit before you
succeed.

- To rule your own spirit, speak to yourself words of
calm.

- Who rules, you or your feelings? You are more than your
moods.

- Passive or violent expression of anger is destructive.
Express it, but reasonably and lovingly (from Ephesians
4:15).

- Attempts to change your ways will *always* meet with
internal resistance – change is always challenged.

- Work towards your goal, but don't be imprisoned by
it.

- True freedom is not the liberty to do whatever you
desire, but the power to do what you ought.

- Whether your bad habit is smoking, drinking, gambling, overeating, violence, compulsive shopping or
overworking, quitting the habit successfully will require
similar techniques.

- Prepare for the wave of desire that will hit you even
after you have quit, and schedule an alternative to get
you through.

- One pleasure-giving habit should be replaced by another.
Have you discovered the Comforter yet?

- To change your actions, first work on your image of
yourself.

- You can speak and think about yourself as you are, which
will only serve to confirm your habit, or you can speak
and think about yourself as you wish to be, which will
assist that new state to come to pass.

- When you cannot believe in yourself, find someone who
does believe in you.

- What genuine need in your life is your bad habit trying to meet?

- Does your method of coping heal the pain or merely hide it for a time?

- 'Part of me wants to and part of me doesn't.' As long as you tolerate ambivalence you will remain in confusion and vulnerable to temptation again.

- Consider often 'What benefit have you gained by doing those things of which you are now ashamed?'

- Your willpower is only as strong as the insight and wisdom that undergirds it. The more wisdom you can find, the stronger will be your resolve.

- Even Jesus struggled with the prayer 'yet not my will, but thine be done . . .'. You are not alone in your battle with temptation.

- Whatever gets your whole attention will eventually get you.

- Have you realised that your 'self', with all its crazy desires, has already been destroyed at Calvary? You don't have to keep wrestling with it now, simply learn to identify with Jesus' own resurrected identity.

- When temptation knocks persistently, ask Christ to answer the door.

- What is the prior need which sets you up for temptation, and why does it exist?

- Before you give in to temptation again, just ask yourself, 'How did I actually benefit the last time I yielded to this dubious desire?'

- What has been learned can always be unlearned; about sexual orientation, ways of coping, personal habits, etc.

- The 'unexamined life' is never the 'abundant life' – it is a crazy life lived in reaction.

Chapter Twenty-Seven

SELF-ESTEEM

Did you know that those who grow up looking into cracked mirrors are doomed to forever think of themselves as 'cracked'? Amusing perhaps, but also very true. Those faulty reflectors may have taken the form of the mother who walked out on you when you were a child, or who could never express her affection for you. It may have been a father who rejected you or constantly criticised you. It may have been school peers who harassed you, teachers who 'failed' you, a partner who was always putting you down or who 'dumped' you. Have you ever considered what damage may have been done to you by such people, or more accurately, by the way in which you have *interpreted* their actions towards you?

Our conclusions are inadequate

From the combined reaction of all these people toward us we come to conclusions about ourselves – who we are – our value, our personal significance – from which in turn we derive our self-esteem. It is their belief in us which first enables us to believe in ourselves, their faith which nurtures our self-confidence, their patient teaching which engenders within us the knowledge of our own worth, and conversely, their unbelief in us which prevents our normal growth and development. Yet whether good or bad, positive or negative, always our conclusions are inadequate, if not utterly wrong, for they are based on the belief that others have the power to tell us who we are, something we must come to realise is not correct.

How do you think of yourself? As capable, intelligent, precious beyond value, totally secure, loveable, socially confident? No, not unless you are one of the tiny minority who were blessed with marvellously able parents and teachers who invested much of themselves and their own wisdom into you, thereby completely validating your existence. It is more likely that you have an image that is much less than that by virtue of those 'cracked' mirrors, and the image they have reflected has been so conditioned into you that now it has its hidden effect on your every thought and action.

Are you comfortable with yourself? Do your own thoughts defeat you before you have even had a chance? How do you escape or protect yourself from such internal pain? Most turn to tobacco, alcohol, television, drugs or heavy 'mind-blowing' music and then finally, when the emotional pain just gets too much, they may seriously consider taking their own lives.

Consider the ugly duckling

At its heart, the crisis is one of faith. Who actually has the authority to tell me who I am? Who can I rely on, who is trustworthy? Why am I so sure that the image which I have of myself is correct? Do you remember the story of the Ugly Duckling? Though born a swan, he imagined himself to be a particularly ugly type of duck, a conclusion which brought a tremendous sense of inferiority and rejection with its associated heartache and frustration. But when did the breakthrough come for the Ugly Duckling? *Not* when he changed his essential being and ability, nor even his performance – that was not the problem. The breakthrough only came when he realised and acknowledged his true identity as a valuable and beautiful swan. With this insight also came the realisation that he had taken on a misbelief on the basis of the way the other ducks had treated him. Yet for this new revelation to have its full effect, he also had to *let go* his old duck-image, and begin to side with the assurances of the swans who were flying overhead. Such a challenge is frightening, for often the old ugly image, while it may cause much pain, seems by its very familiarity to offer more comfort than that which is quite unknown.

The sure foundation

The only sure foundation for our self-esteem is in the knowledge of our Creator and the acknowledgment of ourselves as His special and much loved creation, gathered into the favour in which Christ is held, that we *all* might find acceptance, significance and security. Every other basis is faulty, temporary and unreliable, and leaves us insecure and desperately clinging to our 'survival kits' to bolster such pride as we can muster. In this mindset we may go through life discouraged, defensive, insecure and easily provoked to jealousy. In such pain, we are crippled in ourselves and continually hurting others, thus repeating the cycle in those we relate to. Can you identify your personal survival kit? How do you cope when disappointed yet again by your failure to perform, by others' hostile reactions to you, and by your own inner 'accuser'? Those coping mechanisms are our 'walls' – our survival kit – which must be put aside once we begin to look to Jesus to tell us who we are. We cannot change our feelings, our attitudes or our behaviour until we have an entirely new concept of our true identity, otherwise we would begin to divide down the middle.

Always searching

Without such a foundation for your identity – your self-esteem – you will always be vulnerable. The course of your life may go something like this. As a child you look to Mum for your self-worth. Then when you discover that she can't always be trusted to be positive about you, you may look to Dad, only to find that he has other priorities which he regards as more important to him than you. After that you may have looked to the 'gang' at school and developed all kinds of behaviourisms to gain acceptance by the 'in' group. However it's not very long before you realise that that doesn't work either, but by that time you have compromised your morals, your hopes and ideals so much that the pain is really beginning to set in.

So you look for the love and affection of another boy or girl, and perhaps a whole succession of partners, until you find one who seems to believe in you or make you feel needed and wanted. But by now, you are so insecure that you begin to play games with them in order to 'test' their commitment to you, and this invariably damages and possibly destroys the relationship. Either way, you discover that they can't be totally relied upon either, so you throw yourself into your work, your children, or your sport/hobby, determined to be a success and so finally to be able to feel good about yourself. For a time it works, but then comes a redundancy, a dismissal, a loss of business, sickness, or a child grows up and rebels into delinquency, and again the bubble bursts. Slowly you begin to realise that your life has been a search for validation and significance in all the wrong places, finally disappointed by the realisation that your body is ageing and that the children have got their own lives to live, and may not be there when needed.

Conclusion

The quest must go unfulfilled, until we come to Christ to discover our true worth and identity, *not* by virtue of what we do, or our gender, or who our parents were, or our nationality, but by virtue of our place in Christ as God's own creation, and in what He has done on our behalf. This is the only reliable, eternal mirror into which we may safely look, to discover ourselves in terms of our real security and value – to be released from the crippling effects of low self-esteem.

Further Reading:
I'm O.K. You're O.K., by Thomas Harris.
Romans Chapter 8 (the latter part).
Genesis 32:28 'No longer is your name Jacob . . .'
Created for Love, by John and Agnes Sturt.

Chapter Twenty-Eight

SEX AND SEXUALITY

- In this arena, ignorance is definitely not bliss. All that God gives us is good, providing we participate according to *His* wisdom. If sex for you is not good, make it a priority to find out why.

- Sex without unconditional commitment to your partner is an expression of lust, rather than love, and will release forces of selfishness that will eventually destroy the relationship. Marriage is the only 'safe' context for satisfactory sex.

- Good sex benefits both body and soul, but bad sex is much worse than no sex at all. Early experiences may need to be remembered and reinterpreted before sex can get better.

- Learning how to say 'yes' or 'no' and mean it whole-heartedly is the first step in a happy sex life.

- We are designed as sexual beings, but it is not to rule our lives. Your commitment to your marriage should never be conditional on 'satisfactory' sex.

- Sexual problems begin with inner personal and social problems. Unsatisfactory sex is symptomatic of a prior problem.

- Sexuality is experienced, usually on a subliminal basis, in *all* of our relationships.

- After a frantic day, what have you left to give? Don't try to run on an empty tank.

- Sexuality is delicate and easily bruised. Protect yours by accepting responsibility for it. Inform yourself and work on communication.

- When sex seems like the last chore at the end of the day, it's time to schedule less work and more time for enjoying each other.

- Pain, emotional exhaustion and impatience are the three most common causes for unsatisfactory intimacy.

- That 'spontaneous sex is the best kind' is a myth. Remember to schedule time, just for each other.

- Remember that 'performance' and 'pleasuring' are mutually exclusive endeavours.

- Both partners should spend plenty of time to achieve full arousal. This is the best safeguard against pain and frustration. ('Wham, bam, thank you mam' is a sure path to problems.)

- If you don't know – or won't say – what turns you on, how will your partner ever know? It's up to you to say.

- A man's lack of control doesn't mean that he doesn't love her, or that she's being exploited. Both must learn sensitivity and self-control.

- Don't confuse emotional arousal with physical arousal. Only the woman knows when she is physically ready.

- Anxiety over his performance, high blood pressure, drugs or alcohol are the main causes of difficulty in maintaining arousal.

- Generally speaking, females are interested in the process, while males are interested in the goal. Men should relax and learn to enjoy the process.

- After giving birth, a woman should feel free to decide for herself when she is ready to have sex again. It may be up to six months, especially if she is breast feeding.

- A woman's orgasm originates in the clitoris, so it must be stimulated for an orgasm to occur. Whether this comes from masturbation or penile stimulation is of no moral consequence.

- Good sex involves finding a fine balance between self-lessness and personal pleasure, so that both partners are gratified. A bad balance will, in time, cripple genuine intimacy.

- Physical union is also the time for spiritual union, when the soul of each partner is refreshed.

- No artificial birth-control method is absolutely reliable, so if pregnancy is not an acceptable consequence, then don't.

- Men who accuse their wives of frigidity are usually themselves to blame, because of ignorance, selfishness, harsh words, body odour, impatience etc., and need to be corrected with a gentle but honest comment.

- Generally speaking, men are stimulated by sight, while women are aroused by loving, endearing words, tone, touch and atmosphere.

- The art of lovemaking does not come naturally. It must be learned by understanding, communication and patience.

- Emotional echoes from childhood experiences must always be taken seriously. Get help as soon as you realise something is wrong.

For notes on pornography and masturbation, see chapter 42.

Further Reading:
The Act of Marriage, by Tim and Beverly LaHaye.
Sexual Happiness in Marriage, by Herbert J Miles.

Chapter Twenty-Nine

Sexual Abuse

- Whether to remain in the dark, or face the painful memories and memory blanks and risk the threatening path to emotional healing, is the great question for those who have been abused. The answer will depend on the resources of love and truth available to the victim in the form of friends and counsellors, but he/she should not begin until he/she is ready.

- To remember the disturbing scenes is to relive them, yet it is also to reinterpret them, which is the means of integration of inner child with adult, wherein is the healing. We simply may not bury what is not yet dead (resolved) and time alone has no healing virtue.

- Common symptoms of a history of molestation may be frequent depression, the 'acting out' of what was done, sexual addictions, unexplainable avoidance or loathings, strange feelings of intimidation or fear around certain men or women, perfectionism, fits of unreasonable anger, shame, guilt and excessive self-consciousness, excessive reserve with others, inability to cry, very low self-esteem, sexual frigidity, other addictions, needing to control others, etc.

- When wounds are frozen through trauma, so are feelings – they do not age. To live again, means facing the pain of victimhood, meaninglessness, false guilt etc. and coming through it by re-experiencing the repressed feelings and reinterpretation via the truth.

- 'Where were you, why didn't you stop it?' is the angry question thrown at God. The concept of God as 'Superman' underlies the mistaken belief that causes the

mental tension, and is challenged to its roots by the God
who allows Himself to be crucified.

- That God doesn't always stop it, but goes through it with
  us, tells us that the ultimate threat is not so much in what
  happens to us physically, but in how we interpret it (with
  regard to our own value) and therefore respond to it.
  ('Do not fear those who, after they kill the body, can do
  nothing more . . .')

- The responsibility for what happens remains entirely
  with the perpetrator, as an act of their own volition,
  regardless of whether or not the victim found any
  part of it pleasurable. He activated the victim's natural
  responses in a self-indulgent, premature and destructive
  way. He alone is the perpetrator.

- What is totally beyond a child's ability to understand
  or interpret must be shut out, and therefore is lost to
  conscious memory until later in life when it must be
  reassessed. At that point the feelings experienced may
  still be as strong as they were when first repressed.

- Coming to emotional health depends entirely on knowing the truth about the perpetrator, about ourselves and
  our feelings, and about God. It is not time that aids the
  healing process, but increased insight.

- Simply realising for the first time, why I am the way I am,
  is a huge step forward and a powerful therapeutic tool in
  gaining freedom from the effects of childhood abuse.

- 'If begin to cry, I may never stop' is the very real fear of
  those with a history of past abuse. It's a groundless fear
  and a risk one can take under the supervision of a good
  counsellor.

- 'Who was good and who was bad, who was right and
  who was wrong, and what actually is normal?', are the
  questions that must be asked and answered by those
  abused in childhood.

- 'That your past does not have to define who you are,
  nor control the rest of your life', is the first of many

insights which God alone can give, for you must now accept responsibility for yourself.

• The therapist's role is three-fold: to provide a safe place of unconditional acceptance and understanding, to assist the person to survey the damage by looking beneath the feelings to their source, and to reflect true beliefs back in the face of false ones. (Above all, he/she is not there to preach a premature 'forgive and forget' philosophy, or to tell the victim they simply need to quit dwelling on the past and move on, before the work is done.)

• Any individual is just as vulnerable in life as the measure of truth and true beliefs they have or have not yet comprehended. Children who gain access to 'adult' videos and pictures are therefore particularly vulnerable.

• The unspoken oath of silence within families must be broken, for it controls lives and covers evil by fear of rejection and disapproval, but choose your confidant carefully, it is not for just anyone to know.

• Should the perpetrator and the co-contributors be confronted, even years later? Yes, if at all possible, they must (see Matthew 18:15); to 'speak the truth in love', to bring them to accountability, and to reconcile the relationship. However, this should occur only *after* the victim has equipped him or herself with as much truth and insight and wise support as possible. (A premature encounter with a man in denial will not facilitate healing, the feelings of powerlessness may only be increased.) Someone else needs to be present to offer support and counsel to the perpetrator as well. (His suicide as a direct result of her confrontation will only increase the damage.) Whatever happens, the victim must not assume responsibility for the perpetrator's reaction, neither can the relationship continue until responsibility is accepted.

• 'Why did he do it to me?' is a question that needs to be asked and answered. He did it because he wanted to satisfy a sick desire of his own. He did it because he completely misinterpreted your innocent actions as a 'come-on'. He did it because he or his body (or both) confused intimacy with eroticism. He did it because it was done to him as a child, and now it's the only thing that turns him on. He did it because he is emotionally and socially isolated and cannot relate to the feelings of his victims. He did it because he is quite unable to inter-act with other adults, and you were 'safe'. Ultimately he did it because his thinking is sick, but he is *not* beyond redemption or rehabilitation, and neither are you.

- Though the perpetrator feels remorseful, shamed, guilty, scared and disgusted with himself for what he did, that alone will not stop him because abusing is an addiction that his will power alone cannot stop. Insight, confrontation and accountability may be his only hope of escape.

- A guilt-ridden victim who 'understands' an aggressor, and therefore justifies and excuses him, is in fact indulg-ing him in his evil and becomes an accomplice. This bond of loyalty must be broken by the realisation of his accountability for his own decisions.

- Any person who is left feeling used, dirty, fearful, worth-less, powerless or vulnerable after a sexual encounter has been sexually abused, regardless of how the event took place. There is a sense in which all sexuality in a fallen world contains elements of abuse.

- Whatever behaviour it was that awoke our sexual nature, is what we will desire to return to for arousal later in life, regardless of our moral beliefs, unless help is received. This is why many abused women choose husbands who also abuse them.

- When you loathe something without knowing why, it is because your subconscious has made the connection with the repressed memory, and you must trace it to get back in control.

- Was the overall context of the abuse primarily a dys-functional or socially isolated family? Were the parents preoccupied with their own pain? Such questions help give the victim a new perspective on his or her ordeal.

Assessing the damage done is always with the purpose of planning for future restoration.

- The double-bind for the abused child is 'If I tell it will damage the family because they won't be able to cope with it, and I may be called a liar and hated for it, but if I don't there is no way of stopping it'.

- Rules for confrontation: be specific about the details and the consequences; be clear about your purpose; ask for their admission; express a desire for a better relationship based on truthfulness; and do not be put off your task.

- Misguided Christian counsellors often add to the victims' load by expecting them to forgive and forget, and allowing them to condemn themselves when they find that they are unable to. (The damage must first be assessed before it can be put right.)

- Some label their experience 'abuse' as a defence against accepting their true responsibility and acknowledging their guilt as an aware and morally accountable adult. Counsellors who indulge such thinking do not help their client.

- As with any injury, there are degrees of severity, and no two cases are exactly alike. Beware of presuppositions.

- Before diagnosing 'denial' the counsellor should consider the case for 'counsellor's presumption'. We get what we expect to find.

- The willingness to forgive is a deliberate act, but the act and depth of forgiveness relies upon insights gained which can release from all sense of victimhood. (There are no victims in the family of Christ.)

Further Reading:
Out of the Shadows, by Patrick Carnes.
Escaping the Shadows, Seeking the Light, by Connie Brewer.
Facing Codependence, by Pia Mellody.
A Door of Hope, by Jan Frank.

Chapter Thirty

Victorian Wisdom

- The world knows nothing of its most virtuous subjects.
- He learns much who also studies himself.
- Learn something, even from your failures.
- Law is costly, shake hands and be friends.
- A word before is worth two after.
- One story is good until the other is told.
- Man doubles his evils by brooding on them.
- Credit makes cheap things dear.
- Nothing is cheap if you don't want it.
- Time covers and discovers everything.
- One today is worth two tomorrows.
- Death does not blow a trumpet.
- The beginning, mean and end to all things – God.
- Nothing is troublesome that we do willingly.
- An evil conscience is the worst of the plagues.
- Ill nature sucks poison from the sweetest flower.
- Who never tries cannot win the prize.
- Small beginnings may lead to large ends.
- Second thoughts are often best.
- Always verify your references.
- A waiting appetite kindles many a spite.

- A husband's wrath spoils the best broth.

- Morning is welcome to the industrious.

- Violent passions lead to great depressions.

- He is well paid that is well satisfied.

- Night is not dark to the good, neither is day bright to the wicked.

- Be not the first by whom the new is tried, nor yet the last to cast the old aside.

- Little strokes fell great oaks. Great journeys begin with the first steps.

- Never open the door to a little vice, lest a great one should enter also.

- If you are in debt, somebody else owns part of you.

- Little deeds are like little seeds, they grow to flowers or weeds.

- Time, which is most valuable, is most frittered.

- To cool a passion, take a long walk.

- Books aid thought, they should not supersede it.

- Every day of your life is a page of your history.

- Perseverance overcomes difficulties.

- There is something to be learned, even from the merest trifle.

- Gold is no balm to a wounded spirit.

- There is no darkness so deep as that of the prejudiced mind.

- Solitude is the nurse of wisdom.

- Read not books alone, but men; and, above all, read thyself.

- Walk swiftly from temptation, or it may overtake you.

- Truth is the hidden gem we all should look for.

- Spend more than you make = debt. Spend less than you make = independence.

- Write your own history daily.

- When alone we have our thoughts to control; in our families, our tempers; and in society, our tongues.

- He learns much who studies other men.

- One kind word may turn aside a torrent of anger.

- Hasty climbers have sudden falls.

- When the fox preaches, keep an eye on your chickens.

- Out of debt, out of danger.

- Every man is the architect of his own fortune.

- Man proposes, but God disposes.

- To hope and strive is the way to thrive.

- Short reckonings make long friends.

- Gold has more worshippers than God.

- Never walk one way and look another.

- The child is father of the man.

- He that is down need fear no fall, he that is low, no pride.

- When we think we fail, we are often near success.

- He that complies against his will, is of the same opinion still.

- He jests at scars that never felt a wound.

- Experience keeps a dear school, yet fools will learn no other.

- He that goes a-borrowing goes a-sorrowing.

- Half a truth is often a great lie.

- Approve not of him who commends all you say.

- Having been poor is no shame, but being ashamed of it is.

- Love your neighbours, but don't pull down your hedge.

- It is ill-manners to silence a fool and cruelty to let him go on.

Part 3

Wisdom in Relationships – Family and Everyday

Chapter Thirty-One

ANGER ESCALATION

How to break the cycle of retaliation between couples.

Stage 1

FRUSTRATION BUILD-UP. Either or both cross the line that divides the balance of power *or are perceived to have crossed it*. One gets too aggressive or inconsiderate, or provokes frustration and anger in the other. Power or position or respect is being attacked, or being perceived that way. Most flare-ups are to do with power shifts or betrayed expectations accumulating over a period of time. Insecure, easily threatened people are particularly vulnerable.

Stage 2

FLASH POINT. One 'lashes out' – they have 'had enough', they have taken enough 'garbage', or words to that effect. Such an outbreak is often the result of lack of good communication, and misunderstanding, and may come as a complete surprise to the other. The other retaliates, perhaps with words or mild violence in an attempt to restore the balance of power or to 'punish'. (In the male it is usually to put her 'back in her place'. In the female it is usually to goad him to action or as 'getting even' for bullying.)

Stage 3

ESCALATION quickly occurs, as each one seeks to gain the upper hand, until either real violence occurs or co-operation between partners breaks down altogether (e.g. a lockout, separate rooms, or one partner takes off). This process can occur over days or hours or even minutes. Then others are brought in, perhaps the family or even the police. At this point, though the love is still there, both are angry with each other, as both perceive the other to be in the wrong, so neither will back down by apologising. To do such would be tantamount to becoming a 'wimp' and risking the loss of self-respect. It also feels like condoning injustice. If this state continues, love begins to be eroded.

Stage 4

STAND OFF. By this time there is a point to prove, some power to be held on to, some pride to be maintained. 'We regretted our words and deeds quickly, but refused to apologise because we believed in our cause . . . our "rights" had been violated.' It can only get worse unless they get help quickly.

The Helper's/Counsellor's Way Forward

STEP ONE: Explain to them both about escalation and the absolute need to apologise for the *way* they respond, if not for the cause they are fighting for. Show them how to apologise for the parts they regret e.g. the fact that they shouted or name-called. This enables them to climb down without betraying their sense of justice or self-respect. Otherwise the anger and hostility can only escalate.

STEP TWO: Ask them what they expect from each other to put the matter right. If the other is unwilling to comply, stop and find out why.

STEP THREE: Only when steps one and two have been taken can you then find out how the original violence flared, by talking out the *real* issue.

STEP FOUR: Set up guide lines for future conflict. Teach them how to recognise the warning signs that frustrations are mounting and that pressures are starting to build. They must then sit down and talk about it, thus defusing the situation before tensions mount.

STEP FIVE: Have the wife teach her husband *how* he

may gain her respect and co-operation without resorting to violence. Teach them also that 'flare-ups' indicate an opportunity to dig out some rubbish, rather than a time to hole up.

STEP SIX: Get an undertaking from each one that they will *not ever* repeat the act of violence or shouting which was so inflammatory and that neither will put up with 'no speaks' and 'no touch' for very long.

STEP SEVEN: If they are ready, have them pray for and serve each other.

N.B. In the animal kingdom, if the junior member does not submit, a fight for dominance, which goes to the death, may ensue. That is *not* the way for a couple to sort out their differences. Oldest sisters or brothers may not be able to relinquish their position of dominance for the sake of co-operation in a later marriage. Those women who have been hurt by and therefore oppose male authority may also oppose their husbands simply because of what they represent. The spouse who leaves may in fact *want* to return, but dares not, until there is *evidence* that some changes are being made.

Question: Why does a woman often have to cry before a man will apologise? Perhaps it is because when a woman is struggling to get her own way (rightly or wrongly) a man may consider that he has just two choices. He can either 'give in', in which case he surrenders his 'authority' – his 'position', or else he must struggle to the death of the relationship to maintain his 'place'. But he cannot afford to 'go soft' on the one who is threatening his leadership. His only way out is if his wife surrenders and breaks down in tears. At that point she is no longer perceived as a 'threat' and he can then afford to become vulnerable again in apologising and loving her. The issue, for him at least, is the balance of power, and his own opinion of himself.

Further Reading:
Healing the Angry Heart, by Kathy Collard Miller.

Chapter Thirty-Two

Bonds and Bondages
(see also 'Breaking Soul-ties')

What is a bond? The invisible tie that binds our hearts to the hearts of others. The link by which we influence, and are influenced by others. The prior loyalty we give to others. A 'soul-tie'. The means by which we can empathise and identify with others; the goodwill built up on many shared experiences.

Types of Bond:

Marriage bond. The transference of loyalty is illustrated by ceremony. The bride's new loyalties to her chosen husband (see Genesis 2:24) illustrate the need to 'leave' before one can 'cleave' (be properly joined to another).

Parental bond, particularly of father to daughter and mother to son, e.g. Rebecca and Jacob. Such a relationship must graduate from obedience to mutual friendship. (Parents must take the initiative in this.)

Friendship bond. The hearts are 'knitted together', e.g. David and Jonathan. (If such intense trust is ever betrayed, it can also turn to great hatred.)

Sibling bond. The affections and loyalties amongst brothers and sisters. (Jesus asked 'Who are my brothers and sisters?' His answer indicated the greater strength of those who are 'like-minded' over those who differ, yet are of one 'blood').

Treasured objects are also able to bond with one's heart and soul, to the exclusion of all else, e.g. boats, houses, farms, cars or even pets. (Some men have even been known to 'marry' their motorcycles.)

Devotional bond. Total loyalty to God as God prevents destructive bonds from forming with anything else. (Whatever is not submitted to God in our lives, seeks to *become* our god.)

Emotional bond tied by *physical* intimacy.

A bond becomes a bondage when:

- it inhibits personal growth.
- when loyalties conflict (no man can serve two masters).
- when loyalty goes beyond 'due season', e.g. as in bereavement or adult obedience to one's parents.
- when one party is an emotional parasite draining off energy from the other in a pathological relationship.
- when the friendship is founded on neurotic needs.

The Causes of Destructive Bonds

- Feuds and vendettas of long standing, between individuals or families bent on revenge.
- Manipulation. Controlling another or being controlled by the abuse of loyalty, or fear of being rejected, etc.
- Transference – the 'cross-matching' of personal need forms mutual attraction which underlies cult followings, adultery etc.
- Foster children moved from one family to another have developing bonds overlaid or betrayed, and become unable to develop new ones.
- Married couples unable to bond because of old emotional ties not cut properly, and unfinished business from the past still subconsciously imposing. (*All* horizontal relationships *must* be put right, if we are to truly walk in the light.)
- Homosexuality – where the adult is 'locked-in' to the identity of the opposite parent or the innermost conclusions which helped form their identity in the past.
- Regret causes a person to feel they 'owe' somebody, so that they are always embarrassed by that memory.
- Priorities become confused – one tries to serve two

masters, e.g. God or self, husband or children, and the result is frustration and confusion.
- Inability to respond in faith to Christ because of peer pressure and the need for others' approval.
- The grief process is blocked and one cannot 'let go' the lost loved one.
- Bondage due to vows made. Any vow made to another is in danger of binding one into trouble if it usurps the place and authority of God. The sharing of a secret, a vow, a crisis, or mutual desire for revenge etc., can also become a bond.

We *do* have a psychological impact on each other, we *can* hold each other in a 'soul-tie' which prevents us from acting as truly 'free' individuals. Today many are invisibly bonded by cords they are scarcely aware of, yet they know that there is a subtle force which holds them bound fast. All such negative bonds need to be broken by renunciation, forgiveness and restitution. Often, one's own insecurity makes this difficult, and this must be faced up to and replaced by faith in God's providential care. Also, the company we keep nurtures that which is predominant in our own personalities, e.g. a dominant friend will cause a clinging vine to become more clinging, just as a dependent person will cause a dominant friend to become more domineering. Two who feel they need each other will compromise themselves rather than risk their 'friendship' – this renders them vulnerable to destructive influences. 1 Corinthians 10:14 – 'flee from idolatry' – don't look to a person to meet a need that only *God* can meet. Look to God alone for your self-esteem. Distancing yourself a little may be the most loving thing you can do, both for yourself *and* the other.

Remember

- Christ's position as your centre must not be compromised by any person or you will remain extremely vulnerable to other 'centres'.

- Awareness, rather than aloofness, is the aim.

- Allow for change – you are not today the same two people that began the friendship.

- A friend or spouse is *not*, in any sense, your possession. Be careful when laying 'obligations' on others that they may resent.

- Be willing to let go. Try to identify any reasons that may prevent you from doing so.

An Analogy: It is all right for the moon to orbit around the earth, but it is not all right for the earth to orbit around the moon.

(**Note to helpers** – do not allow anyone to put all their trust in you. Always gently, but firmly, steer them back to God. Remember, He is a 'jealous' God. When you find yourself making their decisions or having your time encroached on beyond what you can volunteer, it's time to back off. The emotionally dependent person needs to grow up, and you need to learn how to say, 'I don't know – but God knows and cares, go to Him'.)

Relevant Scriptures:
Exodus 20:3: 'You shall have no other gods before me.'
Luke 14:26: Every other relationship to be secondary.
John 8:31: 'If you hold to my teaching, you shall be . . . free.'
Galatians 5:1: 'For freedom Christ has set us free.'
1 John 5:21: 'Dear children, keep yourselves from idols.'

Chapter Thirty-Three

TRAINING CHILDREN

- The best gift you can give your children is to have an excellent and loving relationship with your spouse. (A man can't be a good father *until* he is a good husband.) If you don't have a responsible spouse, you *do* have a heavenly Father, and all the resources of your own faith-family (local church) to draw upon.

- Have you completely owned your own decision to have children yet? You can only *love* what you first of all *choose*, otherwise resentment blocks the bonding process. (Freedom is not the ability to choose whatever you want, but the ability to choose for that about which you have no choice.)

- It is a child's right to be loved *and* to know their restrictions. The child needs to feel loved and secure before he or she can love. The love bond, with appropriate restrictions, is the foundation for *all* their behaviour.

- It is a myth that most parents know instinctively how to raise and discipline their children. Simply to hope that they will be O.K. is the shortest recipe for disaster.

- The greatest psychological need of the child is for protective love and discipline. If it is available, then the child faces life with confidence. Discipline and freedom are not contradictory. Discipline must direct a child's natural impulses. Too much freedom will allow the child to destroy himself, and is the most common fault among parents.

- Every child is born with a number of potentialities. Take those potentialities and guide them in the right direction. 'Train up a child according to his/ her own unique talents.'

- Train the young parents in the essentials of good parenting, and prevent neurosis at its beginnings – childhood. This can save a lifetime of corrective training later.

- Emotional stress at home always inhibits a child's natural development. Again, the best gift you can give your child is your own happy relationship with yourself and your spouse.

- Real learning is not competitive; it is done for its own pleasure, and allows us to get closer and closer to the full expression of our total potential. Competition between boys destroys comradeship.

- First look at what your children have done *right*, before pointing out the faults. Praise is the best and *only* setting for criticism.

- If God has given you children, He requires that you pay attention to them. Time, both quality *and* quantity, is *most* necessary. Even a few minutes of focused attention can do wonders, but children learn more by 'being with', than by being 'spoken to'.

- Conditional love and approval (love given 'on condition') breeds insecurity, and insecurity breeds either perfectionists or drop-outs. 'Fathers, do not provoke your children to anger.' Neither allow your children to provoke you.

- 'Can't you do anything right?' is a quick way to kill your child's confidence. Don't attack the person, but the misbelief which is hurting them.

- Parents *must* learn to go to their children and ask for their forgiveness for mistakes made. This enables their children to do likewise in their turn.

- Try never to smack or discipline out of rage or reactive anger – wait until you've calmed down (walk away if necessary) or you'll instil fear and anger in the child's personality. Use your own anger to strengthen your resolve to do it right.

- Of course you love your child, but does he/she *feel* loved? The importance of approving eye and body contact to communicate unconditional love cannot be overstressed. These are two of the most precious gifts that parents can give their children, at *any* age. (Play wrestling and back-slapping kind of stuff is great.)

- If Dad approves of his daughter, only then can she feel good about herself. However when she needs him the most, often he is uncomfortable with her.

- Some difficult temperaments are congenital and are no reflection on your prowess as a parent, but good parenting will assist the child to master his own inclination to wilfulness.

- Give each child a special night when they can have Mum and Dad all to themselves.

- Children's sense of justice means that, as an act of their reason, they will naturally try to take revenge, e.g. tantrums, withdrawal of co-operation, or refusal to eat, and they may need to be faced with the need to forgive and forget, *before* their co-operation can be restored. Often it is a cry of help for someone to recognise injustice in the home.

- Don't compare your children with each other – it will breed discord and frustration.

- One of the most difficult parts of 'growing-up' is learning to accommodate *adults'* failings. Teach them how to appeal your decisions respectfully.

- Children will repeat *whatever* behaviour gets them what they want. This is a priority insight in all your dealings with children.

- Let the mother be firm in her gentleness, and the father be gentle in his firmness.

- If you have taught your children to love Christ, to enjoy people, to respect themselves and authority, and to accept responsibility, you have done well.

- Are you sharing your own hard-earned wisdom with other parents-in-pain?

- One thing worse than parental tyranny is child tyranny. 'Mummy and Daddy are the boss!'

- It's not just the child who needs a good sleep to keep a good mood.

- Sometimes you must make a deliberate choice to be positive about the children, especially when negative thoughts crowd in.

- Good parenting doesn't *always* produce good children, neither does bad parenting always produce bad children. There are *many* other factors at work, not the least of which is the child's own will. Proverbs 22:6 merely describes a general observation. Read it in association with Proverbs 13:1.

- When you are near to panic over a child in trouble, force yourself to stop and think rationally. Panic prayers are not helpful, tending rather to increase one's feeling of helplessness.

- Never allow the child to come between the parents. Mum and Dad should always present a united front, or the child will learn to divide and rule.

- If Mum forces Dad to back down in front of the children, they learn that authority can be overruled. From there it is but a short step to all-out rebellion. If Dad forces Mum to back down, they learn that authority is all about power rather than protection. And remember, no child can serve *two* masters.

- Some children are born with emotional needs that are greater than the parent can meet. Such parents must get all the help they can, *before* they get pushed over the edge.

- When children keep kicking at the fence, both the child and the fence (parents) will be damaged. Parents must work together on discipline. Only love and forgiveness can repair such damage.

- When an adolescent begins to self-determinate, a self-centred person will turn on them as if threatened by an enemy. There's a fine line between rebellion and healthy self-assertion.

- For some children, naughtiness is their only way of saying 'I need attention'.

- *Never* laugh at your children's fears. Recognise the reality of the threat for the child, for *you* are the resource they need to overcome their fears.

- When both parents are absent from the home, they simply can *not* give the children what they are most in need of. Such children will pay a high price for their 'double income' family. In most situations it is more honourable to be poor. Warning signs include no time to talk or go fishing or teach skills or enter into their world. It's simply *not enough* just to provide food, shelter and clothing.

- A street kid's biggest need is usually for a father's guidance and boundaries. They are not comfortable until they find a firm person to give direction and limits that are born out of a sense of their value and worth.

- Education can inform heads, but only God's Spirit can *transform hearts*.

- Parents must renounce their own rebellious attitudes, before they can help their children with theirs. The character of the parent is the final key to the development of the child.

- Mother, beware of smother love. Learn to let them go, while maintaining from a distance responsible supervision of their interaction with others. Father, beware of abdicating your responsibilities, it is *your privilege* to shape your child *today*.

- Why are you hanging on to your little darling? Is it because *you* need to feel needed? Or is it because of your own secret fears?

- What was your strongest feeling when you first saw your baby? It may need to be re-examined to repair a damaged bond.

- Pre-schoolers: Two warnings and then a smack. Smack for deliberate defiance and blatant disrespect. If need be, love will not shrink back from inflicting short-term pain for the sake of long-term gain. Before smacking, *first* be in control of your own emotions, and always warn first.

- It's vital that you teach your children how to share, how to cope with not getting their own way, and how to deal with a bully. But first you must know how yourself.

- Speak well of your children *in front of them* and they will become comfortable with themselves.

- Don't listen to just anybody's opinion of your performance as a parent, be selective about which opinions you value.

- Don't allow your parents to undermine your judgement in front of your own children, or you will lose your authority in their eyes.

- Parents and grandparents must sort out their respective 'territories' and grow closer together through it.

- Every conflict with your child is an opportunity to grow closer together, as *together* you look for a solution.

- If you're down on yourself as a parent, it will seem like *everybody* is down on you.

- Don't ever threaten discipline unless you are also prepared to follow through on your threat.

- Train yourself to respond, rather than to react. Avoid hasty discipline.

- Over a period of time, children start to behave according to your spoken expectations.

- Children do *not* always know what is right for themselves. The parent who believes such a lie will cause their child much unnecessary suffering. We are all dependent on the wisdom and experience of other people.

- If you win the power-struggle at home, you won't need to fight for it in public.

- Rewards and punishment highlight for the child the way it is in life, and helps them relate cause and effect before it becomes life-threatening.

- Consistency, supervision, kindness, courage and clear communication skills are *the* essential qualities to develop for good parenting.

- Remember, we *all* need limits. Love them enough to say *no*.

- Sometimes you must make a deliberate choice to be positive about the children, and sometimes they must do the same about you. It's not just children that need a tongue-taming programme.

- Mum and Dad must back each other in discipline, and share the parenting responsibility, so that each one can take time out and step back a little.

- Dads are much needed when they get home from work if Mum is putting the tea on, and vice versa. What's it like in your house at 6 o'clock? Organise that hour at all costs.

- You only have a short time to enjoy your children, a time that can never be repeated. Don't waste it working for the fickle dollar.

- Children can *record* their experiences, but they need *your* help each day to *interpret* them.

- Each child needs an individual approach in disciplinary matters.

- Assign tasks to your children. They need to know that they are useful and they need to know what their job is and what is expected of them. Communicate your directions clearly and break down the tasks into bite-sized jobs.

- If God has given you children, He will also provide you (both of you) with all you need to parent them, and if you do not have such resources, it can only be because you have not *asked*. Ask Him, and ask each other too.

- Respect for the parents is birthed in the parents' respect for the children. New commands must be undergirded by explanations, or the child is disempowered.

- Restless children come from restless homes – where television is often the only minder. A slow rhythm at home, with Mum in control, *always* produces calmer, more secure children.

- Family pressure, rather than striking the child, is the Jewish way of discipline. Their Rabbis say, 'If a child must be struck, let it be with a feather'! Many times, smacking is a cop-out. Discipline is much more than merely punishment.

- How might your subconscious animosity towards your child be hurting him or her now?

- Are you an 'intrusive' parent? Child abuse can take many forms. Respect the children's privacy.

- Because children are so vulnerable to their parents, they are the most typical victims of damaged human nature.

- The end result will be neither 'nature' nor 'nurture' but a combination of both.

- No matter how successful you become, your child's failure will always feel like your failure. Get all the help you can while you can still influence them.

- If you wrong a child, be sure to apologise or you will lose his respect. For when you lose his trust, you lose him.

- Keep a close eye on the children's rivalry for your

affection. It seeds jealousy that can tear the family apart, and is often born of a misconception.

- The best gift you can give your children is to love your spouse. Next to that it's your encouragement.

- Anticipate a child's natural desire to take revenge by helping to trace the true source of her anger and resolve it.

- Remember that touch-hungry children become touch-hungry adolescents. Don't miss your opportunity to provide your remedy.

- God does not support family cults, and will even enable a child to assert itself if a parent seeks to dominate, and thereby engulf the child's developing identity.

- Do not label a child 'rebellious' who must reassert his individuality in the face of a threatened takeover by an insecure parent.

- When your child is naughty, check first for touch-hunger and lack of focused attention – conditions only you can remedy.

- Removal from the world does not protect children as effectively as explanation and insight. (It is the truth that keeps their hearts safe.) Yet exposure to evil must be supervised.

- Discipline is not the enemy of enthusiasm. Rather, enthusiasm is protected by discipline.

- Labelling people and children is the most natural thing in the world. It is also the most destructive! Children grow into labels.

- Don't 'own' your child's problem for them. They must experience the consequences of their own faulty choices.

- Relationship must come before rebuke, for no one can make another do anything, and children discover this early in their lives.

- Children grow into their labels. Distinguish between

their worth and their behaviour when a rebuke is called for.

- Of course you love your child, but does she perceive it? Can she feel your belief in her? (Beware the myth of marginal 'quality' time.)

- Be sure to discover the limitations of your responsibilities for your children's choices as they grow older, or they will never accept responsibility for themselves.

- The children who learn in order to avoid looking stupid soon quit learning. Learning 'for the fun of it' is self-perpetuating.

- The mistaken belief that some children can never succeed is an evil belief indeed. When a child fails, methods of teaching have already failed the child.

- Childhood resentments form at a subconscious level, and so continue to affect their attitudes in adult life.

- Children who must placate angry, violent adults will, one day, need to be freed from a permanent sense of anxiety. *A wounded spirit who can bear?*

- Your need to be needed can cause you to disempower your loved ones by creating dependence in them. To free another you must first be free yourself.

- Some learn by 'theory before practice', and others learn 'practice before theory', so some are disadvantaged in the classroom and others in the workshop. Neither should take failure personally.

- When a child unquestioningly honours a dishonourable parent, then in adulthood that child will also become dishonourable.

- Power can be withheld or given away. Parents who won't relinquish it breed perpetual children.

- Before exercising 'tough love', consider the possible outcomes, in order to live with the consequences of your 'cruel to be kind' strategy.

- Conflict is natural and a necessary part of life; it's how you handle it that determined whether it will be a positive or a negative experience.

- Do you regret the mistakes you've made in family relationships? It's never too late to apologise and invite forgiveness.

- No one can make you angry. You choose your own reaction. (Why are you threatened?)

- It takes explanations to enable us to internalise external authority, otherwise resentments accumulate into active or passive rebellion.

- The personal growth of a member of the family can be served or crushed by family loyalty. Don't make an idol out of family togetherness.

- Remember that acceptance of the person doesn't necessarily imply approval of their actions. (Otherwise who can love the unlovely?)

- No amount of counselling can undo the damage done by a father who ignores or neglects his son. He must have a male role-model in his life to escape the consequences of his father's evil neglect.

Further Reading:
Parenting the Strong-willed Child, by James Dobson.
Parenting isn't for Cowards, by James Dobson.
How to Really Love your Child, by Ross Campbell.
Discipline While You Can, by James Dobson.

Chapter Thirty-Four

Co-Families

- No man can serve two masters, and no child can obey two parents who have differing agendas.

- Parents must enter into the world of their step-children also, so that the children can learn to enjoy their new parents.

- Be open and up-front with all the children about the reasons for the first marriage breakdown.

- Bonding two families together is difficult, but never impossible if the commitment to make it work is strong enough to pay the price. 'Them' and 'us' must give way to 'we all'.

- Don't expect the kids to have better mental health than you have yourself. Keep working on yourself. Have you accepted responsibility for your predicament? Do you own your own decisions or do you blame others?

- Failure to plan the routine of the family is a plan to fail.

- Spend both quality and quantity time together. Take lots of time for fun and relaxation.

- If the old habits don't work out, don't keep repeating them. Family times, contracts, personal times and Scripture memorisation are all vital in the retraining process.

- Scripture gives stability where there are very few firm guidelines, and it reprogrammes our minds towards self-sacrificial love.

- Unselfish love, communication, humility, forgiveness, honesty, realistic expectations, prayer and persistence will be the resources most in demand, in uniting two families successfully.

- Remember that Abraham, Moses and David were all involved in a two-family setting.

- Be very sure that both you and your family have worked through the grief of ending your first marriage before you contemplate another.

- Ask others for their honest opinion as to where they think that you are in the grief process before you commit yourself to another relationship. They can often judge more objectively than you can.

- Be careful not to overcompensate with discipline for your biological children or favours for your step-children.

- New bonds don't take until all the debris has been cleared away from the previous ties.

- Spend lots of time balancing expectations; spouse with spouse, parent with child, child with parent, child with child.

- When you go on a family outing, go with *all* your heart, or don't go at all. Ambivalent ('I knew I shouldn't have come along') people can spoil any outing.

- Live one day at a time.

Chapter Thirty-Five

CONFLICT

Confronting, done in the context of caring, becomes care-fronting. Ephesians 4:15: 'Speaking the *truth* in love' is the ordained way for relationships to grow.

CONFLICT is a natural and inevitable part of life. In itself it is neutral. We must learn *how* to do it in order to stay in relationship, while remaining loyal to ourselves. Conflict resolution is a precondition to *any* healthy working relationship including marriage, parenting, family, business, church etc.

Many people have a 'fear of conflict' which renders them vulnerable to manipulation. If you care at all, you will have to confront.

Without this skill we cannot be secure enough to risk submitting ourselves to others. We will therefore try to avoid any situation where one or other will have to 'give in' or where conflict is likely. Can you think of examples?

There is a time to *avoid* the conflict (withdraw), to *compromise* (both stand to lose), or to *'give in'* – Jesus did all three at one time or other. But when He confronts He does it for the *other's* welfare rather than for His own. He demonstrates truth *and* love.

N.B. It is not like the assertive aggression in defending our own rights which is so popular today. Preoccupation with one's own rights always leads to anger and alienation.

The aggressive person says 'You have no right to smoke in my presence – get lost–', while the motivation of the 'care-fronter' is 'You are damaging yourself and presuming on our relationship by smoking, and because I care about you *and* our friendship, I must ask you to stop.'

Because most confrontations are done in aggressive anger, and are therefore destructive, some people tend to avoid them. But anger is neutral and must be creatively harnessed. Conflicts also in themselves are neutral, it's how they are handled that is the challenge.

Four Simple Rules:

Care. Be clear. Be gentle. Admit your own fault also.

A relationship is only as good as its *communication*, so continue to improve your skill at it. It is love's medium.

Ask Yourself . . .
'If I were in their shoes, how would I like to be corrected/warned/reproved?'

'How can I best communicate my truth in an honest and uncompromising way?'

Anyone who feels threatened automatically resorts to attacking, blaming and threats – all behaviour that *blocks* good communication. This is why it's so important to speak in a spirit of humility and concern for the other. If you're out to win by putting the other person down, you will *both* lose.

People don't care how much you know until they know how much you care.

Chapter Thirty-Six

DATING

- Whoever you spend time with will inevitably have an influence on you. Keep that in mind when you choose your dates. Is this the kind of person you want to become like?

- Balance expectations for each other and ensure the commitment level is the same, otherwise jealousy and disappointment will cause problems.

- Check your motives for wanting him/her. Are they selfish or is the desire to benefit them as well?

- Don't expect that he/she will meet all your emotional needs. You must be comfortable with yourself before you can be comfortable with another.

- Insist that he or she treats you with respect at all times right from the outset. (People can only love what they value.)

- Never choose somebody as a reaction against family values or conflicts, or you won't be able to back out when things go wrong.

- No matter how strong your morals, your basic drives are stronger, so stay out of each other's bedrooms and isolated places. Remain accountable to those around you, for you are yet human.

- Choose somebody to guide you/advise you during this time, whom both of you respect, and dedicate your relationship to the honour of Christ.

- Get premarriage counselling early on in the relationship

(at or before the time of engagement) in case it exposes factors which change your mind.

- From about the ages of fifteen to twenty-five is a time of transition for both of you. During these years your directions and priorities in life change rapidly in the process of becoming who you will be. Choose your partner slowly.

- Accepting a spouse also involves accepting his or her family. Consider the culture, customs and values carefully. Can you happily become part of these?

- Beware of any displays of selfishness, anger or pride by your date. You will likely be the victim of those same negative emotions yourself some day.

- Promises to improve which your beloved makes are not worth anything. Evidence of change is all that you can rely on for your future security.

- Girls, your opportunity to insist he make those needed changes is **before** you marry him. Afterwards he will have lost much of his motivation.

- The acid test is to ask yourself, 'If I knew he/she was never going to change, would I still marry him/her?'

- If your father or mother has real emotional or behavioural problems, be careful that you don't choose a similar partner, just because they are familiar to you and you can therefore relate more readily.

- Does your evaluation of your own worth limit you to considering only those who appear of the same standing/status? Perhaps your low self-esteem is setting you up for a disaster.

- Be careful of someone with little or no sense of humour – it is indicative of real emotional damage and puts additional strain on a relationship.

- Are you really in love with the actual person, or are you in love with a dream?

- Your relationship will only be as good as your personal

mental and emotional health, no matter whom you date or marry.

- Don't ever pressure him or her with 'God told me' statements that amount to manipulation, nor by encroaching on personal boundaries by teasing, swopping clothes or premature emotional intimacy.

- Dating is the time for balancing expectations and negotiating, *before* commitment takes place. Enter in slowly, with lots of communication.

- Don't tease yourself and risk becoming 'unequally yoked' by dating those who do not share your values, ideals and dreams.

- Never keep a relationship going simply because you're scared of hurting someone by breaking it off. Sometimes you must be cruel to be kind.

- How is he or she with money? Can you happily entrust your own money to him or her? If not, don't consent to marriage yet.

- He or she may be the right person, but is the timing ripe yet for a full-on relationship?

- If you come on too strong, it's much more difficult for the relationship to find an even footing. Human nature is much more likely to appreciate what it has to earn. Conversely, it's difficult to value what we don't have to work for.

- Never be persuaded into a relationship. If you're uncomfortable, back off. If pressured, the best answer is the honest one.

- Avoid a sexual relationship prior to marriage. It sidetracks and short-circuits the emotional energy needed for strong bonding and commitment, and restricts the development of the relationship from going beyond physical attraction. (A relationship built on sex is consequently never able to develop properly.)

- Where appropriate, don't be embarrassed to flirt a little.

It's a natural way of letting somebody know you are attracted to them without risk of embarrassment if its not returned. It should not, however, be confused with seduction or infidelity.

- If your steady date 'dumps' you, learn how not to take it personally. It is no reflection on your value as a person, though it may be a reflection on the correctness of some of your beliefs.

Chapter Thirty-Seven

EXPECTANT MOTHERS

- The perfect first home for any baby is a mother, happy in her pregnancy. Peace comes with the assurance of adequate resources.

- A baby's hearing is the first sense to develop, hence the importance of quiet, contented sound, even while it is still in the womb.

- Fear of bearing a deformed baby is rooted in fear of the unknown, yet *nothing* is unknown to our loving motherly-Father God.

- Always remember that childbirth is a normal function of the female body, and one for which it has been designed.

- While less-than-perfect babies may not be God's *perfect* will, yet God's love and power is revealed in many special ways, in conditions of weakness and imperfection. The key question is 'how will the parents choose to respond?'

- Avoid – as far as possible – becoming excessively emotional while pregnant, by avoiding 'traumatic' thinking. Focus your thoughts on positive things.

- Have you accepted yourself as a woman, and all that that involves? Being comfortable with your pregnancy *begins* with acceptance of your femininity.

- Fear of pregnancy can cause a woman to shut down sexually. Address the *real* cause of anxiety.

- Tears while pregnant do not automatically mean that

something is wrong. Hormones fluctuate dramatically during this time.

- To avoid sibling (and spouse) resentment and jealousy on returning home, involve them all in baby's care.

- The process of birth should not be hurried by unnecessary human intervention. Let the baby come at its own pace.

- Get all the information you can before the day of birth, that you might know what to expect.

- Don't hesitate to ask for extra days in hospital while you regain your strength and establish a good feeding pattern with your baby. There should usually be some latitude in this matter.

- Enjoy your pregnancy. Pamper yourself and your spouse while you can.

- If you aren't happy with your midwife's or doctor's performance, you owe it to yourself and your baby to say so, and/or to find one that you *are* confident in.

Chapter Thirty-Eight

FORGIVENESS

- Grudge-bearers are emotional debt collectors (from Matthew 18:28).

- Grace opposes 'getting even'. God's way is loving confrontation, *preceded* by unconditional forgiveness (from Ephesians 4:32).

- To overcome hatred and bitterness, begin by praying for the one who wronged you (from Luke 6:28).

- Forgiveness involves releasing others from your personal sense of 'justice', then you yourself can receive forgiveness (from Hebrews 10:30).

- God forgave us *before* we apologised. May we in our turn withhold forgiveness until an apology is received? (from Romans 5:8).

- In God's sight the 'offended one' may be in *more* danger than the one 'offending'. Bitterness poisons one's eternal personality, making the victim suffer twice (from Luke 15:28).

- Wounds of injustice and bitterness do not heal by themselves; deliberate forgiveness is the only ointment (from Matthew 18:35).

- Bitterness is a contagious condition. Treat the infection before it spreads to others (from Hebrews 12:15).

- God's kind of love (from agape) is based on a deliberate choice of the will, not merely a feeling. You also can, and must, choose to forgive or at least be willing to learn about it (from John 15:17).

- Release others from your expectations, before they 'fail' you, just as grace has been made available to you (from Romans 5:20).

- Always acknowledge your own faults when mentioning another's (from James 5:16).

- Forgiveness can be a process. The first step? To see your *own* need of it (from Matthew 6:15).

- Living in God's grace means that you don't have to earn His approval in any way, then you can give unconditional love to others (from Romans 5:20).

- Bitterness will not let go the memory of past injustice, but continually tries to 'pay back' the harm done (from Proverbs 17:9).

- The discrepancy between our expectations and what actually happened, will be the degree of our resentment (from Matthew 18:34).

- Pride won't admit fault and will therefore eventually separate the best of friends (from Ephesians 4:32).

- Any relationship needs honesty, plus forgiveness, to survive (from James 2:13).

- Did you vow *never* to be like your father or mother? Your action is actually *reaction*, and your agenda is now set for life.

- Forgiveness is costly, but not as costly as withholding it. You can absorb the loss only when you know that God will balance the books on your behalf.

- As we forgive others, they are then able to change.

- Though forgiving others is difficult, forgiving ourselves is even harder, for we must first face up to our guilt and pride, and allow our self-worth to be threatened.

- Acknowledge your anger and unforgiveness against God, or your spiritual growth will stop. Eventually you will understand why He allows suffering and pain.

- How many unresolved conflicts are you still carrying around from the past which are weighing your spirit down? Unless they are dead they will not be buried.

- Though forgiving others is difficult, there is a Life available to you/within you, which doesn't know what it is to hold a grudge – the life of Christ. Whose life are you manifesting?

- To receive forgiveness from God, you must first find the unconditional love which makes it safe for you to face up to your guilt.

- The right to revenge has *never* been given to man by God. It will only escalate into war. He reserves the right to balance the books *Himself*.

- When the state exercises its muscle, it is not in the spirit of revenge, but to fulfil its divine mandate to maintain law and order – to protect people from themselves.

- When you realise that your antagonist/assailant was also a victim (they were 'weak' rather than wicked, 'sinned against' as much as 'sinning') then – and only then – will you be able to forgive them.

- '*It isn't fair – you betrayed me/ruined my life – I hate you,*' is the corporate cry of the citizens of hell.

- The 'pleasure' of rehearsing the wrongs that were done is a very savage comfort indeed, taking the victim deeper and deeper into darkness. Have you realised yet just how hurt and angry you really are?

- Burying the offence by trying to forget it is no substitute for forgiving the offender. Trauma should never be buried alive.

- No you can't change the past, but you can stop clinging to it once you find something else to cling to. Cling to the One who said 'Father, forgive them, for they know not what they do'.

- No person, nor the injustices of life have any power to harm the essential 'you'. *It is only your chosen response* that can damage you in any real way. Forgiveness comes automatically with such an insight, and such an insight comes when you deliberately acknowledge Christ's continuing care for you.

- Have you discovered your own ability to hurt others equally as much as those who have hurt you? People who are hurting *always* hurt others.

- Forgiveness isn't saying it's not important, or pretending that everything is O.K. It is actually refusing to excuse the offence, but choosing to put it aside. It is remembering, but still forgiving.

- 'If I rely on you for my sense of value, and you betray my trust, then I have only my anger and sense of betrayal to maintain my value, until I can find a new foundation for my self-esteem.'

- The ache of past memories fades when the pain has been redeemed (transformed) into incentive for service and personal growth.

- Is your sense of justice an idol – is it in subjection to the God of justice *and* mercy – or has it become isolated, standing on its 'own'? Principles (elemental spirits) alone can serve us or destroy us.

- You can't forgive another if you feel that you are still vulnerable to their power – that you are still their 'victim'.

- When forgiveness doesn't cost much, neither is it worth much, but who will pay the price until they know their true wealth?

- Though the act may not be forgivable, the person who did it is.

- Begin to forgive by deliberately and repeatedly doing those things you have refused to do in the past; call, visit, and refuse to speak ill of them. Your feelings will catch up with your will sometime later.

- The other person's response to your offer of forgiveness

is their own responsibility, and you must not/cannot try to predict it.

- Forgiveness takes time – the deeper the hurt, the longer the time – but it will come, and the emotional release will be worth it. Meanwhile, act as if you have forgiven them.

- Giving forgiveness and the restoration of trust are two separate issues, but the first clears the way for the second.

- Can forgiveness ever be fully achieved without the conscious recognition of God's recreating activity in the pain? I think not.

- I believe in justice, but first I believe in the willingness of God to demonstrate His ability to transform the worst evil, if we will leave our cause with Him.

- Never forget, the next time you are the victim of injustice, that God demonstrated His ability to 'balance the books', in and through a *miscarriage* of human justice – Calvary – and that it was only Jesus' willingness to forgive His accusers that allowed Him to do it.

- When you apologise, you are clearing out your inflamed conscience, but remember to ask for their forgiveness also, in order to release both you and them. Whether or not they give it, is none of your business, but you *must ask*.

- Far from denying justice, forgiveness takes justice utterly seriously. Justice is first and always the setting for forgiveness.

- The willingness to forgive is a choice, but the *ability* to depends on receiving certain prior insights, for example that the offender was first of all a victim.

- No, life is not fair, but God is, and your security does not rely on life's being just but on God's love for you.

- You must make friends with your past, for it will always

be a part of you. New insight alone will enable you to reinterpret your regrets and leave the pain behind.

• To really forgive yourself, you need to understand fully why you did it, and to become assured that you aren't likely to make that mistake again.

• You can only forgive when you first understand why there are no victims in the family of God.

Chapter Thirty-Nine

MANIPULATION

Manipulation is a most destructive force in human relationships. We should learn:

a. how to recognise it and
b. how to release ourselves from it.

Definition: 'pressurising people to conform by use of a subtle threat or coercion, which causes them to act in conflict with their *own values.*' Wisdom and reason is *always* suppressed when the manipulator is at work.

Nine Kinds of Manipulators

1. **Martyr.** This kind evokes guilt by making one feel selfish and ungrateful. 'After all I've done for you, this is how you repay me,' or 'Remember the favour I did you – well now you *owe* me!'

2. **Bully**. Evokes our fear of violence, anger, pain or conflict, or our fear of being thought of as a coward. 'Threat' is the currency of this kind.

3. **Bludger**. Works on your sympathy, compassion, empathy. To resist one of these is to risk being labelled as 'heartless' or 'cruel', or even (shudder) 'hardhearted'.

4. **Flatterer**. E.g. children may work on your need for affirmation and approval. (Don't ever allow a child to manipulate you or you'll pay for it many times over. Remember, children will always repeat whatever behaviour gets them what they want.) The young girl who is seduced into immorality and then realises that she has been exploited, is also an illustration of this kind of manipulation.

5. **Peer Pressure**. Your fear of non-conformity – need for acceptance, e.g. 'mates' work on your fear of 'disloyalty', fear of rejection, sense of obligation. 'Are we mates or what?'

6. **The Boss**. 'Your job/credibility/reputation is on the line unless you . . .' This works on your insecurity in your position and ability.

7. **The Pouter**. This one uses silence and your need for conversation, communication, and clear air. Such will sulk until you can't stand it any longer and give in to their demands.

8. **The Spouse** who threatens to withhold money or sex or some commodity in order to get their own way. A very dangerous practice in the marriage.

9. **The Pharisee** who for the sake of religious 'unity' expects that you will keep silent to avoid upsetting the religious status quo.

N.B. It is always your *own* fear of the consequences, that is being evoked. Bible examples, Peter – for fear of the temple guard, he denies his beloved Christ at the hour of His trial. Herod, who has John the Baptist beheaded because his wife put him in a bind where he feared 'losing face'. These are two classic examples of the power of manipulation.

Remember that manipulation is the tool of the powerless, the desperate, those who must resort to exploitation to achieve their own ends. It is, in fact, Satan's own means of rule in his kingdom and means of controlling his servants. A 'controlling' spirit, it controls by fear. It works by putting you in a double-bind, setting up an internal conflict which clouds your judgement.

Because it operates on a *subconscious* level, to become *aware* of it is to be *released* from its power – but you *still* have a decision to make.

The price of giving in to it is usually very high and involves: • Loss of self-respect • Loss of other people's respect • Loss of personal freedom • Damage to the relationship • Doing something that will put you in conflict with yourself and cause you many regrets later.

It is important to remember that you are a victim, not

just of the manipulator, but of your *own* fears and needs.
Resentment and anger *always* result.

To Gain Your Freedom

- Identify the areas in which you are vulnerable. What is
  the unspoken threat – why is it a threat to you?

- Identify *who* it is that makes you feel cornered or leaned
  on. (Somebody you tend to avoid.)

- *Confront* the manipulator with what they are doing. (Be
  warned, there may be a violent reaction.)

- *Help* them see that there is a *better way* of gaining your
  response, and that a 'pressured' response is destructive
  to relationships.

If in doubt, ask yourself, 'Is the pressure I feel honest and
upfront, or is it devious and subtle?' Manipulation is a trick
we *all* use instinctively at times, but we must realise that
it will always damage our relationships and that we must
learn *not* to use it.

To 'Peer-Pressure-Proof' Your Child

It is your relationship with, and the wisdom you have
invested in, your child, which is their only defence against
peer pressure. To be accepted, to be liked, is the currency
of decisions made under pressure of peers, and the best
thing you can do for your teenager is to explain to them
the mechanics of manipulation, and build your own relationship with them.

Ultimately, it is only a greater loyalty and commitment to
the will of God which can release us from all our fears, and
lesser loyalties. 'The fear of God is the fear that releases us
from every other fear' (Adams). Acceptance of the work of
Christ is the only way out of an ultimate guilt and fear of
reaping all the consequences of our mistakes in life . . . the
only escape from satanic manipulation.

Further Reading:
Caring Enough To Confront, by David Augsburger.
Telling Each Other the Truth, by William Backus.

Chapter Forty

MARRIAGE
(see also 'Living in Relationships')

- If you want a good marriage, first make up your mind to have it, at *any* cost. A deliberate commitment to this is the foundation for all future decisions.

- The good of the *partner* must *always* be more important than getting one's own way. Relationships are *always eroded by selfishness*.

- To re-found a marriage, as far as possible, past wrongs and harsh words must be righted. Restitution makes way for restoration and humility makes way for restitution.

- Each marriage carries the seeds of its own ruin in the memories and attitudes of the partners. Identify the misbeliefs which reside and deal with them before they take root.

- Identify the fears, prejudices, and any false expectations you bring from childhood – they distort your perception of your spouse.

- An 'equal yoke' joins people of 'like mind', and combines the strengths of those with a common purpose. An 'unequal yoke' will bruise both those it binds. It is simply a mis-identification of one another's values and priorities.

- Good marriage preparation must help to define the differences between two people and prepare them to enjoy those differences.

- 'Let old ties be cut so that new ones can form – old loyalties replaced, in order to be joined.' Forgive old acquaintances the wrong they did you, and give your spouse priority over your original family.

- A marriage *contract* is conditional love, primarily in the interests of self. A marriage *covenant* is unconditional love as demonstrated by God. 'Till death us do part', is missing from the *civil* but not from the *sacred* marriage.

- Love is not just a feeling, or an indefinable 'chemistry', but a deliberate choice. God *commands* us to love out of a deliberate, quality decision, and His unconditional acceptance of us is our inexhaustible resource from which to draw. The feelings will follow on.

- Romance and tenderness die through neglect. *Remember* to nurture each other with little acts of kindness. Compete with each other to make each other happy.

- When desires conflict, negotiate for trial periods – 'your turn, then mine'.

- Husbands who abdicate their leadership leave the relationship to drift into trouble. Let the husband be ready to lay down his own interests for his family.

- Wives who want to dominate their husbands should remember: a man may not be a husband to his 'mother'. Men who behave like children should also remember that a woman may not be a wife to her 'son'.

- Men derive their sense of value from being trusted and admired, women derive theirs from being cared for.

- The partner who must 'give in' repeatedly, may one day 'walk out' unexpectedly, unless they learn to 'speak the truth in love'.

- Good communication is measured by quality rather than quantity.

- Don't leave your partner guessing about your movements, keep in touch. Remember, you are *two people* now.

- Be quick to apologise for those hurtful critical words,

they are the thin edge of the wedge that will eventually force you apart. (Withdraw the thorn before the wound may heal.)

- Never dream of another, lest the idea take hold!

- Remember, if you stop appreciating and caring for your spouse, someone else may start!

- At all costs locate the hidden reason behind those recurring arguments. *Stop talking and start listening*.

- Some people are more courteous to complete strangers than they are to their lifetime companions. How can that be?

- There's nothing good to be gained by playing 'lay the blame'. Cut down your spouse and you damage *yourself*, for you are now 'one flesh'.

- Are you both agreed on the meaning of money? Does it mean security for the future or good times today?

- Own your own anger, and encourage your spouse to own theirs. Nobody has the power to 'make' you angry unless *you* allow it.

- Your love doesn't actually exist or grow, until it's *expressed* in word and deed.

- *Don't* occupy your mind with your spouse's faults or by the time they return home you'll be ready to commit murder. Instead consider your own. This is absolutely imperative, the more so if you have a difficult partner.

- Choose your tone of voice more carefully, for it communicates *more* than your choice of words.

- Can you distinguish between what are selfish self-indulgences, and what are your *legitimate* needs?

- Be careful not to freeze your spouse into their past mistakes. People are not static, they change and grow.

- Consider your role models carefully. Where can you

improve on them? Where do you need to forgive them? Where do you need to ask for their forgiveness? Are their values and standards appropriate for you?

- Be loyal to each other in public, do your dirty laundry at home. Damage done in public is much harder to undo than damage done at home.

- A weak relationship won't sustain excessive demands. Stay out of goodwill-overdraft until love and commitment has been built again.

- If you fall short of your destiny, your spouse will not be held responsible. Only *your* choices alone can shape what you become.

- In a power struggle, sex and money are often used as weapons. This invariably forms a wedge which levers the partners apart. The power of love is 'power for', never 'power over'.

- Estrangement often begins as early as the engagement period, with the first grudge, the first choice *not* to forgive. Escalation of resentment or forgiveness are the only two options.

- Pre-wedding doubts may have been wisdom's last warning, but when God is allowed to change one heart, is *any* relationship beyond salvage?

- Parenthood merely intensifies a relationship. Good relationships get better, poor ones get worse.

- Do not give to a man or woman what belongs to God – your adoration, your security, your entire sense of worth as a person.

- If a marriage is to work, it must be *worked at*. Focusing only on your spouse's virtues releases the needed energy and incentive to both of you.

- Take responsibility for your *own* happiness. Daniel enjoyed God's presence, even in a den full of lions!

- Learn how to recognise when you are being subtly

manipulated, and *always* confront it as a destructive device for getting one's own way.

- *Self*-respect is necessary before you may expect it from your spouse. How can he/she love you if you hate yourself?

- 'You *chose* your love, now *choose to love* your choice.'

- Confront unfaithfulness or violence or drunkenness in your partner *immediately*. Passive 'understanding' is equivalent to aiding and assisting.

- Learn to trust your spouse, but remember they are still human. Absolute trust in people is not taught by Christ. Genuine trust also takes account of human nature.

- Are you putting pressure on your spouse to change? Your 'medicine' might be doing more damage than your mate's faults. *Praise is far more effective than criticism in bringing change.*

- Don't keep picking at each other. Sit down together and communicate your grievance clearly, or else *keep quiet.*

- A threefold cord is not easily broken – invite Jesus Christ in to become that third strand. He is the creator and sustainer of the institute of marriage, and His kind of love must be *learnt*.

- A relationship that breathes is healthier than one that doesn't. Every couple need times apart, from time to time, to avoid emotional claustrophobia. Don't become an 'ingrown marriage'.

- If it's important to him/her, then it's important to you, because you who were one, are now two!

- 'For lack of fuel the fire goes out.' Every time you accuse or attack, you throw another log on conflict's fire.

- There's bound to be some truth in what they say – will it really hurt you to admit it? The next time you feel attacked or criticised, agree and ask for more love and help. You don't *have* to jump to your own defence.

- Spiritual adultery usually occurs before physical. Never share your heart with another, *before* you've shared it with your spouse.

- Partners need to be hugged, long and often. Neglect this need to your mutual deprivation.

- When you can't agree on direction, don't act, but keep talking. And remember, even good marriages do have tense and angry moments.

- Discover and cultivate an interest that *both* of you can enjoy.

- One person can save their marriage alone, if they will commit themselves to that marriage regardless, and if they will discover God's ultimate kind of love in Christ.

- When a wife steps forward to shoulder responsibility, the husband usually takes two steps backwards. (Wives with lazy or irresponsible husbands should *not* take over in an effort to fill the gap and avoid the consequences. Instead a wife should gently offer to assist him with the task, being careful *not* to protect him from the consequences of a slack attitude. Otherwise he will quickly learn to abdicate his position and very soon she will have to carry the load herself.)

- Recipe for disaster: Hollywood idealism plus large doses of 'meism'. Unrealistic expectations of what a marriage should be like is marriage enemy number one. Selfishness follows as a close second.

- Not till the husband is *allowed* to take the lead, will his pride allow him to ask his wife for help.

- You know you're growing up when you can love your partner *despite* your feelings, rather than *because* of them.

- Old soul-ties must be cut by establishing all of ourselves in the present acceptance of Christ, thereby giving up the needs and injustices of the past. Seek help in this matter if old influences persist.

- Accept an apology graciously, or you may not receive any more.

- Your first reaction is usually the wrong one. Don't be content with *rea*ction, become *pro*-active instead.

- Neurotic love totally excludes the actual reality of the 'loved one'. It exists purely to meet the needs of the neurotic.

- Return a soft comment for your partner's hard one, or you'll stoke the fire that will burn both of you, as well as your children.

- Why must you always have it your own way? It isn't threatening to have to give in unless you're already afraid of a takeover.

- Whether a relationship grows or dies depends not on fate or feelings but on choices. Your choices. (Love is something you *do*, not something you feel.)

- Are you over-interpreting their comments because of your own pain? Check it out.

- Love does not maintain the marital commitment; rather it is the marital commitment which maintains love.

- We all need touch and hugs, but first we must take down the walls that have been built too high around our hearts.

- If you leave your partner guessing about your movements, it may communicate that they don't matter or that you don't care.

- Expressing your feelings honestly and doing it kindly are the two fundamental requirements to sustain a good relationship.

- Trying to be a 'good' spouse? First take the time to find out what your partner really needs from you, rather than what you think he/she needs.

- Love for others may begin with something as simple as lowering your expectations for them.

- Hug your loved one soon. Love and affection do not truly exist until they are given expression, and many suffer from 'touch hunger'.

- Different families hold boundaries in different places. If you won't say where yours are, how will others know if they cross it?

- Only the soul assured of its own indestructibility (in the love of God) can really love an adversary or embrace its own self-sacrifice.

- If you don't have any freedom to be yourself, it is not a relationship you are in, it is a cult. You must recall your power or be crushed.

- If you want a better marriage, go to work on yourself, not on your spouse. Changes you make in yourself can set your spouse free.

- Encouragement breeds encouragement. Be sure to give it to your spouse before looking for some yourself.

- Empowering questions are the best way forward when your loved one is really hurting. Why is she/he feeling threatened? Why is she/he angry? What is she/he frightened of?

- If you have traded a measure of your freedom in return for their protection or security, do not then resent their power over you, for *you* have loaned it to them.

- The difficult person in your life is actually God's invitation to *you* to gain greater wisdom and self-awareness.

- 'Peace at any price' is priced at resentment, anger, and ultimately alienation and subjugation.

- Conflict is a natural and necessary part of life; it's how you handle it that determines whether it will be a positive or negative experience.

- She needs reassurance that she has been heard, but 'What

did I just say to you?' is not the way to get it. Better to teach him how to paraphrase, instead.

- A spouse actually 'departs' from the marriage when violent or seriously irresponsible, whether or not they leave. A simplistic reading of 1 Corinthians 7:15 makes the victim out to be the offender.

- Are you in love with your partner, or with your idealised concept of them? (Do you love the person, or merely the person you perceive?)

- The mental health of one partner is often (but not always) reflected in the mental health of the other.

- The stability of a marriage is not necessarily an indication of its health. Even the master and slave will cling together in their mutual need.

- Is there ever a time when leaving one's spouse may in fact be the most loving thing one can do?

- To marry, first find someone who is like you. To remain married, discover that she/he need not be like you at all.

- Making an appointment to spend time with your spouse is not a sign of failure, but the precursor to an enriched relationship.

- The two unrealistic expectations of marriage: that it will annul loneliness, and that one can *make* the other happy.

- When one partner in a co-dependent relationship embarks on a journey of personal growth, the other is forced to make a decision.

- It is a sad thing to see a man make a child of his wife to feed his own ego – as sad as a mother who does it to her son.

- If you continue to cling to your idealised spouse, you will have to ignore who they are in reality.

- If you don't know where or how to draw the boundary,

you'll have no choice but to build a wall. Get some help with your carefronting skills.

- If you won't make decisions, don't complain when others make them for you.

- Lower your expectations for yourself before you dump your anger on others.

'It doesn't really matter whom you marry, since you're sure to find out the next morning it was someone else.' Samuel Rogers (C19th cynic)

Chapter Forty-One

Sexual Morality Before Marriage

To avoid moralistic legalism I list below sixteen reasons against having sex before marriage:

- God, out of His intense love for us and His desire that we be eternally blessed, has said '*No*'. Consequently, to defy Him, is to choose a course that will ultimately lead to our *own* pain and unhappiness and exclude us from His Kingdom.

- Immorality jeopardises the relationship by mixing and confusing love with lust, strengthening selfishness and meism, and weakening a commitment to the ultimate good of the partner – a commitment upon which the future of the relationship utterly depends.

- The drain on time and emotions prevents and interferes with individual and personal growth. At a time when the roots of one's life should be going into the eternal love of God, they are being drawn off into the unreliable personal desires of another human being.

- Guilt, whether conscious or unconscious, will introduce an internal conflict which will bring pain. Such pain causes individuals to try and escape via further sexual stimulation, drugs, alcohol or other forms of escapism.

- The basic principle underlying an enjoyable lifestyle is self-control. Long-term gain is only available via short-term pain i.e. a willingness to forgo immediate pleasure for long-term reward.

- Immorality, being basically lustful, damages love, distorts sound judgement, and alters our basic image of ourselves, the concept that lies at the heart of all that we do and say.

- The physical act of intercourse cannot be separated from the emotional bond that accompanies it, and the change in social status that goes with it. Otherwise the whole person, and the fabric of society, begins to fragment.

- Sex can only be a positive, life-giving experience, *if* it is part of a life-long relationship – in short, a marriage. Such a relationship requires time to adjust to each other and to build reserves of respect, unconditional love, trust, commitment and communication.

- Sex as an end in itself (lust), as with any direct pleasure-seeking, becomes boring, demeaning, and soul-destroying, whether within or outside the marriage commitment. That sense of discontentment and/or shame later becomes a huge obstacle to real sexual enjoyment, usually causing frigidity, impotence, marriage breakdown, and finally disloyalty. (Affairs do not cause marriage breakdowns. On the contrary, marriage breakdowns are what cause affairs.) It is, in effect, a time-bomb, set for a later date.

- A door in the spirit is opened which can sometimes allow demonic activity to disturb and destroy one's peace of mind and sexual contentment. Lust, when indulged, will always breed *more* lust.

- The fabric of society is utterly dependent on the strength of the family unit, and immorality strikes at the very seed of this unit before it has a chance to grow.

- *No* method of birth control is completely safe, and an unwanted pregnancy has a multitude of painful consequences e.g.:

a) A decision to marry, forever undermined by the fact that neither husband nor wife is totally able to own it for themselves, because of the presence of the baby.

b) An abortion, which results in an absolute host of psychologically damaging consequences. (See notes on abortion.)

c)   Solo parenthood and its associated suffering.
d)   Parental and family pain.

- In itself sex is an act of promise of personal commitment, of giving oneself in a real sense to another.
  If this psychological promise is ever broken, one or
  both individuals will be emotionally scarred by the
  betrayal and rejection. To indulge in sex outside of
  giving that commitment is therefore to cheat or defraud
  your partner. It is silently saying, 'I like you only enough
  to commit myself to you as long as it pleases me,' and
  poor self-esteem accepts such a 'secondbest' proposition,
  leaving one partner or another open to being used and
  abused.

- Many relationships start out *unequal*. Neither of them
  ever say what they want or expect out of the relationship – and many never stop to think how it's all
  going to end. If the relationship breaks up, and such
  a breakup remains quite likely, many emotional knots
  tied far too soon will tear apart, endangering one's
  ability to sucessfully bond again. The more closely
  entwined, the more emotionally damaging is the split,
  and our emotional and sexual responses are *easily* damaged.

- Soul ties are eternal. What God unites, no man may
  undo, and so new relationships are left to struggle
  with the ghosts of the past, and individuals are left
  wondering why they don't 'feel' married to their new
  spouses.

- The mind that seeks to indulge itself in sensual appetites,
  as well as pleasing the Lord, is divided against itself, and
  comes into terrible conflict.

Remember:

No amount of religious or moralistic teaching will protect
a young person against the temptation to immorality if
natural, parental friendship and affection is absent. Touch
hunger will simply overpower them.

Relevant Scripture:

Proverbs 4:23: *Guard* the affections of the heart.
Romans 14:23: Unless you are convinced, you are condemned.
1 Corinthians 6:18: Abusing one's own body by misappropriation.
1 Corinthians 7:2: *Avoid* sexual immorality.
1 Corinthians 9:27: Bring your body into subjection.
Ephesians 5:32: This is a great mystery.
2 Timothy 2:22: *Flee* youthful lust.
James 1:15: When lust has conceived.

Chapter Forty-Two

SEXUAL MORALITY FOR YOUNG PEOPLE

I believe there are nine reasons why young people get into immorality:

- The relationship with parents and basic attitudes towards their authority has been damaged through past incidents, and the *resulting* independent spirit of rebellion *rejects* parental guidance and looks for like company.

- Today's sophisticated culture puts couples under great pressure because of an artificially extended time period between puberty and marriage – the gap between 'bodily' timing and 'social' timing. This is largely the result of the extended training which young people in today's culture require, before they may take their place as a couple in society.

- Once two people have committed themselves to each other in a stable relationship, usually announced by the 'engagement', they mistakenly consider themselves married in every personal sense of the word. They misjudge or are ignorant of the emotional, social and spiritual aspects of the bond which sexual intercourse produces.

- The kindness of God's laws have never been understood, and wrong attitudes to authority have been projected over on to Him. Remember that authority is to *protect* from unforeseen danger, not to restrict pleasure.

- Parents have not invested themselves, with their long-term perspectives, into the young person. Consequently the young person can think only in terms of the moment.

- Childhood habits of selfishness have never been corrected by parents, and 'meism' has taken a firm hold, resulting in love being eclipsed by selfish desire (lust).

- Guilt and anger from past events is causing internal pain, for which further immorality and sensuality provides a way of temporary escape.

- Lust fulfilled, at whatever level, invariably breeds more lust, in a descending, frustrating spiral of reprobation.

- 'Sex Education' in schools has in fact been misrepresented as being merely contraceptive and mechanical advice. The fact that it is given in a moral vacuum – a so-called 'neutral' ethical framework – in fact gives the students an entirely unintended message, i.e. that *immorality/promiscuity is O.K.*, as long as one is careful. (The context of the lessons – a class of single pupils – is actually providing the underlying lesson.) The only way to counter this impression is to state clearly from the outset that contraception is a very poor alternative to chastity/self-control, *and then explain why*. (But who has the courage to make such a statement against the tide of popular opinion? One of the most feared labels these days is that of 'narrow-mindedness' or 'prudishness'.)

Further Reading:
Eros Redeemed, by John White.
Eros Defiled, by John White.
Sex and Young People, by Lance Pierson.
Forgotten Factors, by Roy Hession.
Help your Child say No, by Josh McDowell.

Masturbation

- The good news is that nowhere in the Bible is it condemned as wrong, neither do any other objective authorities – e.g. psychologists – consider it dangerous in itself.

- What is condemned is any loss of responsibility for and control over our own mind and thoughts, and an unrestrained self-indulgence in the desires of the body.

- Also the attitude we take to others in using them in fantasy to gratify our lusts, is demeaning to us and to them, and is not an act of love. Instead it cripples our ability to properly relate.

- Surveys find that a very high proportion of young people masturbate (about 90% for guys and 60% for girls). For most the issue ceases to be a problem after marriage.

- Few people actually want to masturbate, most feel that they cannot help it. The key to quitting is:

a) to realise that it is *not* in fact a big deal,
b) to tell someone about your struggle – it will ease your tension and guilt,
c) to nurture the intimacy of your relationship with your partner.
d) to understand it as 'false comforter' in the face of the presence of *The* Comforter.

Pornography

Pornography and 'adult' videos/movies are not for adults, but for sad, lonely people who have got stuck in their social development and aren't able to achieve a fulfilled sex life. Feeding on pornography cripples one's ability to relate properly to the opposite sex and therefore prevents one from ever sexually maturing. It then continues to serve as a frustrating substitute, precipitating greater loneliness and isolation – a vicious, downward, soul-destroying spiral. Lust fulfilled merely breeds more lust, eventually resulting in demonisation.

Where victims are married, help them to restore their relationship. Where victims are single, begin counsel in social skills. Consider carefully the power of curiosity.

Chapter Forty-Three

THE POWER OF PERSUASION

- Neutral in itself, this skill releases great power, for good *or* evil. It is an essential skill for those who would make a dream come true – for those who have any type of commission or task to achieve (Acts 18:13; 26:28).

- Identify the needs and goals of the other party, before you may gain their favourable response. You can persuade anyone to do anything if you can first of all show them how it fits in with their own goals, desires and values.

- Many are the tools of persuasion – analogy, humour, repetition, external pressure, emotion, instruction, art etc. – you can learn to use them all.

- Gaining the confidence to ask something is the first step in persuasion. Then you must actually ask! (Failing to ask for help from others is actually selfish, for it denies them the blessing and satisfaction of helping you.)

- There is usually truth in what your opponent says. If you acknowledge it he or she will be less defensive and much more likely to listen to you.

- Don't move immediately into a conflict mode when you strike opposition – it will only produce hostility, argument and opposition 'Yes and . . .' is more effective than 'No way . . .'

- Allow your opponent to save face – help them to salvage their self-esteem and you'll win a friend for life.

- Try to use an analogy (word-picture) that the other person can relate to, in order to make your true feelings understood e.g. climbing a mile-high staircase, or being trapped down a well; having one foot in the boat and one foot on the dock, or finding half a worm in your apple; changing horses in mid-stream or being hand-cuffed to a corpse.

• All the world loves an enthusiast, and enthusiasm is contagious, but you can't enthuse anybody else if you are not enthused yourself, first of all (from Acts 19:8).

• In all your persuasion, never resort to manipulation. Let your appeal be honest and 'upfront' (from Acts 28:23).

• If you will first entertain them, they will let you tell them anything. A spoonful of sugar helps the medicine go down.

• As a skilled persuader, you can appeal to the best in people, or you can appeal to the beast in people, and you *will* be held accountable.

Chapter Forty-Four

REJECTION

'The pain of rejection is well known to the heart of God.'

Spiritual and personal growth depend on love, acceptance and having a sense of value. However, we live in a 'world of rejection', and it affects everybody to some degree.

Those Severely Affected

A BABY, rejected by its mother, because of poverty, a broken love affair, illegitimacy etc. An abortion may have been desired or even attempted. She may have been prevented from, or resisted, bonding after childbirth, by the physical barrier of an incubator, or anger, or sickness etc.

THE FOSTERED CHILD, rejected by both parents and foster parents.

THE SCHOOL EXPERIENCE, where the child is teased and humiliated by classmates for being different in any way.

THE ILLEGITIMATE CHILD, whose presence pressured mum or dad into marriage, drawing resentment and rejection from either one of them.

THE WRONG-SEX CHILD, who has to try and be the 'other' in order to gain approval.

THE JILTED PARTNER, rejected by spouse. This applies particularly to women as they tend to place their self-esteem in the care of a man. Bitterness often results. (Genesis 31:32: Jacob unwittingly places a curse on Rachel. Genesis 35:18 – 'Son of my sorrow'.)

THE OVERHEARD COMMENT, when parents are heard to ridicule or comment unwisely and the child overhears, misinterprets, and never lets on. Words spoken in the past about our value continue their influence over us. Their power depends on the influence of the speaker – father, mother or teacher. Low self-esteem, feeling second class or inferior, is caused chiefly by parents. Can you hear your parents' words to you in any of these phrases? 'You were/he was, an "accident", a mistake.' 'You clumsy, stupid little . . .' 'This one was supposed to be a boy/girl.' 'We'd all be better off without you.' 'You're a useless little so and so, why aren't you clever like your brother/sister?' 'You'll always be a loser.' 'Sometimes I wish you'd never been born.' 'I'm going to send you away.'

The Bible defines a curse as a statement releasing destructive power. Iniquitous words – 'Life and Death are in the power of the tongue, and they that receive it will eat its fruit.' Words of rejection create a 'point of entry' for the spirit of death. They release a destructive power over our lives. Remember, 'Children are excellent recorders, but poor interpreters'.

Consequences of Rejection

Fear of rejection • Fear of people • Fear of declaring loyalty to Christ • Fear of confrontation • Rejecting others (your children included) for the same reasons for which you were rejected • Striving to prove the statements untrue, by false fronts, developing a competitive nature etc. or else living out that statement, believing it to be right, even long after the cause is removed • Anger towards one's own children may also stem from rejection • Also rebellion, stubbornness, alcoholism, guilt, suicidal tendencies, a death wish and nightmares • Illnesses such as nervous and skin disorders, allergies, stomach-ache and headache • A 'foolishness', or block to natural intelligence, confusion, and dullness of mind • Insatiable need for praise, affirmation, security and approval – will put tremendous pressure on others for constant attention.

REMEMBER:
When people reject you, they are telling you more about themselves than about you. They are projecting their own

pain onto you, but you must not accept it. God has no second-class kids. 'He don' make no junk.' It is actually rebellion if you continue to think of yourself as unloved or rejected. You must begin to change your self-talk. God believes in you, you are made in *His* image. He would have died for you, even had you been the only one who ever lived. Christ was rejected by God and man, to take our experiences of rejection upon Himself, that we might be accepted.

Psalm 68:5–6: Father to the fatherless, families for the solitary • Psalm 139:13–18: Before we were born He ordained our days • Isaiah 53:3: Despised and rejected, a Man of sorrows • Matthew 10:30: Even the very hairs of your head are all numbered • Mark 12:10: The stone the builders rejected . . . God's acceptance of us • Mark 15:34: My God, my God, why have you forsaken me? • Ephesians 1:4–6: Adopted, accepted in the Beloved • 1 Peter 1:2: He chose us to become His children.

Steps to Freedom

1. Renounce your sense of rejection. Forgive those who rejected you, and actively seek to restore friendship with them.

2. Rebuke the spirit of death or inferiority that has been oppressing you. Try to identify its point of entry. Ask God's help.

3. Speak new words of life over yourself, opposing and contradicting the old words and thoughts of rejection. Your feelings are telling you lies. They merely reflect your subconscious beliefs.

4. Seek to love someone else out of their own sense of rejection.

5. Remember: 'stink' thinking will always be followed by 'stink' feelings.

Further Reading:
Rejection, Cause and Cure, by Derek Prince.
Set Free, by Betty Tapscott.

Chapter Forty-Five

LIVING IN RELATIONSHIPS

- You don't have to defend yourself against every 'attack', for God Himself is your vindicator. Why don't you agree at once, and acknowledge that you are guilty of more besides? (from Psalm 17:2).

- Family bonds become bondages when personal need gets too tight a grip (from Genesis 2:24).

- Your own false guilt, false loyalty, fear, and fear of rejection, are the manipulator's tools by which to control you. To be free, first face up to your fear (from John 8:31).

- Use anger to attack the *problem*, never the person, lest you damage them (from James 1:19).

- Accept people right where they are, rather than wait until they have 'arrived' (from Romans 5:8).

- Reconciliation with offended friends always has priority over attendance at church (from Matthew 5:23–24).

- Love continues to hope for others (from 1 Corinthians 13:8).

- Judge only another's actions. Only God may judge their motives (from Matthew 7:1).

- Aggressive goodwill can turn your enemies into your friends (from Romans 12:21).

- Always test the authority which you submit yourself to lest you wind up serving wolves (from 1 Thessalonians 5:21).

- Reserve robs us of our future friendships (from Proverbs

18:24). Putting up walls to protect ourselves robs us of love and intimacy.

- Love takes the initiative wherever it sees the need (from 1 John 4:7).

- Love equips itself to better help the needy (from Luke 11:5–6).

- Release yourself from manipulation by exposing your *own* secret fear or false sense of guilt (from Matthew 14:9).

- Don't freeze others into their past, and don't allow others to freeze you (from Philemon 11).

- We cannot love others while defending ourselves – the one negates the other (from 1 John 4:18).

- Don't decide until you hear both sides, or you will be guilty of prejudice (from Proverbs 18:17).

- Love doesn't avoid confrontation – doesn't take the soft option – the easy way out (from Ephesians 4:15).

- Love doesn't say 'You're failing so I'm leaving'. Love seeks to stay involved – to stay 'in relationship' (from Luke 10:31).

- Those who reject you and put you down are revealing more about themselves than about you (from John 12:48). Don't take it so personally.

- The 'fear [respectful awareness] of God' is the only resource that will enable you to overcome your 'fear of people' (from 1 Samuel 15:24).

- Pray for your offenders' well-being, before confronting them in love (from Matthew 5:44).

- Love and encouragement must always be the context of correction (from Revelation chapters 1, 2 & 3).

- Though you can't change another, you can always

change your own response by increasing your degree of insight (from Matthew 7:3).

- Rebuilding affectionate love begins with a deliberate choice, and continues with honest and real communication (from Hebrews 10:24).

- Wives who want to 'train' their spouses should remember, a man cannot be a husband to his 'mother'. Husbands who want to act like a child should remember, a woman cannot be a wife to her 'son' (from Ephesians 5:22).

- If you don't respect yourself, may God help your neighbour! If you can't live with yourself, may God help your spouse!

- People don't care what you know, till they know that you care (from 1 Corinthians 13:2).

- Giving to them that ask is not always an act of love. What you give may hurt or even destroy them. For you it may simply be the easy way out, the soft option (from James 4:3).

- 'Love your neighbour' does not mean 'indulge him in his *foolishness*', but it may mean sharing in the painful consequences of his decisions (from Philippians 2:7).

- To depend on one's work, spouse, house or children for self-esteem, is to be in a very vulnerable place (from Matthew 7:24).

- 'What's to be gained by laying the blame?' Will it make you feel better to condemn another? (from Galatians 5:15).

- Honouring one's parents (both natural and 'in the Lord') is a prior condition to the blessing of God (from Exodus 20:12). It *includes* an awareness of their faults.

- When walling others out of our lives in order to protect our inner child, our own hearts become walled in, and we become unable to love.

- 'I can destroy my enemies by making them my friends' (Abraham Lincoln).

- Man asks 'Where are you at?' God asks 'How far have you come?'

- Are you applying pressure on someone to change? How then will they 'own' that change for themselves? Space and respect is always the context for genuine change.

- Pressurising someone to change? Be careful lest the 'medicine' do more damage than the 'ailment'.

- Love involves, first of all, spending time.

- Everything you have ever done or said has affected someone in some way. For your every action there is always a reaction in someone else, because we live 'in relationship'.

- People who choose pleasure as their first priority actually become unhappy. People who serve others in love discover that pleasure overtakes them.

- To know what to tolerate and what not to tolerate in others, just remember your own accountability to those in authority over you.

- Tolerance may be a sign of maturity and personal security, but more often it is a sign of apathy and indifference.

- Can you work in a team or do you 'go it alone' if you can't get your own way? Childhood responses must be re-examined.

- Tolerate your differences to achieve a common goal, and in the process you will learn to appreciate those very same differences.

- Two can walk together until one begins to walk in another direction. Then it's time, not to walk, but to talk.

- The kingdom of God is too small to avoid anyone, even your enemy. You cannot run for ever.

- The limits of toleration must be dictated by the original objectives of the group. Reconsider the constitution.

- Speak softly when angry, or the conflict will simply escalate (from Proverbs 15:1).

- Anyone can 'ventilate' their own opinion, but can you grasp another perspective?

- 'An eye for an eye' will eventually blind the whole world. Beware of the 'justice' of man.

- Don't turn a blind eye to misunderstandings between friends. Instead you must call for discussion on what exactly went wrong. 'Blessed are the peace-makers.'

- If the offended one leaves the group, never say 'we're better off without them'. You needed their gifts also, and separation, though it may be necessary, is always a loss.

- Submission to Christ requires mutual submission amongst His members, the family of believers.

- Don't associate only with those who believe the same way you do, or how will you ever learn anything new?

- When you start by saying 'you always . . .' or 'you never . . .' truth will not be found in your next statement, and you inflame the situation.

- Everyone needs a good listener. Such a person is vital to one's mental health, if only to validate one's feelings.

- Face up to your fear of losing love again, or you will lose it anyway.

- Those who appreciate their own self-worth can accept a compliment easily. Real communication results from a spirit of respect for yourself and for the other person.

- The company you keep will affect you, *especially* if you are unaware of it.

- Seek for others the good you desire for yourself, and goodness will overtake you.

- Television soap opera acts like a dummy to 'satisfy' lonely people's need for social involvement but from a safe distance.

- Love will first of all face the wrong-doer with the full *consequences* of their actions, then forgive and forget regardless.

- It is your relationship with Jesus Christ which can enhance every other relationship you are in.

- Can you disagree without being disagreeable? Learn how to care-front, with kindness.

- Love doesn't say 'It's none of my business'. Love risks getting involved.

- The state you are in is inextricably linked with the state of your personal relationships. Resolve the internal conflicts by rebuilding external relationships, and vice versa.

- Caring is a powerful force. If no one cares, you are truly alone. Loneliness is the call of God to acknowledge His love and companionship.

- The most effective way to change those around you is to change *yourself*. They will be easier to live with when they are able to be less defensive around you.

- If you deeply believe yourself to be inferior or a failure, how can you ever receive love?

- Your first reaction is often the wrong one – become pro-active instead.

- To truly listen to another, one must first be willing to be vulnerable. To be vulnerable first requires inner security. The insecure therefore cannot 'hear' you fully or deeply.

- Don't wait till you're angry before you say what needs saying.

- The shift from child to adult takes place when we move from 'reactive' to 'proactive' action in our relationships.

- In order to forgive, remember that the offender/perpetrator is, or was also, the victim of someone else.

- No one can put pressure on you unless you allow them to. (*Why* do you allow them to, in spite of yourself?)

- Don't say 'yes' when part of you is saying 'no'. It will always cause a back-lash. Stop and resolve the ambivalence now.

- People can only accept correction after their self-esteem is properly secured. Until then, 'attack or justify' is all they can do.

- Don't try and change others. Work on yourself instead. Your response to others is always *your* responsibility.

- Be honest with people for their sake, not just your own, and remember: their response to you is *their* responsibility.

- Why are you so vulnerable to manipulation? Their approval is not vital to you. Neither should you fear their reaction if you have to say 'no'.

- Praise and encouragement is much more effective in changing others' behaviour than is criticism, but which do you use on yourself?

- Happiness does not come from getting your own way all the time. Better to learn how to content yourself.

- Are you pressuring someone to change their behaviour? Remember that their self-image may also be pressuring them to resist you.

- In all your coping, first learn how to cope with not getting what you want when you want it, without accumulating resentment.

- If you don't care for your own needs, you'll soon be unable to care for those who need you.

- Monitor your thinking, and choose to dwell on the virtues of your difficult friend, or negative feelings will surely follow.

- Presenting a nicer appearance to others is not the way to deal with the ugliness I perceive within me. Trace it, face it, replace it.

- Regulations without explanations always disempower. Giving explanations with regulations produces friends rather than servants.

- Don't be afraid to honestly, passionately, persuade, for who will change their mind until they can see the danger?

- Co-dependence occurs when one person becomes focused around the pain of another and cannot let go. (Sometimes you just have to walk away and find a new focus.)

- Don't run from the pain. Rather, get some help to face it and resolve it, or you will never enjoy true freedom.

- The willingness to forgive may be a choice, but the ability to do so comes after gaining greater understanding.

- Your feelings are not a reliable guide to tell you about others. Feelings merely reflect your subconscious beliefs.

- Who should own the problem? You must discover, along with your responsibilities toward others, the limitations of those responsibilities.

- Asking empowering questions is the best way forward when the argument is going nowhere (e.g. 'Why are you on the defensive? What are you afraid of?').

- Until you apologise for those things you regret, the offended one cannot release you from the past.

- It's not enough to simply label someone as lazy, strange or hopeless. Instead we must ask, 'Why is she/he like that?' and avoid the guilt of the judgmental.

- Historic reality is not today's reality, and we need to reinterpret (reframe) the people we have judged from past times.

- Social passivity, once identified, needs to be opposed by

'joining in'. Like a muscle, one's social skills need regular exercise.

- Self-sacrifice that is healthy is born of humility, never inferiority.

- Did your exit from the family leave you feeling perpetually guilty? It's a brave thing to defy the family patriarch or matriarch, but for some it becomes essential.

- Does your 'help' empower or disempower the recipient. Better to teach them than to take over. Better to equip them than to deal out 'charity'.

- Power 'over' and power 'for' represent two quite different kinds of power. Which kind is displayed at Calvary?

- If you represent authority or God in your job you'll be the object of transference whatever you do. Don't take their reactions personally; it's not about you at all.

- If you feel threatened by your father, how do you cope now with people in authority? Are you still 'in reaction'?

- To be more aware of the other person, first become more aware of yourself. Without self-awareness, self cannot be laid aside.

- 'What will others think?' is a symptom of the disease called *living our lives through other people's eyes*.

- When somebody wants to pretend that everything between you is fine when in reality it's not, just remind them that they cannot paint over the rot.

- To avoid isolating myself, I should assume that other people like me unless they tell me otherwise.

- Blowing up, clamming up and sidetracking the issue are all defences that frightened people resort to. They will need more insight before they can come into honesty.

- The difficult person in your life is actually God's invitation to you to gain greater wisdom and self-awareness.

- Even though Adam had a perfect relationship with God, yet God Himself acknowledged that it was 'not good' that he should be alone.

- Feelings of being 'the odd one out' are not invoked by others but by our past experience, and should be opposed at every level.

- Nobody can make you happy, neither can you make another happy. For happiness is a consequence of choices which no one may make for another.

- Don't rely on others to give you your self-esteem, nor leave it in their hands, or you'll never risk being really honest with them.

Chapter Forty-Six

SEPARATION AND DIVORCE

- God's ultimate goal for us is peace through reconciliation. Separation is the very last and final means when every other course has been exhausted.

- Will the ploughman release the harness when one beast heads for the cliff? It must surely depend on the strength and resources of love and wisdom of the other.

- The ethics of divorce involves the tension between legalism and hope. Life is not always served by slavish adherence to vows made ill-advisedly, but slavish adherence can be transformed into a life-giving challenge.

- When you simply can't persist with them any longer, remember, God still persists with you!

- Every marriage rests and relies on two individual, free, wills. But what is the power that can change those wills? It is the power of God's love.

- A marriage destroying two people gives God less pleasure than a separation that saves one, but both are less than what He planned.

- When in pain, it's easy to make a poor choice. 'Don't leap off the train when it's travelling through a tunnel.'

- Affairs do not in themselves cause marital breakdowns. Rather, marital breakdowns contribute towards affairs.

- Separation is a process which begins when couples choose not to forgive, and should ultimately end with forgiveness, regardless of whether or not they come together again.

- Not divorce, but the breakdown of love, is what primarily hurts lives of both adults and children.

- Divorce is never the easy way out that it often appears to be. It is more painful than expected, because it is never really over.

- Surveys have revealed that most (though certainly not all) couples, with the benefit of hindsight, later regret their divorce, but by then it's too late to turn back.

- God will continue to love you and care about you, even if you choose divorce, but both you and your children will still have to live with and suffer the consequences, because that's the way life is.

- Some people will try harder to get a car fixed than they will to mend their marriage. Would you dump the car because the first mechanic couldn't fix it? Yet that is what many do to their marriages. Either pride, or shame, or fear of change, or apathy prevents hurting people from getting help.

- For some, the first step in facing up to their own needs is to leave their spouse, but for others, avoidance by escape has become a way of life.

- When people in neurotic marriages get divorced, they often finish up in the same sort of relationship as before, because the partner is not the real problem. Get help to resolve problems in your own life before you attempt a second relationship.

- What does it do to a person's character when they revoke an irrevocable commitment? And more importantly, what does it do when they make an irrevocable commitment without the necessary resources of wisdom and maturity to sustain it?

- There are some who, as they are, simply will not make the choices necessary to continue living in a relationship with anybody. Who but the person leaning on the love of Christ can live and grow with such as these?

- For love to grow, it must be in a voluntary environment. A high-debt predicament demanding two incomes and six or seven-day working weeks is not a voluntary environment for either partner.

- A believer should not, but sometimes must, seek a divorce, but never without doing so in consultation with senior believers (see 1 Corinthians 7:10). Beware of pursuing a divorce on your own judgement. 'If you don't move out of the marriage the right way, you'll have problems later' (Hayford).

- The implications of the scriptures on commitment force us to face up to the pain and deal with the causes, rather than run.

- If one divorces, for the purpose of remarriage, then one is guilty of adultery – fullstop! It's wrong to be dabbling in another relationship if you are still working through a divorce. Beware the double bond.

- Moses' law on divorce was a compromise because of human hard-heartedness, but new-covenant forgiveness can soften hard hearts.

- In a situation of marital unfaithfulness, if the offended one lives by the law (refuses to forgive) then the marriage must die by the law.

- 'Neither the scripture, nor the church, should be made to condemn those who have already divorced, and cannot find their way back. The truth is always liveable and freeing' (Hayford).

- Let the believer who must leave, either remain single or actively seek reconciliation, if the other partner has not remarried and is still able to change.

- Ministers should never unquestioningly agree to remarry a divorcee, unless their ex is already remarried, for reconciliation may still be possible.

- *Question*: How long should you wait for him or her to change? *Answer*: As long as you can, by the sustaining grace of God 'Blessed is the one who endures to the reward.' You're not going through it for nothing (see James 1:12).

- A wife does not have to submit to cruelty, violence, drunkenness, or kinky sex demands. To do so is to deify a single isolated scriptural instruction about submission, and is both legalistic and foolish. To such a woman, God gives the protection of her father, the police and/or the church seniors, and such protection is hers to insist on.

- Marriages made before faith in Christ was discovered may not be dissolved simply for that reason; God still seals them as the divine overseer of His institution.

- Don't talk to others about your partner's faults, or you will make reconciliation much more difficult.

- Total reliance on God's mercy and forgiveness in the face of Matthew 19 is not always a comfortable way to live, but it may certainly be preferable to the living hell of a disastrous marriage.

- Where God commands, He will always provide the resources to enable compliance.

- The need for counselling is utterly essential, and such counsellors are qualified by their mature compassion and caring acceptance of both partners, rather than by their religious 'status' or dogmatic viewpoint.

- Grace will be increased to you if you:
- keep your eyes on Jesus and don't give up.
- remember that many have been through what you are going through.
- remember that Jesus will never 'leave you to it' (unless that is what you insist upon).

Further Reading:
Divorce and Remarriage – Four Christian Views, edited by Wayne House.

Chapter Forty-Seven

Breaking Soul-Ties

Past relationships do, on occasion, continue to cause discomfort despite one's own desire that they no longer have any effect or influence in one's life. This discomfort can become quite severe for a number of reasons, until the root-cause is identified and dealt with in a manner that is appropriate.

Five Possible Roots of Unwanted Soul-Ties

THE KNOWLEDGE OF UNFINISHED BUSINESS e.g. the need for apologies, restitution, talking through past misunderstandings and putting matters to rights. Contrary to one's fear that this contact may increase the bond, it in fact enables it to be dissolved and is in accord with Christ's teaching that we should try to be reconciled with our enemies. Sometimes a social visit (together with one's present spouse) is all that is needed to 'free the stuck needle'.

THE NEED TO GET RIGHT WITH GOD – for the needs and habit-patterns which led one into the foolish decisions in the first place e.g. rebellion against authority, rejection, lust, low self-esteem etc. What in fact may be happening is that the past experience has not yet been redeemed – it has not been transformed into a lesson learned, and therefore still has the pain of meaningless experience about it, and one continues on, quite vulnerable to the same experience repeating itself again. The past must be *faced up to*, not blocked out, and the experiences integrated into who we are *today*. The Christian *does* have a new nature, but in order to adopt that new identity, the old must first be laid to rest. This is in accord with Paul's encouragement to 'forget those things which are behind . . .'

TO FACE UP TO AN UNMET NEED in one's present relationship, which *was* being met by someone from the past, or which one intuitively suspects could be met by someone who is known now. The mind and imagination continue to return to such a figure in the search to find fulfilment. The result may be a confusing mixture of excitement, guilt, embarrassment and desire. The possibility of transference taking place, and the consequent destructive relationship occurring, is very real. The answer is to be open with one's spouse about such struggles, and to continue to work towards a relationship where both learn how to meet the needs of the other. This may require the help of a counsellor, or psychologist. Furthermore, the truth is that only our Creator and Saviour can meet *all* our needs anyhow, and that to look exclusively to a man or woman to do so is actually a form of idolatry which needs to be faced up to and worked through. No man or woman can fill the void within us which God has reserved for Himself.

FRUSTRATED GIFTING. There may be a need to look and see whether there isn't some gifting or ability which we have been given, but which, for one reason or another, is unable to find expression except through thoughts of what might have been. Such a force, if denied, begins to put pressure on us in subconscious ways, so that we find our minds constantly taking paths which don't feel right, or which lead into forbidden territory. Dreams can become agitated, and emotions exhausted as the hidden tug-of-war continues. Say, for example, one has been gifted with a vivid imagination. Such a gift would normally find expression in story telling, or writing. If, however, one has been discouraged in the past by, say, a teacher's bad report, that imagination may sour to become simply negative fantasising, with no form of positive expression. Yet the gift is, in Paul's words, 'without revoke', which means that it will not go away, but will merely find its expression in some distorted form. What was given to be a blessing, has now become a curse.

ATTENTION Where someone has paid you some unwelcome attention, which has nevertheless aroused a desire, then the feeling of embarrassment may make one distinctly uncomfortable, especially if one must continue in their company by reason of work or circumstance. The best attitude to take is to simply acknowledge one's own feelings and 'humanness' of response, and to say to oneself, 'Yes, it happened, so what? It's only a big deal if that's how I think of it.'

N.B. Never try to use the name of Jesus like a Christianised abracadabra. To break emotional bonds with something less than informed insight will do only harm, unless God is doing something very special in that person's life.

Chapter Forty-Eight

PARENTING TEENAGERS

Parents Guide to Survival – Some Dos and Don'ts

Do

DO insist that when they challenge your judgement, they do so with *respect*.

You must insist on that, for God requires it of them.

DO be sure you've actually heard what they are saying before you jump in.

DO try to equip them *before* they are faced with a crisis.

DO look out for unresolved conflicts and hidden resentments, and *take the initiative* in keeping communication going.

DO insist that when they express their anger, it is in ways that are constructive, and not destructive.

DO respond to them according to their behaviour. If they act like children, then treat them as such. If they act like adults, treat them accordingly.

DO compliment and admire them whenever they do well.

DO re-assure them that it is not their fault when you argue with your spouse.

DO encourage them to find their own identity through learning to serve others rather than by indulging themselves.

DO take the time to find out if they are resentful towards

you, or God, for any broken promise or perceived injustice.

DO teach them to be grateful for all that is done for them, and to *express* it.

DO teach them to see the events of life from others' perspectives.

DO seek to explain the principles behind the rules.

DO get permission before asking direct personal questions.

DO remember that kids become rebellious for *very real reasons*.

DO face up to any of your own unfinished business from adolescence.

DO find out what is hindering them from total commitment to the Lord.

DO remember that, as long as they remain at home, it is on your terms, not theirs, so don't be afraid to insist that they live considerately. (It is their co-operation which you want, not their approval.)

DO share your private world with them: it's part of the process of making friends out of one's children.

DO lay down an inflexible rule – no television during meals.

DO get to know their friends, and keep in contact with their friends' parents.

DO keep in close contact with their teachers.

DO explain that when you check on them, it is motivated by love, not distrust.

DO remember that acceptance of your teenager does not necessarily mean that you must approve of their actions.

Don't

DON'T be threatened by a challenge to your judgement – they are seeking to make your wisdom their own.

DON'T run them down, it will destroy their self-esteem and incentive.

DON'T be afraid to admit fault and take the intiative when apologies are necessary. (When you apologise to them, they are then able to apologise to you.)

DON'T be afraid to display affection: your child needs expressions of your love in order to develop emotionally.

DON'T adopt the 'do-as-I-say-because-I-said-it' approach, it will only foster resentment.

DON'T keep on threatening. Warn clearly, then be sure to carry out your warning. ('I cannot and will not continue to tolerate your bad behaviour.') Flexible limits are often the problem.

DON'T minimise their comments and views or insist they surrender their judgement.

DON'T panic when they 'try out' different identities, but caution them when necessary.

DON'T expect too much from them while they are learning a skill that took you a lifetime to master.

DON'T expect that your teens will have to go automatically through a rebellious period.

DON'T assume you know the real reason for a teen's rebellion. Don't reject their friends. Don't assume that they don't love you.

DON'T think that they can't see your *real* priorities.

DON'T take your frustrations out on them – they will know it and resent it.

DON'T favour any one child.

DON'T forget how *you* feel when you are forced to do something.

DON'T forget to explain the *reasons* as well as the rules.

DON'T allow them to monopolise your phone. If they will not heed a warning, then pull the plug and walk away.

DON'T allow them to push your buttons, or push your limits around.

DON'T assume that 'one size fits all'. An older adolescent cannot be controlled in the same way a child can.

Conclusions

If you are worried about them, then *tell* them that. Get in agreement with your spouse about their limits before you try to enforce them. Have you tried to enter *their* world yet? Do you use violent language, smoke and drink alcohol, enjoy soft-pornography, and flout the laws of the road? Perhaps your 'delinquent' child is simply carrying on the family tradition.

When an adolescent child remains delinquent after repeated warnings, put them out of the house, to protect the rest of your family, and to cause them to face up to the responsibility for their own choices. (To reassert control over the family, sometimes you must give up some control.)

Remember:

- We *all* need limits. Love them enough to say *No!*
  No amount of religious or moralistic teaching will prevent teenage immorality if natural parental friendship and affection is absent.

- You can regain dominion in your family when God has dominion over you!

- Your children are not your unpaid servants.

- If you don't know how to cope with not getting your own way, then neither will your children.

  'Insanity IS hereditary . . . parents inherit it from their kids!'

Chapter Forty-Nine

YOUNG MUMS

- It takes a few days for mother's milk supply and a good feeding pattern to be established, and the new mum may need some ongoing support during this time. (And don't neglect nipple preparation or you'll pay for it later.)

- Don't expect mother-love to be automatic. Give yourself time to bond.

- After birth, give your body a year or two to feel like 'you' again, but remember, you don't have to have a beautiful body to accept yourself or be attractive to your husband. It's how you are in yourself that determines your true beauty. Let go the old image gracefully, if it's no longer realistic.

- A placid, contented home helps make for a placid, contented baby.

- Before you go out to work, remember that poverty of heart, rather than poverty of pocket, is poverty indeed for the baby.

- The mental health of the baby begins with the mental health of the mother. Happy, confident mothers usually breed happy, confident babies.

- Mothers often pass on to their child the same kind of environment that they were brought up in. Is that what you want?

- Young mums need a peer group to relate to, not to compare their child's development (children develop at their own rate) but for their own peace of mind.

- The best thing a father can do for his unborn baby is to love and care for its mother.

- Don't feed a child who is 'on the run'. Sit them down and teach them table manners, but remember, spilt food is easier to wipe away than the effect of overly harsh words.

- A flat mattress is less dangerous than a cushy one, especially when baby rolls on to its tummy. (Before five weeks, babies have no reflex action to turn their heads to the side, if constricted about the face.) Lay the baby on its side.

- The best gift a couple can give their baby is their own happy relationship.

- Medicine has its place, but when the baby is cross or teething, your first resort should be hugs and cuddles.

- Constantly crying babies can also make the mother unhappy. Let friends and family reassure her that she is doing well.

- Hot water burns like fire; turn your water heater down to 65 degrees Celsius.

- Visibility is limited when you're backing a vehicle. Fence off the drive, it should never be part of a toddler's playground.

- Play is children's *work*. Allow them the time and stimulation.

- The first five years are crucial to baby's character formation, and can never be repeated. Stay home if at all possible. It's more important to have a happy family than a fine house with a big mortgage.

- Look again at the world through your child's eyes and rediscover the adventure of life.

- Allow yourself 'time out' each day, and you will preserve good relations with your toddler. If you don't care for your own needs, you'll soon be unable to care for those who need you.

- Take time to play with them, even at the expense of

getting the housework done. Each day, look for the fun that baby provides you.

- Supper time is crucial and sets the tone for the whole family. At any cost, get it organised, or you will *all* pay a high price.

- Don't discipline out of frustration or anger, try distraction or removal first. But remember, you can never be the perfect mother, and nobody expects it of you either. 'Good enough' is good enough.

- Dressing babies in wool and cottons, rather than nylons, keeps them warmer and prevents the 'cold and clammies'.

- When baby begins to crawl and walk, get on your knees to check out the dangers quietly waiting at toddler level. (Sharp corners, unprotected fires and heaters, table cloths, jug cords, cactus plants, heavy unsteady furniture, and the contents of drawers and cupboards at floor level should all be considered.)

- Babies don't cry just because they are naughty – what are they in need of?

- Being a mum is easier if you keep it simple. When baby cries, check that:
  - Baby is fed.
  - Baby is warm – not too hot/cold.
  - Baby has been changed.
  - Baby has been loved/cuddled.
  - If baby is still crying, either leave him/her and do something else, or take him/her for a walk.

- Listen to others' advice, but trust also in your own instincts. Nobody else knows your baby as well as you do.

- Don't be embarrassed to keep at a distance those with colds and flu, and those who are smoking, for your loyalty to baby comes first.

- A date for immunisation against dangerous viruses is an

important date to make. Whooping cough, diphtheria, poliomyelitis, hepatitis B, measles, mumps, rubella and tetanus are the big ones.

- Mum is in danger when her bad feelings outweigh the good ones and seem to last longer, and when there's real dread at coping with another day. Tell someone.

- Better to sit on boxes than have Dad doing overtime at every supper time.

- If you see any of these signs it's time to get help quickly:

  - Raspy coughs, wheezes, or if baby finds it hard to breathe
  - Two normal feeds refused
  - Vomits more than twice
  - Sunken eyes and dry nappies
  - Several runny, extra-smelly bowel movements
  - An unusual cry for an hour or more
  - Baby is hard to wake up
  - Baby has a convulsion or fit
  - A runny discharge from an ear
  - Baby is unusually floppy or extra hot or cold

- If baby is not improving 24 hours after a doctor's inspection, ask the doctor again.

Part 4

Wisdom for Christians

Chapter Fifty

THE CHARISMATIC EXPERIENCE

- To be 'baptised in the Holy Spirit' is variously under-stood from the New Testament as: to be immersed • to be anointed • to be empowered • to be supernaturally endued • to receive the pentecostal experience • to be released in • to give complete expression to the Holy Spirit (old English 'Holy Ghost').

- The New Testament considers this baptism a normal experience for all 'believers' at the time of or subsequent to their introduction to faith in Christ. Look again at Acts 19:2.

- The most obvious evidence of having experienced such an anointing is attested to three times – in Acts 2:4; 10:46; 19:6.

- Your conversion-to-faith experience may be likened to receiving the seed of God's Spirit into your life. The release-of-the-Spirit may be likened to having that seed germinate and fully express itself above the surface.

- With your mind you may hear and understand the gift of grace, but when baptised in the Spirit you can actually feel that grace flowing through you.

- One can pray in and with the limitations of the mind for just so long, and then one may desire something more satisfying. Reflect on 1 Corinthians 14:14. The degree of your hunger for God is the real issue here.

- There is no source of eternal life to be found in the mind. It is out of your *innermost being* that the river of living water will flow (from John 6:63; John 7:37–39).

- The Holy Spirit, Holy Breath, Comforter, Spirit of Truth, Advocate, Helper, Spirit of Grace, Spirit of Jesus and Promised One, are all scriptural names and descriptive terms given to the same Spirit of God.

- Where are you centred, in the limited rational workings of your mind, or in the unlimited subconscious realms of the Spirit? Praying and singing in the spirit (by inspiration) reorientates you around your true intuitive centre, healing the heart and de-throning the mind, restoring it to proper relationship with the spirit/Spirit.

- Have such gifts and practices ceased? Check the original terms of the promise (from Luke 11:13; Acts 2:39).

- The conditions to receiving such a touch from God are the same as for receiving Christ in the first place; namely acknowledging your own spiritual hunger and thereby humbling yourself, asking for Him to come, and actually receiving as He begins to respond to your faith. It is *not* conditional upon your personal worthiness (from Luke 11:13).

- Up until this experience, one lives in a 'natural' world. This touch may be the first introduction to a *supernatural* God, who wants to perform miracles *through you* (from Acts 1:8).

- God's children err in these matters for two simple reasons: they do not know what the Scriptures actually say, and they do not know – are not familiar with – the power of God (from Mark 12:24).

- Just as laughter and tears help express the emotions, so do tongues help give expression to the spirit, but remember that if you had never wept yourself, you would have no way of understanding what a weeping person is feeling (from 1 Corinthians 14:14).

- The proud and 'rational' mind is ever the chief opponent of what it does not understand. It can serve you or tether you to the status quo. But you *will* understand the experience *after* you have received it.

- Impartation by the senior believer laying hands on the junior is the scriptural but not the only way to be baptised in the Spirit. The promise is to any who will accept this message. The laying on of hands is helpful merely as a point-of-contact by which your faith may be activated (from Acts 2:41).

- If you are ambivalent (double-minded) about this gift, do not expect to receive it from God, no matter how much He wants to give Himself to you, for He cannot violate His own principles (from Hebrews 11:6).

- Although there is one initial baptism, there must be many successive fillings, as the need arises. Don't rely on past anointings, come *each day* for a fresh touch or you will surely 'dry up' in time. Being filled is to be a process, as well as an event.

- The Old Testament teachings from Moses' Tabernacle and the Three Feasts of Israel teach that the progression towards the Throne of God is marked (and confirmed in Hebrews 6:1–3) by the following steps:
  a. Turning in repentance from futile self-righteousness.
  b. Exercising faith in the sacrifice (Christ).
  c. Water baptism (washings) to express that inner change/new loyalty.
  d. Baptism in the Holy Spirit (entering the Holy Place) as the door into supernatural power and revelation.
  e. Realising our place in Christ far above earthly limitations (entering the Most Holy Place). How far have you come so far? What misbelief is blocking your progress?

- Can you identify three things which you do only when you speak in an unknown tongue? (from 1 Corinthians 14:2–4).

- Any charismatic experience which does not result in renewed love, joy, peace, holiness and power is not to be trusted. The Holy Spirit will always live through you and seek to equip you *for others*.

- All Word and no Spirit and you'll dry up. All Spirit and

no Word and you'll blow up. With the Word *and* the
Spirit, you'll grow up. (Old Pentecostal saying.)

• The 'pentecostal' experience is simply the experience
  which occurred for the disciples 'fifty days after the
  passover'.

• You may be a pre-pentecost or a post-pentecost disciple,
  but each disciple is told to pray until they receive the
  Promise; it is not offered as an optional extra (from
  Luke 24:49).

• Are you fully convinced that you have already received
  such an anointing? If so, then you may speak in tongues
  whenever you are ready and willing to do so, but first
  you may have to face up to some hidden fear, religious
  tradition or compromised loyalty.

• When we learn how to agree with God we invoke
  the presence of the Comforter almost immediately. He
  comes where truth is acknowledged.

Chapter Fifty-One

CHURCH LEADERSHIP

- Pastoral ministry and demanding public service is not for couples with vulnerable marriages or disorderly families. The pressures will damage the bonds and embitter the family members.

- Don't promote spiritual ability or public ministry before or beyond character development or self-discipline. If you do, the results will always be tragic.

- Insecure shepherds will attack their own sheep whenever they feel threatened. Christ calls such men 'hirelings'. A true shepherd will *lay down* his reputation and his own defence for the sake of his sheep.

- Disillusion the congregation's unrealistic expectations before they become disillusioned all by themselves and cannot handle their disappointment.

- Leadership requires, above all else, objective thinking, an understanding of the goals of the whole group, and the ability to hear opposing sides of the argument. Consequently, those who operate intuitively and subjectively should take a supportive role.

- It is a fact of life that foolishness and frivolity are more popular than wisdom and godly instruction. Don't ever be discouraged by small numbers, but do everything out of a genuine desire to serve God by assisting His people.

- The church you attend is whatever *you* make of it, in your own realm of influence.

- Discipline is *not* for the repentant. Such need assistance, supervision and restoration. Discipline is for those who will not acknowledge their fault and change their behaviour.

- To predict how a man will treat his church, consider carefully how he treats his wife and family.

- Never agree to minister the blessing of God to the marriage of a couple who obviously do not have the maturity or commitment to sustain it, or you too will share in the responsibility for their inevitable pain. ('Lay hands on no man suddenly,' either in holy ordination or holy matrimony. The issue for you is not 'are they suited?' but 'are they ready?'. Always agree to marry them on condition that they successfully complete a pre-marriage counselling course. Then, when you're satisfied that they can handle conflict non-destructively and that they are forewarned about what inter-personal difficulties might lie ahead, give them your blessing. To do otherwise will compromise your integrity, and your position, and will bring disrespect to your office.)

- When specific leadership decisions are challenged, general confidence in one's ability or care is often the real issue.

- Never forget that Christ also has a sword of division and a whip of ropes, and that He has a special hatred for harsh unyielding rules (legalism), intolerance on religious grounds (sectarianism), and a feigning to be what we are not (hypocrisy).

- To judge wisely, look past subjective opinion and get to the facts – what is the real issue?

- A hands-off approach by leadership is appropriate for the mature group, but young believers need supervision in order to know: what's required of them • where they are going • when they over-step the mark • how to find satisfaction in their own contribution and come to believe in their own abilities.

- Stress the virtue of tolerance in your community and you will prevent many unnecessary hours settling petty squabbles and clarifying misunderstandings.

- When you can pray in public, but not when you're alone, it's time to stop all that you're doing and take stock of your life.

- To receive wise correction with gratitude is the pastor's dream for his people. Yet how few adults will take it without becoming offended. Rebellious children grow into rebellious adults.

- Remember, until you are assessed as sympathetic, people won't risk sharing their weaknesses, their problems, their hopes and fears with you.

- When someone shares with you a valid criticism of your conduct, you have a limited time in which to respond in some way, beyond which you automatically lose credibility in their eyes.

- As a leader, discover the people's own goals, then help them achieve those goals with encouragement, suggestions, resources and programmes.

- Once people have become offended and angry, it becomes more difficult for them to take the risk of considering a different viewpoint . . . to trust enough and relax enough, to come off the defensive, even to humble themselves and admit they were wrong.

- Many people need simply to be hugged and held, but never hug the opposite sex in private counsel. It's far too dangerous for anyone.

- Never share your heart with another, when you haven't first shared with your partner. Spiritual adultery always occurs before physical, and is a warning for the alert that something is wrong.

- Your church must learn to love the unlovely, by focusing on invisible qualities. Who do you model in high profile positions?

- Members must understand your group's constitution when they join, or they may have grounds to sue you if you ever need to censure their moral behaviour.

- Before *you* may have authority, you yourself need to be *submitted* to authority.

- When God calls you to a task, don't consider the cost, instead consider the rewards.

- Provide opportunity for people to be open and honest about negative things, but always in a positive context.

- Give yourself and your family permission to be human.

- Anger, fear and guilt often operate at a subconscious level, and are not readily available to conscious scrutiny. Thus they can be relentless taskmasters which produce relentless activity, yet leave no trace of a real cause.

- Does my congregation really expect that of me, or is it coming from myself? Is it an external or an internal expectation?

- Are you driven by circumstances or rational goals? Intentional work is more rewarding than reactive.

- What is your emotional stake in your own expectations? Is your self-esteem riding on achievement? The gospel is good news for those who preach it also.

- In a potential marriage breakup, for the pastor the real temptation is to do nothing – to think 'it's their decision, what can I do to stop them?'

- Remember your original vision.

- Try and extricate yourself from those areas where you are being totally relied on, by having others try out the task.

- Don't lose your spontaneity, allow nothing to become predictable.

- Don't allow the group to exist for its own sake.

- You are not there to please people, but to please God. Fulfilling your calling comes before fulfilling other's expectations.

- Accept the fact that there will *always* be those who will misunderstand you. Can you expect better treatment than Christ himself received?

- The super-successful pastor does not make a good role model. Instead of encouraging you, he may discourage you.

- Not how many hours you work, but how many people you involve, is the measure of success.

- Why *should* you know all the answers? What would happen to teamwork if every player was a Captain?

- Don't spend your life building your denomination, it won't last two seconds past your last heartbeat.

- 'God's work, done God's way, will never lack God's supply' (Hudson Taylor).

- In all your searching for the truth remember: the only place one can truly think freely is *outside* the institution's walls.

- Learn to value those feelings of inadequacy and powerlessness, for it is through them and in spite of them, that God works and reveals *His* power.

- There is no hierarchy at the foot of the cross.

- Don't preach from your pulpit ten feet above contradiction – even Christ was vulnerable to His disciples' challenges.

- Aim to dispense life before you dispense information. The presence of God is better demonstrated than explained.

- Jesus spent one third of his time with His disciples, one third with His Father, and one third in the market place, and He calls us to follow Him.

- When an institution that is voluntary in membership can no longer define its own conditions of belonging, that institution in fact ceases to exist.

- *Never* correct someone in public, if you can do so in private.

- To gain pastoral contentment:

    a. Do what you're gifted at – what you enjoy – what God has equipped you to handle. Train others to do what you don't enjoy or what creates conflict. (Do what you do best, and delegate the rest.)
    b. Stay within your income at all times.
    c. Remember, a man is about as happy as he makes up his mind to be. Godliness, with contentment, is great gain (1 Timothy 6:6).

- Whatever you teach or preach, do it directly, simply, and with *all* your heart.

- Victims often *can't* come for help. The shepherd must go and seek them out.

- Address the root cause *before* asking for a change in behaviour or you will rapidly push them back into the works of willpower. Address attitudes first, *then* action.

- Don't shoot your wounded, one day you may be wounded yourself. Discipline is not for the already repentant.

- When you're going in one direction, and your congregation are going in another, remind them that God is working one way, not two, and leave the implications for them to sort out.

- Even the most inspirational of worship must begin with the people making some active choices. A conscious act of the will always undergirds expressions of love, but celebration follows insight.

- In worship especially, the spirit and the mind must learn to work together.

- Those who expect to be rejected, find it in every comment and every glance. They must renounce all self-hatred and learn to re-orientate themselves around the acceptance of God.

- Most people would rather run than face up to up themselves and be discomforted. Their excuse may actually be a cop-out, a way of saying, 'I'm not yet ready to make that commitment or to face that fear!'

- You can't *make* people do *anything*. Your commands are really invitations which people are always free to accept or reject. Power is always on loan.

- Don't ask or demand more from your people than they have understood. In God they trust, but from you they first need to know why.

- Conflict is an inevitable consequence of ministering the truth to those who prefer error. The whole Bible is about such conflict. Don't become a domesticated pastor.

- Don't be surprised when you go to correct someone, if they turn on you in anger. None of us surrenders our own judgement easily.

- Beware those who stay at home, and wait for Pastor to call. They will isolate themselves, and then rail at whoever 'for not caring'.

- *What* will happen in any group depends primarily on *who* is in authority. (The identification of the kind of people that the leaders are is of the first priority, if you would try to anticipate the course that the group will take.)

- Always get permission before asking a direct, personal question.

- Don't be surprised at verbal abuse – in fact beware when everybody speaks well of you.

- Don't get rid of all your opponents, you need them to keep you on track.

- Humble yourself before others take it upon themselves to humble you.

- Acknowledge praise with thanks, then deflect it to those who have supported you. You cannot praise them too much.

- Don't be surprised that the battle just continues on, expect it and plan for the long haul.

- Don't expect a pure church, even Jesus and Paul had a mixed multitude.

- Identify the difference between godly and ungodly suffering or you will be confused and double-minded as to the true source of your affliction.

- Not the multitudes, but the few you take on to maturity, will extend your ministry.

- Send the fearful home, they will discourage your heart and the hearts of your workers.

- Establishing one's own personal disciplines must always remain a priority for those in leadership.

- Advertise your meetings by fostering a desire to know the answers to life's difficulties. Create curiosity.

- Train up faithful women to help you, and to enable you to avoid the dangers of counselling the opposite sex.

- Remember that what God orders, He pays for. What *you* order, *you* must pay for.

- If (because of a shortage of workers), you promote a person before they are ready, you will increase, rather than decrease your workload. God does not change his mind on qualifications for leadership, just because there is a shortage of leaders.

- Do you discipline your staff, or teach them to discipline themselves?

- Fit the style of leadership to the maturity of those you lead – open or structured, autocratic or concensus.

Lies For Church Leadership to Identify and Discard

- It's *all* up to me.

- Though *I've* got a poor self-image, my *church* can have a good one.

- The size of the church reflects the worth of the pastor.

- I should always have the answers.

- The more knowledge people have, the more they will put into practice.

- I can believe God for miracles in my services, without meditating on His Word to build faith.

- One bad apple can't spoil the barrel.

- Criticism is always against me personally.

- God's servants should be doormats.

- More training will make my frustation go away.

- I should always be doing more.

- I should be like that 'successful' pastor.

- I have something to offer or boast of that wasn't freely given to me.

- My church's doctrine is the whole truth, and doesn't include any error whatsoever.

- I can get a harvest without doing the work.

- Unity will come while focusing on our differences.

- I can avoid care-fronting people and expect that the trouble will just 'go away'.

- I am wasting my time when counselling people who aren't ready or willing to co-operate.

- A couple with untamed tongues and selfish attitudes can marry in the happy expectancy of a long and happy marriage.

- As a minister of Christ I can marry an ill-prepared couple and not share in the responsibility and pain of their divorce.

- Any other motivation for service to God, other than gratitude that He has already done everything for me, is acceptable.

- God doesn't utterly hate the politics of seeking power.

- I am better than the people I serve.

- Only the people with faith can get healed.

- A technique, method, or seven-point sermon can substitute for the presence of God.

- I can live in my intellect and still be perceptive in the spirit.

- There are more important things than introducing people to Christ.

- I must be more concerned about *my* reputation than about the people I pastor.

- My conflict is primarily with people, rather than with the spirit which has blinded their minds.

- People can give me the run-around without my permission.

- I can rebuke one in front of another, and still retain their trust.

- I can work without taking a day of rest, and not burn out.

- I can neglect my personal prayer life and not grow weary in well-doing.

- I can resist temptation regardless of the state of my own marriage.

- That I don't need supervision.

Chapter Fifty-Two

COUNSELLORS

Build hope by setting out the conditions of blessing. (The first condition is prayer – James 5:13.) We are responsible, moral agents who will reap the consequences of our own actions, and this works both ways. (Even if we are helpless to change, we are not helpless to get help.)

Always respect the responsibility of the individual's 'Power to Choose'. Ultimately, they, and nobody else, are responsible for what they become, because only they can choose their own reaction.

Assist those who will meet the conditions of change. Simple, easy conditions to be sure, but they must invest something of themselves in their own progress. Do they want your help?

Share your faith in them. Love is the primary incentive to change. Speak hope and encouragement. This is 'priming the pump', or 'jump-starting'. It is the one essential gift that parents must give their children.

Desire for right and wrong are present in all of us – praise the good and warn the evil. Deal evenhandedly to bring them to the turning point.

A sense of threat and their defences go up. Check your own attitude. You can't help someone who is on the defensive with you. What put them on guard? Neither can you help if *you* are on the defensive.

Come alongside as a 'wounded healer', not from above. Don't be afraid to be vulnerable – confess your own frailty. When pointing out another's fault, acknowledge your own. We don't minister *to* sufferers but *with* them.

All heavy exhortation has a reverse side – the power to crush. 'Try harder' is a terrible thing to be told when you are already exhausted. Get to the root misbelief, then the behaviour will change.

Warning – people are fragile; especially bruised people. Tread softly, speak gently, when walking in people's hearts.

Where people are already under pressure, tread cautiously. If they are trying to silence their conscience, they will certainly try to silence you as well.

No one pays the price, until they desire the product. Your 'product' is the blessing of God. Are you walking in its fullness yourself? (Do others desire what you have or do they pity you?)

People don't care what you know, till they know that you care. It is simply the fact that you care that first qualifies you to share your truth. Who you are as a person is just as important as your skills. Before all else, counsellors are burden bearers.

Who or what is controlling/manipulating the counsellee? Who have they given their own power to? They cannot serve two masters.

Beware the presumptuous statement. As a person of authority, your words can create or destroy. Judgemental, erroneous statements, and prejudiced conclusions which allow no disagreement are just 'not on'. Your statements are better framed as questions.

Repairing a marriage? First, restore the friendship. The trust has been betrayed; it must be restored very gradually by instruction and forgiveness, and a renewed commitment to courting.

Always sandwich correction between layers of praise. Ours is not to condemn. Praise and encouragement will prevent condemnation and despair from taking hold.

People need friends rather than 'analysis'. Analysis can be degrading and threatening if done with a motive other than compassion. Beware the counsellor with an agenda all of his or her own.

First ask 'What is hurting you?' Then ask 'What do you think the answer is?' Then help to explore the alternatives. Use their wisdom, but 'what is going wrong' must come before 'why?'

Do you communicate the gift of grace or the law of sowing and reaping? Do you attract people or repel them? Do they sense mercy or judgement around you?

People need to express their inner mind, and check their own conclusions by talking it over. It may be the first time they have been able to gain any insight into the problem. Listen with all the resources you have at your disposal.

Even little acts of love and care do mighty works. A 'thinking of you' card – a little gift – confirms their worth and reminds them of God's love and encouragement.

To hear the real issue, don't just listen to the words. What do you sense as you listen? What is this person trying to express? What emotion emanates from them?

When rebuke is called for, remember compassion. In judgement, remember mercy and be sure to get your facts straight first.

As a Christian counsellor, you are to follow THE Counsellor. Listen to God, follow your God-given leads, and act on His principles, as found in Scripture.

Only your knowledge of the truth gives you authority in confusion. There are many alternatives to choose from, but only Scripture reveals the path that leads to blessing.

The first compulsory qualification for the counsellor is compassion. A sense of their pain enables the bond to form by which you may lead them. Without empathy you will do only damage.

Grace is the antidote for discouragement and guilt. Love and acceptance when we least deserve it, and the power to do God's will, is freely available 'in Christ'. (Few counsellors have a good understanding of grace.)

Unreal expectations are the most common cause of anger. Their expectations must be lowered to be realistic, or else the true root cause of the frustration should be identified.

Be alert to the various meanings of a word. Some terms are loaded e.g. Father, devil, prosperity, God, exorcism, church, Christian. Stop and define your use of them.

Do not condone idolatry in the form of child worship. Guilt and unresolved issues in their own minds cause a parent to become dependent on and over-protective of their children. They must let go, or they will suffocate the child's proper development.

Begin with people as they are now. Don't wait till they improve or conform to your requirements. Grace is unconditional acceptance, and gets in on the ground floor to approve of who they are, not necessarily what they do.

To overcome a life-dominating problem requires a restructured life and restructured thinking, e.g. alcoholism, drug-addiction, homosexuality, crime. A new, non-tempting, non-familiar environment is called for.

People feel better when better organised. Encourage structure in the form of goals, homework and planning, in order to monitor progress and take hold of the situation.

Choices, more than circumstances, determine our predicaments. Blaming others enables us to avoid the responsibility of our own lives – it also removes from us our power to change.

The cause of most troubled relationships is simply plain selfishness and personal defensiveness! 'Meism' develops where parenting was poor. It oppose the way of love and is rooted in the misbelief that 'nobody greater than I is looking out for me, therefore survival of self is my priority'.

Is it God they are rejecting, or a hideous concept of Him? Our concept of God distances us or else attracts us and draws us on. Father or Judge? Saviour or sadist? Knowable or mystical?

Those who are trying to change others need to concentrate on changing themselves. We must learn that we should celebrate our differences and work on ourselves.

What is your relationship with the counsellee? Who do they remind you of? You must first become aware of your response to them, so that you can consciously place it to one side.

You can't lead anybody any further than you have come yourself. Keep seeking to develop your own wisdom, insight, and spiritual authority, in order that you may be of more help to others.

All your good advice will count for nought unless the counsellee can 'own it' for themselves (can fit it into their own belief structure). Until they have made it work for themselves, they are merely doing it for you, and when you leave, their motivation to continue will cease.

Pray aggressively to identify and overpower the evil influences which attach themselves to and cripple their victims. Our struggle is not primarily with people so much as it is with the buried misbeliefs which are disturbing their proper function. The nature of the affliction prescribes the type of treatment.

Addiction/drug usage is a secondary problem – attend to the broken relationships and internal pain first, e.g. rejection, unforgiveness, anxiety, fear, inferiority, anger etc. These came before the addiction, and must be dealt with before the secondary problem is tackled.

Some behavioural problems are caused by the direct influence of unclean spirits which the victim mistakenly owns as their own nature. Identify and evict the squatter that the whole house may be available for the owner's occupation.

Emotional troubles begin in families. Treat the whole family to cure the patient. In physical illness the complaint is limited to the patient in question, but with emotional troubles the causes are often in the relationships surrounding the person. Reconcile the family first.

Medication and drugs are no substitute for love and care and tuition in healthy thinking.

Don't play God, enlist all the help available. Other members of the family, welfare workers, church members, etc. – all have a role to play.

Adult problems are merely childhood problems which grew up with us. Much of a counsellor's work is helping the client resolve the unfinished business of childhood and adolescence.

Beware of focusing overly on the negative. The more we focus on others' faults and the situational negatives, the further we get from the available resources, and from God.

To advise is to disempower. Not to advise is to betray their trust. The one thing worse than non-directional counselling is that kind of advice-giving which the counsellee is completely unable to 'own' as their own.

Every counsellor in this world must experience failure. Remember Noah – he faithfully preached 120 years and never won a single convert! Do what you are called to do and leave the results to God.

Those who forget the past are condemned to repeat it. The purpose of probing into childhood is not to blame anyone, but to find out how we got to where we are, so we can compensate for the damage done to our belief structure.

Self-doubt is vital to the counsellor. All diagnosis remains 'best guesses', based on one's own knowledge and experience.

All significant psychiatric problems are 'over-determined'. There are always a number of contributing factors which will need to be teased out.

Do not revere psychiatry. It is trapped in empiricism. It cannot heal evil for it dare not name it, and it cannot study what it dare not name. Outside of the church, truth is determined by one's peers.

It is hard work finding answers to your leading questions. Give the counsellee plenty of time and space to do the work of thinking very deeply about their replies.

The Bible is psychotherapy for sick thinking. Those who are most evil are least likely to submit to psychotherapy. To them it seems like suicide.

Uncrucified compassion is the primary cause of burn-out in counsellors and care-givers. The rescuer must not lose his or her own power.

Chapter Fifty-Three

DIVINE JUDGEMENT

- Divine judgment is best understood as the *breaking-in of reality* upon delusion, as when the accumulated consequences of our actions force us to realise we have been 'living a lie'. (For example when one is shocked into reality by the notice of debt accumulated on one's credit card.)

- The ugly duckling was judged at the moment he realised he was actually a swan. His judgement meant both death and new life to him as it pulled him out of his 'pretend' state.

- What is the fate of a swan who continues to insist he is really an ugly duckling? In this persistent repression of his true identity, he is his own judge, tormentor and destroyer.

- Are you angry at those who avoid you because of the lies they were told about you, or merely grieved at the stalemate of the relationship? Isn't that also God's own attitude to humanity?

- At the point where a rich man is torn from his wealth and a proud man is torn from his status (or a beautiful woman is separated from her beauty) by physical death, they are judged, for their sense of identity is all bound up with *this* life. Their separation by death is also their judgement, for it is the consequential break-up of the foundations of their identity.

- Better to suffer judgement in life than judgement at death. A little tremor can prepare us for a major earthquake, if we will rightly respond to it.

- There is so much grace in the worst of us, and so much self in the best of us, that none of us is well placed to judge the rest of us.

- Judgment is the final *separation* of right beliefs from mistaken beliefs, truth from lies, reality from delusion, the love-life from the self-life. With which beliefs have you come to identify yourself throughout your own life?

- At death I hope that my judgement will be complete, for there is a part of me I want to forever disown. I do not want it to inherit heaven, for fear of spoiling it.

- Orthodox concepts of judgement are *interpersonal* (between persons) and fundamentally flawed. Neo-orthodox views understand it as both event and process, and that it is ultimately *intra-personal* (between the natures of the individual).

- That which is born of God will return to God, whether acknowledged and developed or not, for it is incorruptible, regardless of the vessel it dwelt in while in time. Those natural desires whose interests are purely selfish (which have never been redeemed) will ultimately destroy the subject in their unrestrainedness (from Jude 18–19).

- Universalism cannot coexist with divine justice, but remember that although *all* are loved and forgiven, it does not mean that all will acknowledge it or enjoy it.

- Like a mist in morning sun a wrong belief masquerading as the truth is judged at the moment the truth is fully revealed. Is it a belief you have built your life around?

- Why should God be offended or angered at those who are 'put off' His rule because of the way authority has been misrepresented to them by parents etc. as being threatening to personal growth? Rather than angered, He is sorely grieved at their destruction as they push through authority's safety barriers to their own hurt.

- Always remember that the most powerful judge in the land does not in fact decide anybody's fate. Rather, he merely insists that the offender inherit the real results and consequences of his own choices. Your day-by-day and moment-by-moment choices are in fact becoming your judgement.

• Daily we see people who already have one foot in hell, yet they often live in the same *ultimate* reality as those who already have one foot in heaven. (Sometimes even the predicaments are the same.) It is surely our *responses* which determine what we perceive and become.

• Hell has no external walls! Those in torment are there by their own habits, as they have habitually searched for pleasure and comfort without reference to God, truth or wisdom.

• People are 'damned' only when they can finally no longer separate themselves from the mistaken beliefs which they have adopted throughout their lives. Ultimately their fate is the same as the erroneous conclusions they have insisted on identifying themselves with, and they themselves become part of the lie, and therefore share in the same fate as the Father of lies.

• What you believe to be the truth is of eternal significance, therefore test all beliefs, and hold fast to what is true, lest you be swept into delusion – the realm of anti-reality.

• Feelings reflect our subconsciously held beliefs. Indulging those feelings produced by mistaken beliefs is therefore the route we take into torment.

• I knew a child of God whom God did not label 'gay', but everyone else did, in spite of the boy's objections. In time he was pressured to believe and so fulfilled the lie, and became identified with it, but God has not yet changed His mind. We must learn to judge (distinguish) between the creation of God and their chosen, mistaken beliefs.

• When a person condemns herself because of mistaken thinking, a faulty conscience or a wrong concept of God, even God cannot release that person (from Luke 6:37; Matthew 6:14; Romans 14:14, 23).

- If all human evil is finally dealt with in the death of Christ, then those reliant on this can live in expectation of ever-increasing life, rather than ever-increasing indulgence in the desires of human nature (from Romans 8).

- God shows mercy to all, for it was He who disabled all through disobedience (from Romans 11:32), yet every individual will still have to respond to the divine inquiry into their lives.

Chapter Fifty-Four

EVANGELISM

- 'People really *do* want to hear what I have to offer them in their predicament.' This should be the thought of your mind as you offer to share what is most precious to you – the God-given 'God-man'.

- 'I'm moved by your situation, may I pray with you right here?' A response such as this reinforces the fact that we do not offer a philosophy or method, but a Person – the Divine Person of Jesus Christ.

- There are no coincidences for those whose desire is to be used of God. Every chance meeting is in fact a divinely set-up appointment.

- Their philosophy may sound great, but will it help in time of trouble – will it satisfy the deepest longings of their heart? Does it assure them that they know, and are known by God?

- Yes, nature is beautiful, but you can't have a meaningful relationship with a sunset, neither does it offer a way out of endless regret, guilt or despair.

- Their concept of God: did it come from God or did they invent it themselves? A God made by oneself is not to be trusted in the hour of trouble. It will last only as long as things go well.

- Though many have tried to find God at the last and have been unable to, nobody ever repented of being a Christian on their deathbed.

- Every day, people show that they don't have to understand something to believe in it.

- Great knowledge is not a major factor in who are successful evangelists and who are not. Loving boldness and enthusiasm about Jesus is.

- There is only one cause for their misery – sin, and sin only has one conclusion – death. Let them know that 'in Christ' they have already died, and now it's time to arise in *His* life.

- Make friends with your sense of inadequacy, it will always be with you, and reminds you to live out of His ability.

- Love them and serve them, to earn the right to be heard.

- To be salt and light in the community, commit yourself to regular community involvement.

- 'Absolute surrender' is the only way in to a transformed life, and will free us from the fear of ever falling away. Christ must become president, not just resident.

- You cannot lead someone who is in pain to God, if they think that God is the cause of it. First dismantle their objections and false concepts, then lead them to Jesus.

- Remember Peter's denial of Christ and then face up to your own fear of man.

- We learn to conform to others' expectations in our conversations in order that social relations may remain untroubled, but such conformity will effectively cripple our witness when it becomes our first loyalty.

- Be bold! Christ already has enough 'secret agents'.

- If you cannot or will not be a witness to Jesus, you should face the fact that you are not the means of people finding peace with God – in fact, you are the greatest obstacle. You can only be successful in evangelism, if you are first of all enthusiastic about your relationship with God yourself.

- Try never to miss an opportunity to steer someone who

is enthusing about the creation towards the Creator. You are chosen to help them to make that connection.

- When salt has lost its savour, what good is it? When a messenger is afraid to tell the message, how will anybody benefit?

- The fear of man is not a spirit, but a culturally conditioned attitude which must become outdated and replaced by the fear of God.

- Your direct honesty with people about the state of their souls will not turn anybody off Christ, it will merely expose their already present attitudes, and may well wake them up in the process.

- Before you can help somebody discover the truth, you must risk offending them. If you will not take that risk, you can only conform to their pleasure, and you may well end up reinforcing their delusions.

- How people respond to an alarm is their responsibility. Your responsibility is simply to sound it.

- Remember that what is good news for the guilty will be irrelevant to the grief-stricken, and what is good news for the grief-stricken will be irrelevant to the homeless. Christ is good news for men of every race and situation, but we must match the message to the people.

- 'Woe to you when all men speak well of you, for that is how their fathers treated the false prophets' (from Luke 6:26)

- For the majority of people in the Western world, the issue is not actually one of works vs. grace, which the cultists may struggle with, or 'natural' religion vs. divine revelation – the problem for the intellectuals and liberals – but a preoccupation with the physical, material life which simply renders them apathetic toward eternal realities. The whole question of God seems simply irrelevant, until they are forcefully and shockingly confronted with the supernatural demonstration of His power.

- Have you *earned* the right to correct or rebuke them? People will not give that power to you *until* you have gained their respect.

- When you approach a community to make an impact on it, don't bypass its key people. Go *first* to the leaders and inform them of your purpose and methods, for they also are God's servants (albeit unwittingly) and God will honour your courage and integrity with their co-operation.

- Get in agreement with your partner concerning your mission before anything else.

- How others respond to your invitation is *their* responsibility, not yours, but in what form does the invitation come?

- They can only make a genuine response to your offer if they also feel free to refuse. There is a world of difference between an invitation and a command.

- May your every contact with people leave them a little closer to the truth, a little closer to Christ, no matter where they are.

- Though there is only one way to God, there are many ways to Jesus. Can you identify the way that your seeker is coming?

- Lifestyle alone is not scriptural evangelism, for unless your lips declare salvation, the world will not comprehend God's righteousness. Your reputation will not help them to find Jesus.

- Effective witnessing begins with the assurance that God *can* and *wants* to change a person's life.

- That child needs to be saved every bit as much as Hitler did.

- Learn to see people the way they *could* be, rather than the way they *are*. Distinguish between who they are as children of God, and the things they believe which may not be of God.

- If you don't have a sense of humour – if you can't laugh – who will want to be around you?

- Don't allow yourself to be intimidated, or fear will eventually bind you up.

- If you don't respect the people you are witnessing to, they will know it and close up immediately.

- Don't make any promises that you can't keep.

- People will usually treat you according to how you think of yourself. If you come in as an old friend, that's how you'll be treated.

- How will you ever be an effective witness to the world if you don't begin with your own neighbour?

- Every day in a hundred ways, there are opportunities to tell your community about the Lord.

- If you will simply tell enough people how to be saved, you cannot help but get results.

- Wherever people gather is a good place to share Jesus.

- All you really need to witness effectively is the love of Jesus in your heart and the way to Him in your head.

- The *message* is always more important than the *method*.

- If you carry a Bible with you and use it, people will not easily misunderstand your purpose.

- Discipline yourself to focus on your one purpose, leading them to Christ alone.

- Start each day with the intention of sharing Christ with somebody.

- Sometimes you have to ignore their words and just keep talking to their hearts.

- *Clichés* are no substitute for insight and understanding.

- *Zimsum* is the Hebrew word for the self-restriction of God. He has restrained Himself – self-detained in His

prison of love – so that He might not disempower His
children.

- God often chooses to meet with those outside the covenant community, which is always an offence to those
within (from Luke 4:28).

- That God should reveal Himself in a particular person, at
a particular place, at a particular time, is both the greatest
blessing and the greatest offence of Christianity.

- 'All paths lead to God' – until one path leads to Jonestown
or Waco. Then we must begin to discriminate.

- The heart and key to the Christian message is the
vicarious nature of the life of Christ. Yes, He died for
you, but He also lived and performed on your behalf.

- Do not insist that repentance occur prior to receiving
Christ. It is rather the awareness of His love that enables
us to change our ways.

- Because conversion occurs from the inside out, it can
really only make sense to a fellow believer. (Essence
follows existence.)

- Beginning religious instruction with an emphasis on
improving performance is *not* the gospel.

- It is the recognition of who Jesus is 'on our behalf'
and therefore who we truly are, that truly marks the
'born-again' experience.

- When a person becomes a Christian, they automatically
enter into an identity crisis. (You are not who you
thought you were.)

- Trusting in the performance of your own life, far from
putting you in good standing with God, will actually disqualify you from divine favour. There *is* a better way.

For inspiration, read Arthur Blessitt's *Street University*.

Chapter Fifty-Five

Exorcism

Five Steps to Successful Self-Deliverance

1. Correctly diagnose the cause

Symptoms which may indicate the presence of a spiritual 'squatter' or 'unclean' influence as opposed to mere human disfunction and acts of self-indulgence, are:

- Compulsive, obsessive, recurring, bizarre and obscene thoughts or actions. These may well include a sense of losing control over one's own thoughts and actions and an altered sense of consciousness, e.g. repeated thoughts of blasphemy, bestiality, sexual perversion and brutal violence • Recurring suicidal impulses, and tormenting and mocking voices in the mind may also indicate alien activity • *All mind torments* and violent swings of mood are also indicative.

- Physical sicknesses and diseases are occasionally directly attributable. (May include cancer, asthma, migraines, epilepsy, allergies, paralysis, psychosomatic disorders, rheumatism, tumours, neuralgia – even appendicitis. Authorities are deeply divided over symptomatology and etiology.)

- History of occult practices.

- Involvement and fascination with mysticism.

- The practice of passive mind meditation techniques.

- A history of sexual deviancy of any type, or abortion.

- Addiction or attraction to hard-core pornography.

- A history of acute alcoholic, drug or nicotine addiction.

- Repeated compulsive thoughts of hatred, murder, violence and rebellion.

- Deep involvement in martial arts.

- Acute fear, anxiety attacks, phobias.

- Compulsion to run out of charismatic services without knowing why.

- Sudden undiagnosable attacks of pain.

- Compulsive religious practices, cult (works-based) doctrines, eastern religions.

- Direct or family involvement with Freemasonry.

- Chronic confusion of thoughts and loss of memory.

- Persistent desire to return to any unclean habit.

- Preference for incense-laden atmosphere and preference for hard-rock music.

- Personal attachment to charms, amulets and symbols of idolatry, including Madonna statuettes. Symbols of violence and rebellion

- Referral to tarot cards.

- Inability to acknowledge Jesus as Lord even when the desire is present.

- Gossip and slander rampant in the church.

- Altered states of consciousness which do not yield to the will of the person.

More obvious symptoms include:

- Fear and hatred in the eyes and expression.

- Social isolation.

- Glazed or bulging eyes.

- Constant weariness or depression – a deep sense of heaviness.

- Chronic restlessness and/or talkativeness.

Such symptoms may indicate a very mild demonic influence (oppression) or they may indicate a 'nest' of considerable strength, even, on very rare occasions, approaching the state of complete possession.

2. Meet the conditions upon which deliverance rests

Acknowledge your failure and rebellion, and come to the end of self-reliance. Admit your desperation and yield your life completely to the will of God. If you are still making excuses for your behaviour, you are not yet ready. 'God delivers us from our enemies, not our friends' (Derek Prince). Identify, confess and renounce all that the Bible calls sin, including unforgiveness, bitterness, occult involvement, rebellion against parental, church or government authority, past immoralities, etc.

This may also involve a period of fasting (spending meal and entertainment times in prayer and heart-searching). It must be a total yielding of yourself to Christ as your Lord and Saviour and a new awareness of who you are in Christ. (You only have authority over the spirits in the measure that you submit yourself to the Lord of all spirits.)

Destroy any object which symbolises spiritual power and learn to do the opposite of what those desires want. (As you refuse to feed the demonic presence, by refusing to co-operate with them in your thoughts and actions, and consistently opposing their every desire, their hold is loosened and their power is weakened.)

3. Discover your authority 'in Christ' from the Scriptures

Learn to identify yourself with His death and resurrection by faith, and become bold and strong in it. This is vital, as the devil does not take any notice of 'wimpy' prayers or commands. The person born-again by the Spirit of God has a life within them which does not know any defeat. That is the life we must learn to stir up and live out of. 'It's fun to cast out devils when you know that in Christ you can't lose' (Liardon).

Phil 2:9–10: Name above every name • Heb 11:6: God rewards the seeker • Mark 16:17: In my name • James 4:7: Submit to God • Luke 10:19: Given you authority • 1 John 1:9: If we confess . . . • Mark 9:29: Requires prayer • Matt 12:29: Bind the strong . . . • Matt 18:18: Whatever you bind • 2 Cor 10:5: Casting down • 1 Peter 5:8: Roaring lion • Joel 2:32: All who call • Eph 1:19: His mighty power • 2 Cor 4:2: Renounce • Rev 12:11: By the blood • Matt 17:21: Faith from fasting • Gal 5:24: Have crucified • Gal 3:13: Jesus took the . . . • Is 26:3: Perfect peace • Rom 6:11: dead to sin • 1 John 4:4: Greater is He • 1 John 3:8: For this purpose • Gal 6:9: Don't get discouraged • John 8:32: Truth shall make . . . • Deut 3:22: The Lord shall fight 2 Cor 7:1: Let us purify • Col 2:14: Sin cancelled • Matt 28:18: All authority is given • 2 Tim 1:7: Not a spirit of fear • Is 58:6: Loose the chains of . . .

3. If possible, choose a suitable time, place and helpers

- Acknowledge the protection of the angelic hosts and the blood of Jesus.

- Authoritatively, powerfully and insistently command the known spirits to leave, in the name/power of the Lord Jesus.

- Command that any other spirits leave also. (There are usually several in a group!) Do not allow them to be violent or to scream, but limit all their activity to leaving. Pray strongly, ordering it/them out as you do. Continue until deliverance and relief comes. No difference means no deliverance. You may be shocked at what reveals itself – things you thought were part of your own character – simply continue to demand their departure.

- Never argue or 'pussy foot' with them. On rare occasions

the demon will try to speak lies, using the victim's own voice. They usually begin by insisting that they will never leave – yet as you continue to pressure them, they will flee enraged.

Deliverance in progress is often evidenced by coughing, trembling, pressure on the throat, retching, moaning, shrieking, growling, roaring, bringing up phlegm, breaking out in a hot flush, or simply a deep sigh accompanied by a new feeling of relief. Often they are expelled from the nervous system. The more anointed, illuminated, and prepared you are, the easier and faster the deliverance will be accomplished. Praying strongly (either in the spirit or in your native language) is vital. You must *hate* that thing with a holy anger. Don't be afraid to shout or kneel – what we do in the physical is bound up with what happens in our hearts.

Upon deliverance there will be a new sense of lightness and relief. Now pray for a new infilling of the Holy Spirit with expressions of praise. If the tormentor proves strong or stubborn, the individual should renounce it by its character, and begin to claim their freedom by faith. Remember the conflict is between Christ and His disobedient servant, the minion of Satan – you are merely co-operating with the Holy Spirit by enforcing *His* lordship over all creation including the opposition.

5. Hold your deliverance, by being filled with the Spirit

Make no room in your thoughts for lies. Daily refuse the will of Satan, and accept the will of God. Don't be surprised or disheartened if a counter attack comes, but strongly assert your freedom in Christ, and cast down every habitual imagination which opposes the Word of God. ('Whatsoever things are pure . . .' Philippians 4:8.) Continue to receive and submit to pastoral and/or parental supervision, as this is vital. Deliverance may be a single event or it may be a process, depending on the depth of your repentance and the strength of your resources. It is God's will that you

be free as soon as you are able to hold your freedom. If
full deliverance seems too slow, read Exodus 23:29–33,
Deuteronomy 7:20–24, Ezekiel 34:25–31, Galatians 6:9.

Prayer Guidelines for Deliverance:

I acknowledge Jesus Christ to be my Lord and Saviour.
I confess and renounce every act of rebellion and sin
that I or my parents may have committed, and which
may have brought bondage or domination to my life,
and I ask for forgiveness and healing. (At this point,
take time to name such things.) I repent of any action
or attitude which does not glorify Jesus Christ. I now
claim the release and freedom promised by Jesus
Christ, that He may be Lord of my whole life, and
Satan, I command you to leave me entirely, you no
longer have any right of access to me, or any power
over me, and I insist on gaining total freedom from
all your influence. Your property – my carnal nature
– was condemned and buried with Christ, 2000 years
ago. I now enforce Christ's victory over you.

Pray along these lines strongly and persistently until relief
comes.

The Holy Spirit will also help, revealing hidden and subconscious memories and events which have allowed the
destroyer access in the past. When these are revealed, the
root cause can more easily be broken and the shadows
expelled more easily.

WARNING: There is a very fine line between positive
spiritual discernment and negative superstition. Get clear
in your own mind which is which.

Further Reading:
Pigs in the Parlour, by Frank Hammond.
Evicting Demonic Squatters, by Noel Gibson.
Demons Defeated, by Bill Subritzky.
God's Chosen Fast, by Arthur Wallis.
The Devil Did Not Make Me Do It, by Paul Miller.

Chapter Fifty-Six

THE 'WORD-OF-FAITH' AND PRESUMPTION

- Faith says like Peter 'Lord if it's you, bid me come to you on the water.' Presumption just leaps from the boat in the hope that if Jesus said it to Peter, He's said it to everyone.

- Fear looks and shrinks back. Faith looks and then listens for God. Presumption doesn't look *or* listen, it just leaps!

- If you merely state the troublesome situation as it is, you simply help confirm the status quo. But if you acknowledge sensory reality (things as they stand) and heavenly reality (things as they are 'in Christ') then God's changing power to heal, save, and set free is actualised.

- Faith does *not* deny the reality of sickness and need, but it also acknowledges that these things cannot dwell where the perfect will of God is being done. One or other must yield. Which it will be, is up to you and the words and actions you choose.

- You need not deny the reality of sickness, poverty or tragedy to walk in overcoming faith but, as a joint-heir with Jesus and freed from the curse, you can deny them any place in your life (from Galatians 3:13).

- To speak of yourself as you would like to be, rather than as you are, is not presumptuous, providing it is within scriptural bounds; it is learning to agree with God, and see from His viewpoint. The whole world was created from 'things that are not'.

- There are two kinds of knowledge, sensory knowledge

and revelation knowledge. The one can only call things as they *are*, the other calls things as they *can be*.

- Presumption says 'Name it, then claim it.' Faith says. 'If He didn't spare even His own Son, neither will He withhold any good thing to those who love Him. Let us now prepare our hearts and speech to receive.'

- A 'hard-up', need-orientated mindset has been formed by the world and its 'limited' resources, and is confronted directly by God's promise to supply all of our needs out of His abundance.

- Faith focuses on the promises of God, unbelief focuses on the problems of the moment (from Isaiah 26:3).

- Unbelief pleads with God for our needs to be met. Faith acknowledges what God has said is already ours 'in Christ' (from Matthew 6:8).

- Believing that one receives must come before receiving, but the mind loyal only to sensory knowledge always rebels at this; it is folly to it (from Mark 11:24).

- The natural eye sees what is on earth, but only the eye of faith can see what is in heaven.

- To speak of things as they are 'in heaven', while we are yet still of the world, immediately throws into sharp relief the contrast between the two realms, and who can bear it?

- The 'word of faith' is the language of a people whose eyes are on the realities of heaven, but those who have settled for the status quo must either oppose it or admit that they are wrong.

- Hope looks always to the future, but faith grasps it *now*. It calls the things that are not as though they are (from Hebrews 11:1–2).

- The word-of-faith sets the stage for God to act, the word-of-the-world merely confirms things as they 'are' (from Romans 10:17).

- Intellectual assent is not faith, faith requires an active committal to obey what is revealed. It is existentialism at its finest hour.

- Speaking about the future as if it were present reality can have a hollow, mocking sound, but it quickly exposes, by contrast, the true nature of the problem – usually unbelief and disobedience.

- Unbelief says 'It cannot be done.' Faith says 'God's work, done God's way, will *never* lack God's supply.'

- The word-of-faith is often seized upon by those who have difficulty facing reality, as a way of legitimising their escapist attitude, and by the insecure, the stubborn and the strong-willed who see it as a means to control their environment in a way that pleases them. Thus comes the 'hyper-faith' and 'name-it, claim-it' ridicule.

- As long as you are still *trying* to believe for your miracle, you haven't yet heard from God – but you will be coming to His attention. Get closer yet.

- Taking medication does not inhibit the miraculous power of God, but what is your confidence *really* in?

- God will never condemn you for stepping out into new realms of faith, no matter what the result, but running before you can walk always results in heavy falls. (Remember though that withholding vital medication from dependants without medical clearance is considered by society to be criminal negligence.)

- Be aware of the fine line between faith in God, and a faith in your own faith which precludes God. The distinction is very subtle, and hyper-faith can be found in both the liberal and fundamental emphasis.

Twelve Clear Ways To Distinguish Faith From Presumption

1. Presumption is motivated by the desires of self. Faith is motivated by love for Christ and His people.

2. Presumption substitutes formulas for relationship.

3. Presumption claims things that are beyond one's faith/
    maturity level.

4. Presumption claims on the basis of one's own actions,
    rather than on the basis of faith in Christ's promises,
    e.g. *because* I am fasting, or refusing medication, God
    must heal me.

5. Presumption confuses revelation knowledge with sen-
    sory knowledge, a 'faith' fact with a 'physical' fact, and
    errs towards the teaching of Christian Science.

6. Presumption seeks power over others without regard
    to their personal sovereignty or moral responsibility.

7. Presumption uses Jesus' name like a magic formula,
    rather than as permission to *act on His behalf* – by His
    specific commission.

8. Presumption treats the promises of God as uncondi-
    tional. Faith is born first and last out of a *relationship*.

9. Presumption teaches that God would lead His people
    into indebtedness, and calls the loan 'His provision',
    but *faith owes no man* (from Romans 13:8).

10. Faith is *delegated* authority, presumption operates under
    no authority (from Matthew 8:9; John 15:7).

11. Faith expects whatever is *promised*, presumption expects
    whatever is *wanted* – and knows no restrictions (from
    John 15:7).

12. Faith acknowledges that the kingdom of God is not yet
    come in fullness; presumption leaves no room for hope
    or failure.

Chapter Fifty-Seven

MIRACLES

- If you need a great miracle, then locate a nucleus of people who will pray and lay hold of God together with the spirit of the needy one until the faith of God penetrates the darkness and the power comes.

- It's not long prayers but believing the promises of God that gets the results. God responds to *believers*, not beggars.

- Healing is 'of God', but there is a skill in getting that life-stream to pass from ourselves to others, which includes calling for repentance and appropriate action.

- Unconfessed sin always obstructs the power of God. 'When our hearts do not condemn us, then we have confidence toward God.'

- The power of the Holy Spirit can become as real as electricity. You receive such an anointing from God through faith and prayer, and when supercharged with it you minister it to another directly through laying on hands or some other point of contact. It's that simple.

- If the seeker has no faith, instruct him or her so that some will arise, and then exercise your own, to invoke the manifested power of God.

- Before the *power* must come the *wilderness*, where the Spirit can bring you to death to self. No real *seeking* after God means no real *power* with God. 'The secret of failure is the failure of secret prayer.'

- The Spirit and power of God is attracted into the spirit of a person by *believing prayer* and the *spoken word* of promise.

- 'Great faith is the product of great fights, great testimonies are the outcome of great tests, great triumphs can only come from great trials' (Smith Wigglesworth).

- For God, there is absolutely no difference between healing a headache and replacing a limb. And He wants to do both.

- Great faith comes by growth and exercise. 'First the blade, then the ear, then the corn in the ear' (Smith Wigglesworth).

- God will pass by a million people to touch one who is believing Him for His provision.

- The only appropriate response to the arguments of all those whose faith is purely in reason and homemade gods is a genuine demonstration of the ready power of Christ to 'break in' on His own creation.

- The Bible makes no sense at all if we remove from it all reference to the miraculous. It loses all integrity of identity and meaning if we try to impose upon it our own worldview.

- In our 'believers' meetings, we must become satisfied with nothing less than the tangible, manifested, presence of God. Yet the Spirit of God will not share our loyalty with a 'safe' all-overriding agenda.

- Without the manifested power of God the Church cannot compete with secular entertainment, but without someone to speak forth the Word of Faith there will be no power.

- If you can't yet believe God for a miracle, then believe Him for whatever you can. We must all begin somewhere.

- You may talk, sing, pray or write about the power of God, but if you will not pray and believe God yourself, you will never *demonstrate* it.

- Only when you are truly subject to the *Creator* will you have dominion over the *creation*.

- It actually requires no more faith to work miracles than to speak in tongues or to prophesy. *Any* faith pleases God.

- Always continue reaching for the manifestation of the supernatural (signs following) in your ministry and remember, your prayers – in fact your every word – will either charge the atmosphere with faith or unbelief.

- Faith must grow by Word, Spirit and exercise, and every child of God has the potential for the miraculous.

- When notable miracles follow your instruction, you'll no longer have to go looking for people to instruct.

- You should oppose negative unbelief at every level. Jesus is always ready to move, but He's waiting for you to tear down the negative forces that bind you.

- Signs and wonders don't get people *regenerated*, but they certainly get their *attention*.

- *Television* and *ignorance* of the promises God has given in Scripture are the major short circuits of the Church's power today.

- Locate and fellowship consistently with people of faith and power, for the company you choose will always influence you.

- 'The day is coming that when people say "there is no God" some will simply pray miracles into manifestation in reply' (Liardon).

- 'Each day, go into the realm of the spirit, for that is where the move of God is taking place' (Liardon).

- You must be willing to do *whatever* God tells you when the healing power begins to function.

- Note carefully: wrong thinking is the *only* tool that Satan has got to prevent you from exercising the power of God.

- 'If you are all absorbed with earthly things, you cannot lay hold of heavenly power' (Smith Wigglesworth).

- Pray through your apathy, then through your unbelief, then through your fears, repeating the promises of God, releasing your faith through actions of obedience.

- To step out in miracles you will first have to face your fear of looking foolish. Only an intimate relationship with the Holy Spirit will give you that kind of trusting courage.

- To believe God to do the impossible in a public meeting, you must first build expectancy and focus the people's eyes on Christ, not on yourself.

- Can you find a group of believers who will not be satisfied with words, social intercourse, celebration, liturgy or religious tradition, but who utterly insist on seeking a genuine manifestation of His presence? They are a rare group in any place, and God's Spirit searches the whole world to find them.

- 'The prayer of faith can come after just one day of prayer and fasting, and even children should be taught how' (Harry Greenwood).

- 'Automatic church does not invoke the Spirit's power or bring His approval! He is only as active as our belief in His promises to provide.'

- When God uses you to perform an amazing miracle, you should say 'Well I finally managed to get out of His way'.

- Don't isolate yourself from the family of Christ in seeking your miracle, for you are part of the body of believers.

- To display the power of God, first let go every vestige of personal ambition.

Further Reading:
The John G Lake Sermons, edited by Gordon Lindsay.
If You Need Healing Do These Things, by Oral Roberts.
Christ The Healer, by F.F. Bosworth.
Cry of the Spirit, edited by Roberts Liardon.
All Things are Possible, by David Edwin Harrell Jnr.

Chapter Fifty-Eight

PROGRESSING 'IN CHRIST'

- All the blessings of God (not His love) are conditional upon your co-operation (from Deuteronomy 28).

- Every believer experiences two natures. The first is self-centred and therefore fearful and selfish. The second is made in the image of Christ and knows only faith and love. Which life do you identify yourself with?

- Sorrow and suffering always follow ignorance of, or rebellion against the truth. Find and conform to the universal laws as they are in reality (from Proverbs 5:22).

- Before making a decision, learn to link the choice with its consequences. Prudence means thinking ahead (from Proverbs 14:8).

- God merely reveals the realms of blessing and cursing; it is our choices which determine our destiny (from Deuteronomy 28).

- The truly repentant person abandons all excuses and accepts responsibility for their predicament. Then they may continue living in the full assurance of God's forgiveness (from Psalm 32:5).

- The blessings of God – share them to increase them, or withhold them to lose them (from Acts 20:35).

- Christ is the Gift we have no part in shaping. You cannot receive Him on your own terms (from Luke 6:46).

- Are you spending your life searching for what you lacked in childhood? In Christ, you lack nothing (from Psalm 23:1).

- To reap the rewards, first do the necessary work (from Proverbs 10:4).

- God is enabled to un-mess our messes – whenever He's placed in charge (from Luke 15:17).

- We are healed, that we in turn might become healed helpers (from 2 Corinthians 1:4).

- 'God is my vindicator' – my reputation is His affair alone (from Luke 18:7).

- By justice and mercy, evil is removed and hope is renewed (from Proverbs 16:6)

- Admission of guilt reveals forgiveness and grace, but obedience brings peace and prosperity (from 1 John 1:9).

- God's love is unconditional. Every independent effort of ours to earn it will obscure its reality and leave us under a futile burden of 'performance' (from Matthew 11:28).

- Genuine repentance is always followed by genuine fruit – a life of daily obedience (from Luke 3:8).

- As Christians, our daily guidance is to allow the life of Christ to express Himself more readily through *our* lives (from Romans 8:29).

- God commends *willingness* more highly than success, *yieldedness* more highly than effort (from 1 Samuel 16:7).

- God's laws and delegated authority are not to *threaten* us, but to *protect* us, and to nurture us in our growth (from 1 Peter 2:13).

- In human terms, God is more 'saddened' by the rebellious, than 'angered' (from 1 John 4:18).

- To overcome a life-dominating habit, e.g. drug addiction, crime or homosexuality, calls for a totally restructured lifestyle . . . new thinking, new surroundings and new companions (from Hebrews 12:13).

- Restitution of wrongs done in word and in deed precedes restoration of relationships (from Luke 19:8).

- Just as faith is fulfilled by action, so understanding is fulfilled by obedience (from James 1:22).

- God is not the *author* of every human predicament, but He is the *master* over it (from Luke 8:24; John 10:10).

- Our submission gives God permission to intervene on our behalf (from Luke 1:38).

- Assurance of salvation comes with personal change and spiritual growth (from Luke 19:9).

- The Spirit will, with our co-operation, search our character, corner by corner, to completely fill us with Himself (from Romans 12:2).

- Do you conform for exterior motives (from outside pressure)? That is legalism. Faith allows you to own your own behaviour, by releasing you from the burden of performance (from Psalm 40:8; 1 John 4:18).

- Don't allow false statements to go unchallenged, or they will become self-fulfilling prophecies (from Proverbs 18:21).

- Exposure and confession break the strength of obsessive sin (from Psalm 32:5).

- Depressed people feel better when they are better organised (from Proverbs 6:6). It helps them to regain the reins of their own lives.

- It is our *own* choices, rather than circumstances, which determine our future (from Luke 15:18).

- Scripture; don't just read it – you must *apply* its principles in your life before it will do you good (from James 1:22).

- The first condition to finding God is the acknowledgment of your own helplessness/failure (from Luke 18:13).

- Does your situation look hopeless? *Look again at Christ* and His promises (from Romans 8:35).

- Only faith enables you to touch God, and everyone has a measure to invest. What will you do with your deposit? (from Romans 12:3).

- Only Christ-conscious people can walk on troubled waters (from Matthew 14:30).

- We are *all* destined to learn obedience by the things which we suffer (from Hebrews 5:8).

- Face it or escape it is often the question – but first assess your resources (from 1 Samuel 30:1–8).

- The problems and troubles of life are to pressure you into God. Let them serve you well (from James 1:2–5).

- 'Confession' is accepting the responsibility, and paves the way to receiving God's unmerited love (from 1 John 1:9).

- Behave the way you would like to be, and *that* is how you will become (from 2 Peter 1:5).

- 'The only legitimate motive for Christian service is gratitude – gratitude that our service is entirely unnecessary for us to be accepted by God, through Christ' (Luther).

- Sin is always the setting for the revelation of grace. Justice is always the setting for the revelation of forgiveness (from Romans 5:20).

- True repentance is the exhaustion of self-effort. Coming to the end of yourself (from 1 Corinthians 1:29).

- Sow a belief, reap a thought. Sow a thought, reap an act. Sow an act, reap a habit. Sow a habit, reap a character. Sow a character, reap an eternal destiny.

- When you fail, God can get your full attention.

- No, God is not angry with you, or punishing you, but you must realise that if you (from or your parents) threw the ball, it must bounce back (from Galatians 6:7).

- In Christ we are dead to sin, but the power of sin is not yet dead.

- Righteousness through 'trying harder' ends either in pride or disillusionment/discouragement.

- Find peace with God by adopting *Christ's* righteousness as your own, and do not seek purity by the power of your resolve.

- To experience the power of sin, just try to conquer a habit all by yourself.

- The Christian life is not a do-it-yourself clean up – no self-generated righteousness belongs 'in Christ'.

- Not self-exertion, but insight into the vicarious (on behalf of) nature of Christ, sets us free from guilt and self-hatred (from John 8:32).

- We are 'cursed of God' only when He reluctantly releases and abandons us to our headlong pursuit of self-gratification. (This is the spiritual state of death, for it has no relationship with the spirit of sacrificial love – the self-giving life of God.)

- Every deed, whether good or bad, has its return. Only the power of God can interrupt this elemental cosmic law and that cancelling power is revealed at the cross of Christ.

- When we deliberately do wrong and suppress our conscience, we side with those who preferred the darkness and silenced Christ by crucifixion. There is *no one* who is righteous!

- What is forbidden is most desired – and efforts at self-denial can actually strengthen the desire still further (from Romans 7:6).

- We can choose freely only when we are free to choose. Grace sets us free from the tyranny of law and rule and will power (from Romans 11:6).

- Jesus says, 'I don't want you to be as good as you can, I want you to relax in my perfection, so that I may live my life through you.'

- Fear and anger result from having our basic beliefs

about life threatened or demolished, especially if we have nothing to replace them with.

- Tackle disasters one piece at a time, and look for what can be learned from the experience. Thus you will transform every tragedy.

- What benefit did you gain from indulging in that which still tempts you? Stop and reconsider often (from Romans 6:21).

- I can tell where you will journey to in the afterlife by the kinds of preparations you are making today.

- An honest mistake is not a cause of shame, but repeating it might be.

- The desires that you have previously fed are the ones that will dominate your life in the future.

- Our responses to the events of life reveal what is hidden deep in our hearts.

- If you work like a great saint, but hope like a great sinner, you can't go wrong.

- God knows that nothing is gained by obtaining your pressured, reluctant obedience. The recoil will soon follow.

- It may be all right for someone else, but is it right for you?

- One day plus another always has an accumulative effect. What are you accumulating in the spiritual realm?

- True freedom is not the liberty to do what you please – that will only result in enslavement to selfish desire. Freedom 'in Christ' is the power and desire to do God's will.

- God says, 'When you say you love me, you are in fact acknowledging that I also want and need you – and I do. I am vulnerable to your choices, I am threatened by your inclination to bury your treasure – my awakening life within you (from Matthew 25:28).

- How readily entertainment substitutes for repentance in the churches today. It will hide the pain but never heal it.

- Anxiety and fear, anger and depression, are usually indicative of simply too much disagreeing with God (from Isaiah 26:3).

- You cannot 'try harder' to please God and live in His grace at the same time. The one negates the other.

- Beware of a spiritual life which increases rather than alleviates guilt.

- Salvation always includes increasing mental, emotional and social health, but a 'born again' experience is not a shortcut to the abundant life.

- Don't equate salvation with church attendance. There are many anonymous believers who simply haven't yet made the connection between their own merciful God and Jesus.

- Guidance is not like walking a tightrope. If you truly love God and people, then do what you will and it will please Him.

- Do not confuse faith with fatalism. There are no straight lines between God and circumstances.

- The authority of man tolerates no challenge. The authority of God says, 'Come now, let us reason together . . .'

- The boundaries that God gives are our friends, for they safeguard us against becoming enslaved to our own desires – for sex, food, stimulus, etc.

- God is not a tease! That which He requires of you He first of all gives you. Those desires He gives you He can also fulfil.

- My performance says nothing about my essential value as a person. My value can only come from the fact that I am wanted by God.

- Live one moment at a time, and live it to the full. Seize

the opportunity. It may not come again; it is a holy moment.

- When you are trying to please God, remember that Jesus has already done so on your behalf. (There are no brownie points left for you to have to earn.)

- Trusting in the performance of your own life, far from putting you in good standing with God, will actually disqualify you from divine favour. There is a better way.

- It is the recognition of who Jesus is 'on our behalf' and therefore who we are, that truly marks the born-again experience.

- Did Jesus ever refuse to heal the sickness of anyone who actually reached out to Him? Do His actions still express the will of God for us today?

- Making relative truth into absolutes ends in legalism. Making absolute truth into relatives ends in liberalism. Avoid doing either.

- The pain of change comes from the difficulty of betraying and opposing one's own long-held beliefs, once they are found to be wrong.

Chapter Fifty-Nine

Pauline Wisdom

The points that follow have all been distilled from Paul's
Epistle to the Romans.

Chapters 1–8

The Law of Sin and Death and the Law of Life 'in Christ'

1. God's indignation is upon all those who suppress
their instinctive knowledge of the truth, both Jew and
Gentile.

2. It is on you also, for no one is completely obedient.

3. This includes the Jews who actually have God's laws,
so – we obviously need a new basis for righteousness.

4. Actually Abraham had already come into it – faith in
God's faithfulness/promises.

5. a. Jesus' death and resurrection as humanity in One
(the Son of humanity), gives us His access to these
promises.
b. Just as in and by one (Adam), death came to all, so
in and by One, all are made righteous.

6. a. Your old self-seeking nature has been condemned
in Christ.
b. So don't now serve it; instead serve Christ as one
back from the dead.

7. a. This is illustrated by the death of one's spouse.
b. The Law exposed and strengthened my corrupted
nature, so . . .

   c. I realise that my corrupt nature (which is not the
      real 'me') is in fact my adversary, bringing death
      to me. What am I to do?

 8. a. I need to realise that Jesus has made a new life and
       identity available to me, and now . . .
    b. I am to live out of this new spirit, the law-of-life
       in Christ.
    c. Through suffering we are to focus ourselves on the
       Promise.
    d. Since it was God Himself who rescued me, who can
       ever harm or oppose me now? (My own cause no
       longer needs to be my primary concern.)

Chapters 9–11

How The Jews Fit In

 9. a. Yet the Jews, as God's chosen people, are still
       missing out. (They are not Abraham's *spiritual*
       descendants however),
    b. because they are trusting in their *own* efforts.

10. a. They are trying so hard . . .
    b. perhaps they will see and desire what the Gentiles
       are grasping.

11. a. Yet their rejection is neither permanent nor complete
       – it is so that God could adopt you . . .
    b. And soon God will reveal His mercy to them also.
    c. In fact God has confined all in disobedience, that
       He may have mercy on all.

Chapters 12–16

The 'How To'

12. a. In view of these things, here is how to live.
    b. Whatever you do, do as for the Lord. Love, share
       with all – enemies included.

13. a. Civil authorities are God's delegates – serve them
       too.

   b. Live on the edge of eternity, by loving one another.

14. You're *all* trying to please God, so don't put others down.

15. a. The issue now is not 'is it lawful or not?' but 'will it help or hinder another in their growth in faith and love?'
   b. So Gentile Christians are to accept each other wherever they are 'at', just as *God* has accepted you as you are.

16. Greet my friends – withdraw from false teachings – blessings.

Chapter Sixty

SICKNESS AND CHRIST

- It's not God's will for you or your family to be sick. Jesus healed all who reached out to Him (from Luke 6:19; Acts 5:16).

- It is not the shepherd, but the *thief* who comes to rob, kill and destroy (from John 10:10).

- If it is *really* God's will for you to be sick, why do you yet seek treatment for your illness? Aren't your beliefs in contradiction? (from James 1:8).

- Sickness is never an occasion for guilt, though it may be inviting some self-assessment.

- Would you, as a parent, discipline your children with a disease? Of course not! So how dare you believe that your heavenly Father is less of a parent than you? (from Luke 11:13).

- Healing (from both yours and your family's) has *already* been provided for in the atonement. Now it is really up to you to appropriate it, by prayer, fasting and seeking insight into the cause (from 2 Chronicles 7:14).

- When you erroneously believe that your sickness comes from God, you give the destroyer unrestricted access to your life! God's people perish through lack of (from sound) knowledge (from Hosea 4:6).

- Even the destroyer serves God's purposes, but only in those who have rebelled against God's word of warning and correction (from Deuteronomy 28).

- Does God 'allow' your sickness? Yes, He must, if *you*

are allowing it, for 'in Christ' you have been given dominion over *all sickness*. We should begin to exercise that dominion.

- There are many reasons why you may be sick. It may be as a result of your lifestyle, your sin, your forebear's sin, an accident or a by-product of medication. Regardless of the cause, sin and sickness entered by one man (Adam) and has been dealt with by one man (Jesus Christ) who is waiting now to heal you. Your apathy and unbelief is now the *only* obstacle to His power. However, your apathy and unbelief will block God's healing power (from Matthew 13:58).

- 'Saved' in the original Greek means: 'healed, delivered, made whole' (from Acts 14:9).

- God is the ultimate healer. Doctors cannot heal anyone, they merely help the body to help itself, but automatic recourse to drugs and medicines prevents God's people from developing their faith, in calling upon His power (from 2 Chronicles 16:12).

- When medical people do their training in a 'supernatural void', then their cures are also void of a supernatural God (from John 5:44).

- Will there be sickness in heaven? 'May Thy will be done on earth, *as it is in heaven*' (from Matthew 6:10). But the kingdom is not yet fully come.

- The 'elders' mentioned in James 5:14 are not those voted in by the political process of man, but include *any* man or woman who can counsel and pray *in confident faith* for your healing. A rare person.

- Our own fears often give the destroyer his right-of-access to our lives (from Job 4:14). So can entirely unrealistic expectations.

- When you or your children are sick, doctors, psychiatrists, medicines or church meetings should never replace the need for a word from Christ (from Matthew 8:16).

- Christ's will is to heal you, but He may also with-hold it until you first of all seek Him fervently (from Matthew 11:28).

- No matter how much faith you have exercised already, you haven't crossed the bridge until you've reached the other side. Don't quit until you've got what you need (from Mark 10:48).

- If you can have faith for your soul, you can have faith for your body!

- While you are relying on medication, can you truly believe God, or are you merely experimenting?

- Prayer must not be a substitute for actually believ-ing God's promises. Some are great beggars but poor believers.

- The Law of the Spirit of life will set you free from the law of sin and death, if, as an act of your will, you place yourself in union with it.

- Remember, there are instant and gradual healings, just as there are instant and gradual conversions. God wants us whole. His healing salvation (soul and body) is both process and event.

- One of the Talmud's prescriptions for healing is to repeat Psalm 91 seven times a day.

- Are you more conscious of your sickness than of the power of God? Whatever gets your attention, eventually gets you!

- 'Stop grizzling – you are not in trouble, you are in your destiny. This is your opportunity to grow up and learn how to overcome' (Liardon).

- You will only have complete dominion over sickness when God has complete dominion over *you*. In hope we look for that in a coming age.

- If you can't believe God for great healings, begin with colds and headaches. Overcoming sickness is a process which begins here and is completed in eternity.

- Don't begin your thinking with Paul's 'thorn', or you will turn New Testament experience upside down, and make the exception into the norm.

- Objections to divine healing must be identified and answered before one can be released from double-mindedness. Nevertheless, the tension between healing and non-healing will remain until the perfect day.

- Even when you have no faith, remember that faith comes – it is the faith of God.

- If the sickness is to test you, when will you pass the test? When you have gained the desired level of hope and patience, will the sickness then be removed?

- God uses sickness and disability to demonstrate His power, but the power of God is not displayed where it is not earnestly desired.

- Believing God for miracles is a mighty task, and few there be that qualify. The grace of God remains our strength meanwhile. Even miracles are not greater than unconditional trust in God. It is hope, not healings, which remains the anchor of our souls.

- On this earth there will always be tension between what is and what ought to be.

- That faith healers wear glasses and eventually die reassures us that all miracles are only a foretaste of what is to come.

Chapter Sixty-One

Social action and Politics

- Authority must never be separated from responsibility. Power and accountability *must* abide together.

- Political murder and political theft is murder and theft which is sanctioned by the judiciary, e.g. abortion, excessive taxation, and land 'appropriation'.

- Today's Western holocaust is loneliness, parental delinquency, greed, apathy, and moral relativism.

- Is it really justice that you seek, or merely your own cause?

- Never confuse the task of the Church with the task of the state. The Church reveals the rescue of God in this world, whereas the state is to maintain law and order. Its task is divinely legitimated only by the presence and work of God in the Church.

- The use of force rather than dialogue to achieve good aims always backfires. Permanent change must come from public support, i.e. willing change, and willing change comes with public education of the same facts which inspired the leaders to legislate in the first place. Good government is open government and relies on good media.

- Once government becomes insensitive to the public will, and is allowed to continue in it, degeneration into totalitarianism is inevitable. A nation of chickens eventually produces a government of foxes.

- To use physical force in the name of Christ is always a contradiction in terms. Christ's power is not 'of this world'. The state however, 'bears the sword' as necessary to fulfilling its mandate to maintain order and justice.

* Laws can be wrong and laws can be cruel, and those who live purely by the law are both wrong and cruel. Justice is always the aim and object of the law.

* The Church not only may, but *must*, oppose a corrupt state, in her service of Christ, for the Church alone gives the state its divine legitimation.

* Christianity needs to be freed of overt heavenly-mindedness, to be more authentic in the world, but the rule of the kingdom must be internalised, before it can be socialised.

* There is never a total separation between the Church and the state. They are bound together in mutual service, the state to supervise the society in which the Church exists, the Church to give divine credibility to the state.

* Theology should *never* become the tool of ideology, nevertheless religion is more often an instrument of power than a corrective of it.

* The way things are now should *never* determine the way things ought to be in the future. The rules and principles determine the nature of the game, not vice versa, or the result will be chaos.

* The revelation of Christ crucified redefines our understanding of power and success, and challenges our use of human force to achieve anything.

* The follower of Christ always sides with the oppressed, but the oppressed are always found on *both* sides.

* The Church is paralysed in a society which believes that religion is purely a private matter – that the gospel has no social implications.

* Which is better; to protest and resist and risk death, or to survive at any price in endless regret and inner conflict? If 'survival' is your highest priority, you are vulnerable to control by a Hitler, an Eichmann, by *any* bully who

appears. You will either side with them willingly or reluctantly. 'If you board the wrong train, it's no use running along the corridor in the opposite direction' (Bonhoeffer).

- To remain silent when we should protest, to co-operate passively without resistance, makes us accomplices to the very evil that threatens us, and dishonours the command to love our enemies.

- The state destroys the life of its own people when it seems to reward them for immorality and idleness. It must not protect its people from the consequences of their own wrong decisions, or their foolishness will become unrestrained, and the innocent will be burdened also. Even a Third-World peasant who earns his own support is better off and happier than a beneficiary who has lost all self-respect.

- The world is not corrected by the Church when the Church is full of the world.

- The fire of love, vision, hope and justice – don't allow it to go out. Return often to your dream, your goal, your vision. The desire we feed is the one which will dominate our lives.

- **Some wisdom from Gandhi:** 'We must proclaim our equality under God.' • 'We must publicly attack the symbol of injustice.' • 'A magazine is necessary to unite a community.' • 'For this cause I am prepared to die, but for no cause will I kill.' • 'Through our pain we will make them see their injustice and we will destroy their resolve. Force has no answer to non-violent, non-co-operation.' • 'They can have my dead body, but not my obedience to injustice.' • 'Violence will inflame their wills; firmness will open their eyes.' • 'If the government afflicts one minority group, then every minority group should combine to resist.' • 'The highest authority must have clear reporting of the true state of affairs. Direct your efforts at the leaders.' • 'I do not advocate passive resistance, it must be active and provocative – the function of a civil resister is to provoke response in order to make the injustice visible.' • 'I want to change their minds, not kill them for weaknesses which we all suffer from.' • 'Put away your revenge, what do you gain by killing each other?'

- Evil, seen too often, can eventually be embraced by every man who has no foundation of objective morality to hold to.

- The nature of democracy is rule by consensus, and the nature of consensus demands that we be willing to work within a compromise situation. In a group with many differing belief systems, no one group should be able to force their minority opinions on the rest, no matter how much they may be convinced of the justice of their cause. If your minority group could force change on the populace, then so could the opposing group. Both truth and democracy rely on good media.

- Coalition governments, formed entirely by proportional representation to give all minority groups a voice, can become too faction-ridden to govern. Leadership is only as strong as its unity of purpose.

- The greater the crowd, the less the restraint. Mob rule is survival of the most violent. Never unleash public anger until your organisation is strong enough to harness it.

- The Church can only help if it truly reflects the Spirit of Christ. Consider Ireland: one of the most religious countries in Europe, yet walls have had to be built to separate one set of 'Christian' people from another.

- The essence of unity is the acceptance of diversity. Such a philosophy enables each group to be secure in the knowledge that it can survive and grow. Unity comes in the *accommodation* of difference, not the suppression and conquest of one side by the other.

- 'Respect for the past, taken to extremes, will paralyse our attitude toward the future' (John Hume, MP, N. Ireland).

- What happens to the family when the Welfare State takes over the role of the father?

- Why does society insist on preparation and tests to qualify for driving a car, flying a plane, getting a mortgage or a gun, and yet expects absolutely nothing for marrying or parenting, the two basic institutions on which society itself is utterly dependent?

- One man, one woman, *can* make a difference in any place or nation. Romania discovered that the overthrow of a tyrant can be sparked by one priest preaching a sermon on liberty. Alabama discovered that one black woman who got tired of being pushed around and refused to give up her seat on a bus, and one young man who insisted on his right to attend a white university, could reverse a hundred years of discrimination.

- Let the minorities pool *all* their resources to resist the threat.

- Use the law, and document every action, every injustice, every consequence of every decision, to feed the media, who can then gather your allies and help turn the tide of ill-informed public opinion.

- Remember, youth will always respond faster to a call for national change than will the aged.

- Every movement for social reform needs a song, a poem, and a photographer.

- Businesses only understand boycotts, especially the vulnerable ones.

- Where legal remedies are not available to the people, redress, right or wrong, is usually found in the streets.

- Anger is always the immediate response when confronting intimidation, manipulation and prejudice in people.

- 'The Christian's goal is not to strive to *rule* in society, but to *serve*. While God's rule *is* authoritarian, it is also *voluntary*. Non-believers need never fear the loss of civil rights under a Christian government' (Charles Colson).

• We do not need to be saved primarily from the tyranny of oppressive governments, but from the tyranny of revenge, rebellion and hatred – the tyranny of *self*.

• The kingdom of God is the kingdom that has come and the kingdom that has still to come. It is both 'now' and 'not yet'. It is a spiritual 'rule', not a physical 'of this world' realm.

• A pervasive sense of powerlessness and impotence paves the way for political 'saviours' and an all-powerful state.

• Remember that perfection will always elude us in this life, so we can resist the dictator who gains power by promising us Utopia.

• Religion is *never* just a private matter, for what we believe about morality, ultimate authority and the meaning of life, directly influences every decision of social consequence we ever make. There is no such thing as 'neutrality'.

• Humanists fail to understand the spiritual void and moral bankruptcy of man, and Christians often fail to understand the political dimension of their faith.

• A Christian government will teach the people how to seek reconciliation rather than revenge.

• Never risk an eternally accusing conscience by supporting prejudice and bigotry, no matter how popular the cause. An offended conscience can be your cruelest and most persistent opponent.

• Society needs protection, first of all from *itself*. It loves alcohol, yet condemns the horrific acts of drunkenness. It loves its regular television dosage of soft pornography, yet condemns rape and sexual harassment. It loves tobacco, yet condemns drugs and fears cancer. It loves making laws, but is paranoid about censorship. It loves to avoid taxes, but howls aloud if any service is cut. It loves all the benefits of a 'high tech' society, but blames everyone but itself for mounting unemployment. It loves to protect the trees and the whales, but turns a blind eye to the 'termination' of its unborn children.

- Righteousness can never be *forced* on a family or nation. Members of Christ's school are all voluntary.

- In a totalitarian society, the only place one can be truly free is in prison.

- Let the political activist who is soft on abortion commit Proverbs 24:11 to heart 'Rescue those being led away to death; hold back those staggering towards slaughter'.

- The state often encroaches upon the Church, because it needs religious legitimisation for its policies, and an independent Church is the only structure that rivals the state's claim for ultimate allegiance.

- When a man wants ultimate power, he must first provoke a national emergency, then demand the need for instantaneous action, in order to suspend all constitutional rights.

- A church is not free if it cannot pronounce judgement on the evils of society. It must jealously guard that freedom.

- A government's first duty is not to *avoid* evil, but to *restrain* it.

- Give a bully an inch, and you will pay in blood to retrieve a yard. Resist *every* ultimatum, *every* form of manipulation, immediately. Make no deals with terrorists, for their sake, as well as your own.

- The method of reason and discussion is only preferable to the use of force if both parties' goals are reasonable. There are many, however, who are not motivated by any 'reasonable' motivation. Never lose touch with the true nature and irredemptability of human evil.

- A government may be good, or popular, but it cannot be both, until the people are educated to wisdom.

- A belief in every and any god is a belief in no god at all. Religious pluralism, in seeking to remain neutral, in fact denies all values. It is actually more exclusive than Christianity.

- Does the state or the Church have the right to codify morality, or does final choice belong to the individual? Removal of the transcendent abandons the law to float fragmented on a sea of relativism.

- Social anarchy results when nobody is prepared to maintain a standard of right and wrong. Without objective values, no one has a superior claim over anybody else. When we forget God, we are left to the reign of relativism, and therefore chaos. This in turn sets the stage for totalitarianism.

- Constitutions only work insofar as they reflect a common unity of ideals and aspirations.

- If a people have nothing for which they would die, then neither do they have anything for which to live.

- The paradox of our century is that 'free' nations are now denigrating the traditional role of religion, while those nations that have long been tyrannised are longing for religious reality.

- In remaining optimistic about human nature, human-centred philosophies turn a blind eye to centuries of terror and depravity.

- When government fails to curb greed and violence, and instead confines its activities merely to protecting individualised values, it is in fact trying to privatise divine law.

- Whoever has access to the media can win the minds of the people. Media stations are the new military targets in revolution and war, the real prize in the battle for public support.

- When His disciples complained that Jesus had offended those in authority, He merely replied 'Don't worry about them, every plant that my Father did not plant shall be uprooted'.

- Tyrants and ball teams have this in common, neither put *themselves* out. They have to be *put out*.

- Wait and pray till feelings are high, then do something symbolic to highlight the injustice and trigger the response to turn the tide.

- Martin Luther King, on justice and human rights issues: 'If *we* are wrong, then our constitution is wrong. If *we* are wrong, then the Scriptures are wrong. If *we* are wrong, then almighty God is wrong.'

- Going to the law must never become a luxury, out of reach for the average person. When this occurs, the state has failed to fulfil its divine mandate of maintaining justice.

- The first principle of democratic government can easily degenerate to 'don't rock the boat' in order that each may entrench itself in power.

- Never underestimate the power and willingness of the media to distort truth, for they always have a hidden agenda.

- One simple idea that feels right can mobilise a nation.

- There is nothing very positive about locking non-violent people away, and even less about letting them back out into the community without any support or resources.

- Patriotism/nationalism is fine as long as it is non-aggressive. The cry 'My country, right or wrong', precedes international grief.

- I believe in justice, but first I believe in the power of God who wants to demonstrate His ability to transform the worst of evils, if we will acknowledge the pain and leave our cause with Him.

- Never forget, as victims of injustice, that God demonstrated His amazing ability to 'balance the books', in and

through a miscarriage of human justice – Calvary – and
that it was Jesus' freely given forgiveness that allowed
Him to do it.

- If a Christian in the police force may bear arms to stop a
homicidal killer loose in the community, then a Christian
may bear arms to stop a crazed nation attacking others,
and a Christian may bear arms to stop his own crazed
government from attacking its own people.

- If you would not try to stop a drunk driver from killing
pedestrians purely by prayer, why then resort purely to
prayer to stop a tyrant?

- In a situation of injustice and oppression, the most 'dangerous' man or woman is the one who will repeatedly
and publicly speak the truth.

- A corrupt government can survive only by intimidation,
a corrupt Church, and the support of armed forces who
will not identify themselves with their victims.

- When a government degenerates into tyranny and
oppression, it loses its divine right to rule.

- We should invite every member of the government to
view the pain first-hand, or else how will they make the
right decisions?

- Three questions to ask of apathetic Christians:
  1. Is Christ of any earthly use?
  2. Is their loyalty to their own comfort, or to the hope
     of a better tomorrow?
  3. Will they bring the abuse of human rights to light,
     or will they 'pass by on the other side' and become
     guilty of passive complicity to evil?

- The belief that 'force can achieve anything' is challenged
head on at Calvary.

The tools of social change

- Prayer, with the application of Matthew 18.
- Publication of the injustice, using letters to the editors
of newspapers, magazines, etc.

- Open protest using slogans, signs, songs etc.
- Letters and telegrams to officers and representatives concerned.
- Articles for print in journals, magazines, papers etc.
- Boycotts of businesses who oppose, and support of those who support.
- Speakers sent to all interested parties and groups.
- Photography to supply visual evidence. (Stills and video.)
- Quotes from leaders and famous people in support of the cause.